Catholic for a Reason

*The editors wish to thank everyone
who assisted in putting this book together, especially
Ann J. Recznik, Edward A. Pankus, Jeffrey Ziegler,
Karyn O'Neel, and Thomas J. Nash.*

SCOTT HAHN AND LEON J. SUPRENANT, JR.

EDITORS

Catholic for a Reason

Emmaus Road ✕ Steubenville

Nihil Obstat
Rev. James Dunfee
Censor Librorum

Imprimatur ✠
Most Rev. Bishop Gilbert I. Sheldon, D.D., D.Min.

Copyright © February 4, 1998
Emmaus Road Publishing, Inc.

Library of Congress (98-070701)
Published by
Emmaus Road Publishing, Inc.
827 North Fourth Street
Steubenville, Ohio 43952
800-398-5470

Cover design by
Kinsey Advertising, Inc., CA

Published in the United States of America

ISBN 0-9663223-0-4

CONTENTS

Foreword i

Abbreviations iv

I. Introduction: The Mystery of the Family of God 1
   Scott Hahn

II. *His* Story Is *Your* Story 15
    Jeffery Cavins

III. Divine Revelation: How God's Plan Is Known by Us 39
     Curtis J. Mitch

IV. The Church as the Family of God 59
    Fr. Pablo Gadenz

V. Justification as Divine Sonship:
   Is "Faith Alone" Justifiable? 87
   Richard A. White

VI. Born Again: What the Bible Teaches About Baptism 107
    Kimberly Hahn

VII. The Family That Learns Together, Yearns Together:
     The Liturgy as Family Pedagogy 135
     Sean Innerst

VIII. The Heart of the Home: Jesus in the Eucharist 159
      Edward P. Sri

IX. Scripture's Revelation of Mary 183
    Timothy Gray

X. The Priest as Spiritual Father 207
   Fr. Pablo Gadenz

XI. The "Real Presence" of the Marriage Bond 231
    Leon J. Suprenant, Jr.

XII. Sacraments of Healing:
     A Return from Exile and a Healing of Heart 261
     Kris Gray

XIII. The Burning Truth About Purgatory 285
      Curtis A. Martin

XIV. Conclusion: Heaven as Homecoming 307
     Scott Hahn

Foreword

A colleague recently suggested that someday, when I retire, I might want to teach a course in Church management. It would only take one session, and the content would be simple: (1) have fewer staff meetings; and (2) make the meetings brief. He was being humorous, of course. Some meetings are important. And without the many good people who work on our parish and diocesan support staffs, not much would be accomplished.

Nevertheless, at least some of the practical problems afflicting the Church since Vatican II might be cured if we simply limited all meetings to sixty—or even thirty—minutes. One of the very few things we actually "own" in life is our time. Unfortunately, as Catholics, we have probably spent too much of our precious time over the past thirty-five years meeting and planning—and too little preaching Jesus Christ and bringing the world to conversion. Now we must deal with the consequences. We're losing souls.

Nowhere is this more urgently clear than in Latin America, where Fundamentalist Christian sects have made deep inroads into traditionally Catholic cultures. It's tempting to write off their success to "unfair" U.S. Protestant financial backing. But that's too easy. The fact is, their enthusiasm for Jesus is contagious. No matter how incomplete their message, these Fundamentalists believe. Their faith has power. Their witness offers hope. Their message responds to the deepest hungers of the heart. The irony is, they're succeeding with only a portion of the truth—such is the power of the Gospel!—while many Catholics, who've been granted the fullness of God's truth, too often fail to share it with the zeal and joy it deserves.

That is why the Holy Father's 1997 Special Assembly for America, which brought together bishops from all over Latin and North America, called again for a new evangelization, and also a new apologetics. Catholics—and by "Catholics" I mean each and every one of us, especially lay persons—need to rediscover their missionary fire. They also need the tools to explain their faith positively and persuasively when challenged by others. The new apologetics must serve the new evangelization and, in fact, be its foundation; in other words, its goal must be to win souls, not merely defeat opponents in theological debate.

From where will the new apologetics come? Well, happily for you, you're holding an excellent example in your hands. *Catholic for a Reason* has all the marks of an apologetics classic: conciliatory in tone; rooted in Scripture; very readable in presentation; and persuasive in its explanations. Or, to put it another way, it reaches both the heart and head. The chapters by Timothy Gray on Mary, Sean Innerst on Liturgy, and Edward Sri on the Eucharist go to the heart of the differences between Catholics and Protestants in a particularly effective way. But every contributor takes the same insightful approach.

Toward the end of his chapter, Sean Innerst observes, "Without memories, minds, and hearts full of the whole family history of the People of God . . . we condemn ourselves to an amnesia of the soul. Lacking those memories, we have no individual or corporate identity." Without an identity, I would add, we have no purpose or future, and this certainly isn't what Jesus intended when He told us to "go therefore and make disciples of all nations" (Mt. 28:19).

For three decades, too many Catholics have suffered amnesia about the urgency of sharing their faith for the salvation of the world. To be better evangelizers, Catholics must first be better rememberers. The core memories of the Christian faith include not only sacred Scripture, but also the lived experience and learned wisdom of the believing community—which we call Tradition. We will do a much better job of preaching Jesus Christ to the world when we wake up as believers and remember who we are; why and what we believe; how we got here; and from Whom our Catholic faith comes.

This book, as you will discover, is an ideal place to start.

†Charles J. Chaput, O.F.M. Cap.
Archbishop of Denver

Abbreviations

THE OLD TESTAMENT

Gen.	Genesis
Ex.	Exodus
Lev.	Leviticus
Num.	Numbers
Deut.	Deuteronomy
Josh.	Joshua
Judg.	Judges
Ruth	Ruth
1 Sam.	1 Samuel
2 Sam.	2 Samuel
1 Kings	1 Kings
2 Kings	2 Kings
1 Chron.	1 Chronicles
2 Chron.	2 Chronicles
Ezra	Ezra
Neh.	Nehemiah
Tob.	Tobit
Jud.	Judith
Esther	Esther
Job	Job
Ps.	Psalms
Prov.	Proverbs
Eccles.	Ecclesiastes
Song	Song of Solomon
Wis.	Wisdom
Sir.	Sirach (Ecclesiasticus)
Is.	Isaiah
Jer.	Jeremiah
Lam.	Lamentations
Bar.	Baruch
Ezek.	Ezekiel
Dan.	Daniel
Hos.	Hosea

Joel	Joel
Amos	Amos
Obad.	Obadiah
Jon.	Jonah
Mic.	Micah
Nahum	Nahum
Hab.	Habakkuk
Zeph.	Zephaniah
Hag.	Haggai
Zech.	Zechariah
Mal.	Malachi
1 Mac.	1 Maccabees
2 Mac.	2 Maccabees

THE NEW TESTAMENT

Mt.	Matthew
Mk.	Mark
Lk.	Luke
Jn.	John
Acts	Acts of the Apostles
Rom.	Romans
1 Cor.	1 Corinthians
2 Cor.	2 Corinthians
Gal.	Galatians
Eph.	Ephesians
Phil.	Philippians
Col.	Colossians
1 Thess.	1 Thessalonians
2 Thess.	2 Thessalonians
1 Tim.	1 Timothy
2 Tim.	2 Timothy
Tit.	Titus
Philem.	Philemon
Heb.	Hebrews
Jas.	James
1 Pet.	1 Peter

2 Pet.	2 Peter
1 Jn.	1 John
2 Jn.	2 John
3 Jn.	3 John
Jude	Jude
Rev.	Revelation (Apocalypse)

DOCUMENTS OF VATICAN II

SC   Constitution on the Sacred Liturgy
(*Sacrosanctum Concilium*), December 4, 1963

IM   Decree on the Means of Social Communication
(*Inter Mirifica*), December 4, 1963

LG   Dogmatic Constitution on the Church
(*Lumen Gentium*), November 21, 1964

OE   Decree on the Catholic Eastern Churches
(*Orientalium Ecclesiarum*), November 21, 1964

UR   Decree on Ecumenism
(*Unitatis Redintegratio*), November 21, 1964

CD   Decree on the Pastoral Office of Bishops in the Church
(*Christus Dominus*), October 28, 1965

PC   Decree on the Up-to-Date Renewal of Religious Life
(*Perfectae Caritatis*), October 28, 1965

OT   Decree on the Training of Priests
(*Optatam Totius*), October 28, 1965

GE   Declaration on Christian Education
(*Gravissimum Educationis*), October 28, 1965

NA   Declaration on the Relation of the Church to Non-
Christian Religions (*Nostra Aetate*), October 28, 1965

DV   Dogmatic Constitution on Divine Revelation
(*Dei Verbum*), November 18, 1965

AA   Decree on the Apostolate of Lay People
(*Apostolicam Actuositatem*), November 18, 1965

DH   Declaration on Religious Liberty
(*Dignitatis Humanae*), December 7, 1965

AG   Decree on the Church's Missionary Activity
(*Ad Gentes Divinitus*), December 7, 1965

PO   Decree on the Ministry and Life of Priests
(*Presbyterorum Ordinis*), December 7, 1965

GS   Pastoral Constitution on the Church in the Modern
World (*Gaudium et Spes*), December 7, 1965

CATECHISM OF THE CATHOLIC CHURCH

Throughout the text, the *Catechism of the Catholic Church* (United States Catholic Conference—Libreria Editrice Vaticana, 1994, as revised in the 1997 Latin typical edition) will be cited simply as "Catechism."

CHAPTER I

Introduction

The Mystery of the Family of God

SCOTT HAHN

With so many books around these days, busy readers have the right to ask: What's so special about *this* one? To put it plainly, this book is written to change the way you think—about everything.

Sound ambitious? It is. But not unreasonable, since what is presented in these chapters has already done exactly that for every one of the authors.

I should know. Not only have I experienced a profound change of mind and heart (as well as ecclesiastical affiliation), but I've also witnessed a similar transformation in the lives of each and every one of the authors, all of whom I've had as students at some point over the last two decades.

More accurately, perhaps, we have all been students together. And we've had the privilege of studying under the world's greatest teacher, Jesus Christ, who faithfully transmitted His lessons to us through the infallible channels of Scripture and Tradition, as they are interpreted by our Holy Mother, the Roman Catholic Church. And so that is all you should expect to find here.

The following chapters are meant to show how the teachings

of Scripture and the Catholic Church relate to each other. At the same time, we hope that you will catch a new vision of the Catholic faith in all of its beauty, symmetry, coherence, and practicality.

So instead of another novel fad, or some new esoteric theory knowable only by an elite and privileged few, these authors wish to share a vision that is "ever ancient and ever new." After all, why settle for the fleeting when you can have the timeless and eternal?

What is this new-old vision? It is the mystery of the Family of God. Sounds simple enough. And in a way, it is—at first. But as you begin reading and thinking more about it, you'll ascend from one level of mystery (the family as "the domestic Church," *ecclesia domestica*) to another (the Church as "the Family of God," *familia Dei*), until you reach the highest and holiest mystery of all: the Blessed Trinity, the divine Family.[1]

Where to Begin—At the Sign of the Cross

How in the world can the average person be expected to attain such lofty heights? Perhaps the best way to begin is to recall something that every Catholic first learned as a child: how to make the Sign of the Cross. We perform this simple act of worship by acknowledging God as Father, Son, and Holy Spirit while tracing the lines of a cross over our body with our right hand.

There you have it, the entire Gospel summed up in about three seconds. We profess the highest and holiest mystery about God, the Blessed Trinity, while confessing what Jesus Christ did on Calvary for our salvation.

We do it whenever we enter a Church, and at the beginning and end of every Mass. Some major leaguers do it every time they

---

[1] See Francis Cardinal George, *Inculturation and Ecclesial Communion* (Rome: Urbaniana University Press, 1990), 262: "Communio, the Church's internal sharing, is rooted in the life of the Trinity and is structured or expressed externally in a diversity of roles in the Church. Another analogue for Church life, the natural hierarchy of the family, provides a model for understanding ecclesial hierarchy." He adds: "The internal dynamics of family, the natural complementarity of its different members, the exchange of services, of education, of the fruits of the personal sacrifice—all enable John Paul II to see the family as a domestic Church and the Church herself as the family of God."

step into the batter's box. For most of us, however, we first experienced it not as something we did, but as something done to us—as babies—by our natural parents, godparents, and the priest, who fulfilled the role of our spiritual father, on the occasion of our Baptism.

At that moment, we were born from above and made to share in the grace of God's own family life, as His beloved children. This is the very thing that we call to mind every time we make the Sign of the Cross, namely, our adoption as God's children and entrance into the divine family of Christ, the Church. It is our identity.

It seems simple enough, at one level. And yet it remains an inexhaustible mystery for the greatest saints and highest angels. In the final analysis, all of theology is reducible to a sustained effort by theologians to unpack the vast sum of truth signified by this one simple act. In any case, it's more than mere ritual.

The Greatest Mystery of Faith— The Trinity as the First Family

For many Christians, the Trinity is simply a dogma that you must accept—if only to avoid heresy. Beyond that, however, many don't give it much thought. After all, they say, it *is* a mystery. And so it is, and more: It is the chief mystery of our faith, from which every other mystery flows.[2]

But what do we mean by mystery? One common misunderstanding is echoed in the definition once offered by a boy in Sunday school: "A mystery," he announced to the class, "is something that we have to believe, even if we know it isn't true."

Not quite. Further, the notion of mystery is not the same thing as a secret or a puzzle. Certainly supernatural mysteries are not knowable by our natural human powers alone. Yet mys-

---

[2] See J.A. DiNoia, O.P., *et al.*, *The Love That Never Ends: A Key to the Catechism of the Catholic Church* (Huntington, IN: Our Sunday Visitor, 1996), 25: "All of the great mysteries of the Christian faith—creation, revelation, incarnation, redemption, communion, the Church, our Lady, and the last things—unfold in the Catechism as elements of the single mystery of the divine Trinity."

teries do not go against our reason and experience, simply beyond them.

In this way, the mysteries of faith are to the mind what light is to the eyes: They make our spiritual vision possible. Moreover, there are *natural* mysteries (e.g., time, space, life, love), just as there are *supernatural* mysteries (e.g., Trinity, Incarnation, inspiration, transubstantiation). Natural mysteries are like the sun, which enables us to see during the day, while the supernatural mysteries of faith are like the stars, which enable us to see at night. If you think this makes faith inferi, recall that, although we do not see as well at night, we nevertheless can see much farther—into the very depths of outer space.

Both sets of mysteries extend beyond the reach of our real— but meager—powers of logical proof and scientific demonstration. However, that doesn't require us to deny the truth and reality of either set. Recall how the axioms of geometry work; even though they are impossible to prove, they serve as the necessary means to build "proofs" of theorems and corollaries. Indeed, there would be no geometry without axioms. Likewise, there would be no philosophy or science without natural mysteries; just as faith could not exist without supernatural mysteries.

Supernatural mysteries of faith may be understood as divinely revealed truths that we believe on the authority of God Our Father. Our faith ultimately rests on God's fatherly goodness, wisdom, and power. This fact underscores the importance of the mystery of the Trinity; for without it, we would not know that God is Father.[3]

We can also see why the Trinity is the highest mystery, for it points beyond all other revealed truths, which only tell us what God has done (e.g., creation, redemption, sanctification). In fact, only the dogma of the Trinity discloses the all-surpassing mystery

---

[3] The Church's ancient formulation of the Trinitarian dogma was based upon the con viction, drawn from the New Testament, that God's eternal Fatherhood is more than a metaphorical image—it is a metaphysical reality. God's eternal sonship necessarily follows, as Saint Athanasius effectively demonstrated against the Arians in the fourth century. Since the Son is the eternal image (*eikon*) of the Father—not in a static but truly

of God's essential identity, that is, who He is—in Himself, from all eternity: Father, Son, and Holy Spirit.

Perhaps nobody has stated this awesome mystery more simply and clearly and profoundly than Pope John Paul II: "God in His deepest mystery is not a solitude, but a family, since He has in Himself fatherhood, sonship, and the essence of the family, which is love."[4] Did you catch that? Notice he did not say that God is *like* a family, but that He *is* a family. Why? Because God possesses—from eternity—the essential attributes of family: fatherhood, sonship, and love. And He alone possesses them in their perfection.

It may be more accurate, then, to say that the Hahns are like a family, since these family attributes are present in my household, but only imperfectly. The Trinity is thus much more than a dogma to be memorized. It provides us a spiritual vision, as well as a practical challenge for families and parishes to live and love more like God.

---

dynamic sense—He must be eternally "imaging" the Father's life-giving act of eternal begetting. This points to the twofold reason for adding the *filioque* ("and the Son") clause to the Nicene Creed: First, because the Son would not image the Father if the Father "spirated" the Spirit apart from the Son; and second, because the Spirit's procession from the first two Persons represents the precise form in which the Son's eternal imaging of the Father is expressed. In other words, the Father's eternal act of "begetting" consists of a gift of life and love, which the Son must eternally image. Thus, the Holy Spirit is properly identified with that divine *Gift-of-Life-and-Love* (as Saints Augustine and Thomas Aquinas demonstrated). Long after the Council of Nicaea (325), in order to combat a variation of Arianism that emerged in seventh-century Spain, orthodox Catholic theologians recognized the need to add the *filioque* clause to the Creed of Nicaea. Their decision was subsequently ratified by several popes. Since the *filioque* clause ensures an understanding of the Son's full divinity, it also reinforces the Son's full equality with the Father. In this way, the *filioque* clause also points to the perfection of God's Fatherhood—as the theological conclusion needed to ensure the full perfection of the Father's eternal act of paternity. It is perhaps unfortunate that many contemporary ecumenical theologians tend to neglect these considerations (especially the last one).

[4] *Puebla: A Pilgrimage of Faith* (Boston: Daughters of St. Paul, 1979), 86. Notably, the Pope goes on to say in the very next line: "This subject of the family is not, therefore, extraneous to the subject of the Holy Spirit."

What Difference Does This Mystery Make?

At this point, someone might protest: Does this mean that all believers have to become professional theologians? Certainly not—any more than a man must become a master mechanic before he gets his driver's license. But if true love leads a man to learn the ways of his beloved, then it should be considered normal for believers to desire to study and grow in the knowledge of God.

The fact of the matter is that theology is not the exclusive domain of professional theologians. Every true lover of God should have a strong desire to study theology—as a true "amateur" (French for "one who loves," from the Latin *amor*). In short, theologizing means loving the Lord with all of our minds (cf. Mt. 22:37).[5]

What difference does all of this make for someone who truly wants to love God? It means that he'll want to know who God really is, above all else, and not just what He has done. After all, how do you feel when another person relates to you, not for who you are as a person, but only for what you can do for them? Perhaps a bit used?

No real love or friendship is possible as long as the other person is unable or unwilling to look beyond your function, that is, to see you as a person. Likewise, it is vital to our spiritual maturity as God's sons and daughters that we learn to look beyond what God has done, to see who He really is: Father, Son, and Holy Spirit.

---

[5] Many people wrongly assume that theologizing necessarily entails doubt, or some negative form of critical questioning. Perhaps that comes from the many theologians who have made a name for themselves by dissenting. In any case, the true nature of theology is stated by Saint Anselm: "faith seeking understanding" (*fides quaerens intellectum*). It is noteworthy that the Latin word for "seeking" (*quaerens*) is also the verbal root of *quaestio*, which represents a common theological form for medieval theologians like Saint Thomas Aquinas. Their understanding of "question" was more closely related to our notion of "quest" than to anything having to do with doubt *per se*. If we follow this classical sense, theology should be understood, quite literally, as a "faithful quest for understanding" (cf. Catechism, nos. 94, 158).

What's in a Name?

The importance of getting this right really hit me one Sunday while attending Mass at a small parish in the Midwest. Standing up front, next to the priest, was the director of religious education, a middle-aged woman religious in a white robe. She began by making the Sign of the Cross, while intoning, "We gather together in the name of the Creator, the Redeemer, and the Sanctifier."

Now I had heard of this sort of thing happening before, but I had never actually seen it. It instantly struck me as wrong, quite apart from liturgical norms, feminist motives, or political agendas. But I wasn't sure exactly why—until three ideas suddenly converged in my mind. First, we were no longer naming God in terms of who He is—in Himself, from eternity; rather we were addressing Him simply in terms of what He has done—for us, in history. Second, although there's nothing wrong with acknowledging God's works (of creation, redemption, and sanctification), nonetheless, the act of *thanksgiving* is a lesser expression of worship than *praise*—which we offer God precisely for who He is. Third, no matter how old creation may be, it's definitely not eternal, in which case God cannot be an eternal Creator (let alone an eternal Redeemer or Sanctifier).

It follows that the Trinity is God's eternal identity. This implies that God's most proper name is Father, Son, and Holy Spirit. Anything else will invariably lead us to a shallower understanding of—and relationship with—our God and Savior.

Perhaps this strikes you as theological nit-picking. Nothing could be further from the truth. The Trinity is not only the most proper name for God, it also reveals to us the deepest dimensions of all God does, whether it be creating, redeeming, or sanctifying. For whatever God does, it flows freely from who He is. We may thus discern—with the eyes of faith—a familial purpose in all of God's words and deeds. In short, the world bears a certain Trinitarian trademark, what older theologians called "the footprints of the Trinity" (*vestigia Trinitatis*).

Applying the Paradigm

Let us consider four doctrinal areas in order to see how this Trinitarian familial perspective may enhance our understanding:[6]

1. Creator and Creation: Seeing creation as the work of the Trinity enables us to see the world differently. God is more than our Creator; He is Our Father by grace. Instead of mere creatures, we are made in God's image and likeness to live as His sons and daughters. Instead of a vast impersonal cosmos, the Father fashioned the world to be our home—a royal palace and a holy temple.

2. Covenant and Law: More than a legal contract, a covenant is a sacred family bond. So God's covenants in salvation history (with Adam, Noah, Abram, Moses, David, and Jesus) reveal how He fathers His ever-expanding family and maintains its unity and solidarity. Accordingly, the laws of the covenant are not arbitrary stipulations forcefully imposed by a superior power, but rather expressions of God's fatherly wisdom, goodness, and love. We obey them in order to mature, so that we can love like God.

When God makes and keeps covenants with His people, He's just being true to Himself—for the Trinity is a covenantal Being.

"Covenant" is *what* God does because "covenant" is *who* God is.

3. Sin and Judgment: More than broken laws, sin means broken lives and broken homes. At root, sin comes from our refusal to keep the covenant, so we lose the grace of divine sonship. We sin because we don't want to love as much as God loves us; it's too demanding. Sin is absurd and deadly—for in sinning, we stupidly prefer something other than the life and love to which Our Father calls us. God punishes sin with death because sin is what kills His life in us. Judgment is not an impersonal legal process, nor are the covenant curses enactments of God's vindictive wrath. Like God's covenant law, the curses are not expressions of

---

[6] For a much fuller explanation and list of references, see Scott Hahn, *Kinship by Covenant: A Biblical-Theological Study of Covenant Types and Texts in the Old and New Testaments* (Ann Arbor, MI: University Microfilms, 1995)

hatred, but fatherly love and discipline; they impose suffering that is remedial, restorative, and redemptive. God's wrath is not opposed to His love; it's an expression of it. God *is* love (1 Jn. 4:8), but His love is a consuming fire (Heb. 12:29). That fiery love reflects the inner life of the Trinity. Sinners don't escape God's love; they get burned by it—unless and until they reopen themselves to it. That is what repentance achieves, and that's what God's wrath is for. Seeing God as Father doesn't lessen the severity of His wrath, nor is a lower standard of justice implied. On the contrary, a good father requires more from his sons and daughters than judges from defendants. And a good father also shows greater mercy.

4. Salvation and the Church: Salvation is not only *from* sin, but *for* sonship—in Christ. We are not only forgiven by God's grace, we are adopted and divinized, that is, we "become partakers of the divine nature" (2 Pet. 1:4). This is ultimately why God created us, to share in the life-giving love of the Trinity. Self-sacrificial love is the essential law of God's covenant, which we broke—but Jesus kept. After assuming our humanity, He transformed it into a perfect image—and instrument—of the Trinity's love, by offering it as a sacrificial gift-of-self to the Father on our behalf. The Son of God "took the form of a servant" (Phil. 2:6) so that sinful servants may be restored as sons of God. As Saint Athanasius declared: "The Son of God became the Son of Man so that sons of men could become sons of God."

By establishing the New Covenant, Christ founded one Church—through His own resurrected body—as an extension of His Incarnation and the Trinity's life. The Catholic Church is the universal Family of God, outside of which there is no salvation. This teaching does not condemn anyone. Rather, it simply clarifies the essential meaning of salvation and the Church. Since the essence of salvation is the life of divine sonship, to speak of salvation outside of God's family, the Church, is to confuse things greatly—since being *outside* God's family is precisely what we need to be saved from.

I don't know about you, dear reader, but speaking personally,

I find this familial approach to theological matters to be more than a little helpful. Having spent many years looking into various philosophical and systematic approaches, I am convinced of one thing: This is a theology that you can take home with you—and one that you'll find when you get there!

I'm also convinced that this "Family of God theology" hasn't come a moment too soon. Look around. Who can miss the signs of the deep crisis facing the institution of marriage and the family? Make no mistake about it, these are not normal times in which we're living. More than ever, the family is being besieged from without, and betrayed from within. And not only the nuclear family, but the Family of God, the Catholic Church.

War, violence, crime, abortion, addiction, perversion, deceit, ignorance, greed, disease. The oddest thing is that nobody really desires these things: But that is to miss the point, for what we *do* desire is what makes these things inevitable.

Fifty years ago, who would have imagined such troubled times? In fact, at least one man did—the pope. Listen to the prophetic voice of the Vicar of Christ, Pope Pius XII, writing to President Harry S Truman in 1949:

> Salvation will not come to the world unless humanity, following the teachings and the example of Christ, comes to recognize that all men are children of the one Father who is in heaven, called to be true brethren through His divine Son whom He sent as the Redeemer of all.[7]

Since then, the same clarion call has never stopped resounding from the chair of Saint Peter. In fact, this great vision of the mystery of the Family of God has been consistently proclaimed and published by each and every pope, along with the writings of Vatican II, and perhaps most profoundly by Pope John Paul II, as Fr. Pablo Gadenz's chapter entitled "The Church as the Family of God" makes abundantly clear. To be sure, Our Heavenly Father can always be trusted to provide what His children need most.

---

[7] From the Letter of Pope Pius XII to President Harry S Truman, published December 20, 1949.

Scott Hahn received his doctorate in theology from Marquette University in Milwaukee, Wisconsin, and is a professor of theology at Franciscan University of Steubenville. He is an internationally known Catholic lecturer and apologist. His latest book, A Father Who Keeps His Promises: God's Covenant Love in Scripture, *was published this year by Servant Books.*

CHAPTER II

His Story
Is *Your* Story

JEFFERY CAVINS

From the time that I was a small boy, I have had an awareness of God, a hunger. As a teenager I looked into philosophy, Eastern religions, music, and back-to-nature lifestyles to try to put life in perspective. At eighteen, I accepted Jesus' invitation to follow Him and dedicated my life to Him. Through rebellion and anger, I left the Catholic Church and worshipped at "independent" Christian churches. In fact, I was a Protestant pastor for twelve years.

Independently I tried to listen to Him and over many years composed a theology similar to a patchwork quilt—insights and perspectives from various books, speakers, and acquaintances that were oftentimes very good. While I'm thankful for all I learned as a Protestant pastor, I became aware that I was not standing on objective truth. Rather, I was standing on subjective truth, the truths of my experience. This left me with a foundation that was no bigger than myself. However, by studying salvation history, I discovered that God, as a loving Father, was trying to raise a family, and that truth was passed on within His family plan. This realization, among others, led me back to the Catholic

Church, the Church founded on Peter and the apostles.

When I returned to the Catholic Church, I picked up the narrative thread of my story. I found the form and direction that gave me freedom and life. Accepting and embracing the Catholic Church brought a deep resonance of peace within my soul. For when I picked up the narrative thread of my story, I found that intertwined within that thread was His story.

In this chapter, we will look at how God gradually revealed Himself to man throughout history, starting with Adam and Eve, then culminating in what would finally become His one holy Catholic Church. Emphasis will be placed on both the role of "family" and the value of "story" in salvation history. These concepts are crucial for personally and corporately embracing and transmitting the Church's message. In addition, we will discuss the importance of understanding the "big picture" within the Bible and introduce a practical way to read the books of the Bible as a single, cohesive narrative.

You are invited to come on this family adventure. Along the way, you will begin to see why God created you and what your future holds. King David, Israel's second king, sums up God's desire to see all people as members of His family when he says in Ps. 68:6, "God gives the desolate a home to dwell in."

Back in the late 1970's, the Pittsburgh Pirates' baseball team was on a roll. The colors of black and yellow could be seen on every street corner in Pittsburgh. Every coffee shop and school was abuzz with pennant prognosticators. To sum up their sense of unity, pride, and identity, the city adopted the pop song "We Are Family" by Sister Sledge. People often use the term "family" to describe those who are so close that they are, well, family. A business where associates work closely together is often referred to as "one big happy family." Pope John Paul II writes that even for those who remain single, the family is the "fundamental community in which the whole network of social relations is grounded."[1]

---

[1] Pope John II, *Letter to Families*, Vatican Translation (Boston: St. Paul Books & Media, 1994), no. 2.

The History of Salvation
Passes by Way of the Family

Pope John Paul II in his 1994 *Letter to Families* teaches that "[t]he history of mankind, the history of salvation, passes by way of the family."[2] In other words, the family is at the center of the struggle between good and evil, between life and death, between love and all that is opposed to love. All of salvation history can be understood as a family story, from the individual family to the Church, to the very Trinity: Father, Son, and Holy Spirit.

The emphasis on family in salvation history begins with the Trinity itself. Pope John Paul II has stated: "God in His deepest mystery is not a solitude, but a family, since He has in Himself fatherhood, sonship, and the essence of the family, which is love."[3] Dr. Scott Hahn, professor of theology at Franciscan University in Steubenville, points out:

> The work of salvation is the work of all three Persons of the Holy Trinity. Our redemption thus assumes trinitarian and family proportions.
> The first Person of the Trinity is now our Father (Jn. 20:17), because of the saving work of the Son, who is "the firstborn among many brethren" (Rom. 8:29), and so the Holy Spirit is "the Spirit of sonship," who causes us to cry "Abba, Father" (Rom. 8:15).[4]

Hahn explains that what makes Christianity unique and definitive is that the Gospel is God's sharing His family life and love with mankind.[5]

As a Father, God's intent is to raise mature sons and daughters, and He does this by drawing us into His family activity as "fellow workers" (1 Cor. 3:9). There are many biblical examples

---

[2] *Ibid.*, no. 23.
[3] See chapter one, p. 7, note 4.
[4] Scott Hahn, "She Gave the Word Flesh," *Inside the Vatican* (October 1997), 62.
[5] *Ibid.*

of coworkers with God in His saving plan, such as Andrew's bringing his brother Peter to the Lord, or the young boy's contributing his five barley loaves and two fishes to what would become the feeding of the five thousand (cf. Jn. 6:9). Within God's family paradigm, the Virgin Mary is a coworker with God in the redemption of mankind. She is acknowledged and honored as being the Mother of God and of the Redeemer, which means "she is clearly the mother of the members of Christ . . . since she has by her charity joined in bringing about the birth of believers in the Church, who are members of its head."[6]

God, who entered human history through the family, also makes parents coworkers with Christ. The family originates in a marital communion described by Vatican II as a "covenant," in which man and woman give themselves totally to each other and accept each other. William Kilpatrick, author of *Why Johnny Can't Tell Right From Wrong*, describes how marriage

> is a shared story: the partners grow in love partly on the basis of shared memories, and partly on the conviction that they are on a journey together. In having children, they bring them into the story and introduce them to the characters—aunts, uncles, and grandparents—who are already a part of it.[7]

It is in the family, Pope John Paul II says, that numerous interpersonal relationships are established: "married life, fatherhood and motherhood, filiation and fraternity—through which each human person is introduced into the 'human family' and into the 'family of God,' which is the Church."[8] Fr. Marcial Maciel, founder of the Legionaries of Christ, observes "how beautiful and what a responsibility it is to know that the motherly and fatherly

---

[6] LG 53, quoting Saint Augustine's treatise *De sancta virginitate* (On holy virginity); cf. Catechism, no. 963.

[7] William Kilpatrick, *Why Johnny Can't Tell Right From Wrong and What We Can Do About It* (New York: Touchstone, 1993), 195.

[8] Pope John Paul II, Apostolic Exhortation On the Role of the Christian Family in the Modern World *Familiaris Consortio*, Vatican Translation (Boston: Daughters of St. Paul, 1981), no. 15.

love you show your children is where they learn their relationship with God!"[9]

Similarly, as children are a living reflection of their parents' love,
the marriage covenant is a living reflection of the self-donation
found in the Trinity and Christ's love for the Church (cf. Eph.
5:25, 32). The family is truly the theater in which the children see
salvation history continue, and it is their primary point of entry
into the divine drama. Pope John Paul II declares that "in coming
into the world [man] begins, in the family, his 'great adventure,'
the adventure of human life."[10] In light of the influence a family
has, it should not come as a surprise that today Satan would tar-
get the family by trying to redefine and divide it.

The Family Has a Story

As a loving Father, God has not only provided us with a family setting in which to grow up; He also has a plan for His family,
a lovingly thought-out destiny. His plan encompasses the whole
world for all time, and by it we gauge our own progress and find
an anchor for life's many storms. Those who are members of the
Catholic Church have stepped into a new corporate and personal
story that can only be understood and lived in the context of family. Throughout history, people have a natural tendency to frame
experiences in terms of a narrative or story. This desire, common
to all of us, is very important for understanding both the Bible
and our own lives. We tend to approach the Bible and life assuming that both will make perfect sense, both complete with introduction, body, and conclusion. We are born, we grow up and find
that beautiful mate with whom we will live happily ever after,
then discover the right occupation, raise 2.5 perfect children, and
finally retire with adequate funds to take us through the golden
years. In the same way, we expect to pick up the Bible and read
it cover to cover with the story line hitting us squarely in the face.

---

[9] Marcial Maciel, L.C., *The Home: School of Evangelization* (Hamden, CT: Center for
   Integral Formation, 1995), 11.
[10] *Letter to Families*, no. 11.

Neither our lives nor the Bible is quite so simple.

Kilpatrick explains that "the same impulse that makes us want our books to have a plot makes us want our lives to have a plot. We need to feel that we are getting somewhere, making progress."[11] Perhaps this desire accounts for our being drawn to novels that take the form of a journey or adventure, such as *The Odyssey, Moby-Dick, Swiss Family Robinson*, or motion pictures like *Love Story* or *Rudy*, the story of an unlikely football hero.

Indeed, stories are powerful. They provide us with a path, an opportunity to make better sense of our lives. Many times stories alert our hearts to the fact that life is a journey, a quest that goes beyond merely surviving. But many find themselves tired, empty, living day-to-day without a story. Kilpatrick observes that when we

> turn our attention to those who attempt suicide, we find that the problem is not so much that they have lost their self-esteem but, more importantly, that they have lost the narrative thread of their lives. Life has become pointless, without plot or direction. We are willing to endure suffering when the suffering has meaning, but meaning is exactly what is absent in the case of a potential suicide. When suffering can be set within a narrative scheme, we manage to keep going; but if life itself is pointless, why put up with its thousand mockeries and cruelties?[12]

Our fascination with stories suggests that there is an ultimate story of which we are an integral part, a story to which we are drawn that is bigger than ourselves. As man's longing for God provides evidence for His existence, so the ultimate story, written by God, is evident by our endless search for a plot that will make sense of our lives. Saint Augustine once said that our hearts are restless until they rest in God (cf. Catechism, no. 30). We could also say that no story will leave us with a sense of completeness and belonging until we enter His story. For His story provides the comprehensive story line by which every life finally makes sense. Ironically, we often find ourselves resisting Our Heavenly Father

---

[11] Kilpatrick, 192.
[12] *Ibid.*, 194.

similar to how a teen may resist being identified with parents at a high school function. We wrestle with those who are there to nourish and teach us.

God Reveals Himself to Man Gradually

The challenge we face today is reading the Bible in such a way that the basic story line of salvation history is clearly seen and understood. We are not talking at this stage about understanding detail, but about grasping the scope of the divine story, the "big picture." It is important to keep in mind that, while the Bible is a book of seemingly obscure details, it is also a letter written by Our Heavenly Father. Letters are written to be understood.

The Bible, although made up of many stories, contains a single story within its pages. Though not evident at first glance, the story is about God and His relationship with His creation, the universe. As the Creator of the universe, God could certainly have said much about the beauty and complexity of the galaxies. However, He limits the field on which this divine story is played out primarily to planet Earth. While the Earth is marvelous and in itself speaks of His power and glory, its role is to be a glorious stage for the greatest story ever told.

At center stage stands man, the most complex creation in the universe and the true object of God's love and affection. Man would betray God, and yet God in turn would die for man, and by means of a covenant bring man into the family life of the Trinity. This is the world's story, invented, orchestrated, and executed by God. By inviting us to be His friends, companions, and, most importantly, His sons and daughters, Our Heavenly Father has made His story our story.

From the very beginning, it was God's intention to walk with mankind in a love relationship, but this relationship was severed through the disobedience of Adam and Eve. The fall of Adam and Eve introduced sin into the human race and has had devastating repercussions down through the centuries. Out of balance with his Maker, yet with the desire for God written in his heart (cf. Catechism, no. 27), man struggles to find meaning in life.

Starting with the very early chapters of Genesis all the way through the Book of Revelation, God gradually reveals His plan to reestablish the broken relationship between Himself and His treasured creation. Only in God's revealed plan does man once again find his intended purpose for being, "because man is created by God and for God; and God never ceases to draw man to himself. Only in God will he find the truth and happiness he never stops searching for" (Catechism, no. 27).

It is important for all Catholics to understand that, when they read the Bible, they are reading a book of history. History is very important to the Christian, for God has revealed Himself through actual human events. There should be no misunderstanding—this is actual history as opposed to cleverly devised tales. Pope Paul VI said, "The history of salvation is being accomplished in the midst of the history of the world."[13] The Bible provides countless examples of how, through word and deed, God has entered the life of His people.

Although God greatly loves all of mankind, we see early on in the Scriptures that His strategy to redeem humanity was to start with one family, Noah's, and then progressively unite more and more people until all of mankind would have the opportunity to be a part of His worldwide family.

Interwoven throughout the family story is a divine method of teaching. The divine plan of Revelation

is realized by deeds and words, which are intrinsically bound up with each other. As a result, the works performed by God in the history of salvation show forth and bear out the doctrine and realities signified by the words; the words, for their part, proclaim the works, and bring to light the mystery they contain (DV 2).

---

[13] Pope Paul VI, General Catechetical Directory (1971), no. 52, as found in Eugene Kevane, ed., *Teaching the Catholic Faith Today* (Boston: Daughters of St. Paul, 1982), 82.

God communicates Himself to us gradually by this method so as to welcome us in stages. The Bible narrates the mighty deeds of God as they relate to the salvation of man. These great deeds of God are understood in and through the lesser deeds of the various biblical characters. For example, the sacrificial nature of God's love is graphically illustrated and better understood in the story of Abraham's nearly sacrificing his son Isaac, found in Gen. 22. In this passage, we learn one of the revelatory names of God, *Yahweh Jireh,* "the LORD will provide" (Gen. 22:14).

Dei Verbum speaks of this gradual self-communication of God:

> [W]ishing to open up the way to heavenly salvation, he manifested himself to our first parents from the very beginning. After the fall, he buoyed them up with the hope of salvation, by promising redemption (cf. Gen. 3:15); and he has never ceased to take care of the human race. For he wishes to give eternal life to all those who seek salvation by patience in welldoing (cf. Rom. 2:6-7). In his own time God called Abraham, and made him into a great nation (cf. Gen. 12:2). After the era of the patriarchs, he taught this nation, by Moses and the prophets, to recognize him as the only living and true God, as a provident Father and just judge. He taught them, too, to look for the promised Saviour. And so, throughout the ages, he prepared the way for the Gospel.
>
> After God had spoken many times and in various ways through the prophets, "in these last days he has spoken to us by a Son" (Heb. 1:1-2). For he sent his Son, the eternal Word who enlightens all men[.] . . (DV 3-4).

Dutch Catholic theologian Han Renckens states the same truth when he says, "[T]his God travels along with people, grows with them from 'my God' and 'God of my fathers' to family God and to a tribal and national God."[14]

---

[14] Han Renckens, *A Bible Of Your Own* (New York: Orbis Books, 1995), 24.

Dr. Scott Hahn often refers to this covenantal progression in his lectures on salvation history.[15] Hahn shows how the Catholic Church is the culmination of salvation history and the fulfillment of the Old Testament covenants with Israel. As we read through the Bible chronologically, these expanding covenant families are significant benchmarks and give the reader a sense of progression. The five covenant families are: one holy family (Noah), tribe (Abraham), nation (Moses), kingdom (David), and one holy Church (Jesus Christ).

The instrument God used to bind Himself to His people was known in antiquity as a *berit*, or a "covenant." A covenant is a sacred family bond, "an agreement enacted between two parties in which one or both make promises under oath to perform or refrain from certain actions stipulated in advance."[16] The result of a covenant is the formation or reinforcement of a mutually beneficial family relationship. The major covenants in the Bible progressively expand in scope to bring more sons and daughters into the Family of God.

Hahn develops his argument by pointing out that God made His first and foundational marriage covenant between Adam and Eve, the first couple. The fruit of their covenant love was children.

The story then progresses to Noah and his three sons, in total four marriages, making *one holy family* with Noah as the mediator of the household. In Gen. 9, God makes a covenant with Noah, but it extends beyond Noah, for God said that this covenant is "with you and with your descendants after you" (Gen. 9:9). The mission of Noah's family would be to guard, reveal, and communicate love. This would become a "living reflection of and a real sharing in God's love for humanity."[17]

Next we find the number of people included in the covenant expanding to *one holy tribe*, with Abraham acting as the tribal

---

[15] Scott Hahn, Lecture, Defending The Faith VI Conference, Franciscan University of Steubenville (OH), June 24, 1995.
[16] David Noel Freedman, ed., *The Anchor Bible Dictionary*, vol. 1 (New York: Doubleday, 1992), 1179.
[17] *Familiaris Consortio*, no. 17.

chieftain. In Gen. 12:1-3, God makes three promises to Abram: land, royal dynasty, and worldwide blessing. These three promises provide a broad outline for salvation history as well as a sure foundation for future generations to recall in times of trouble.

In Gen. 15, God upgrades the promise of *land* to covenant status, letting Abram know that

> your descendants will be sojourners in a land that is not theirs, and will be slaves there, and they will be oppressed for four hundred years; but I will bring judgment on the nation which they serve, and afterward they shall come out with great possessions (Gen. 15:13-14).

This promise of land was fulfilled as the children of Israel conquered Canaan under the leadership of Joshua.

Abraham's grandson Jacob, whose name was later changed to "Israel,"[18] had twelve sons. These twelve tribes of Israel spent four hundred years in Egyptian bondage, where the covenantal expansion plan silently progressed. It was in Egypt that God raised up Moses, of the tribe of Levi, to lead Israel out of bondage to become *one holy nation*. Ex. 24 describes the dramatic scene, with the nation of Israel gathered around Mt. Sinai after leaving Egypt through a miraculous deliverance. There at Mt. Sinai, Moses conveys the words of the covenant he had received directly from God, and the Israelites agree to enter into a national covenant with Yahweh.

In Gen. 17, God upgrades the promise to Abram of *royal dynasty* to covenant status and changes *Abram's* name, which means "exalted father," to *Abraham*, which means "father of many." At this point, God introduces circumcision as a sign of the covenant and promises that Abraham will have a son with whom the Lord will establish an everlasting covenant. God's covenantal plan took a major leap several hundred years later as God began

---

[18] Jacob received a new name from God, "Israel." The name Israel means "he struggles with God." This would later become not only the name of the covenant nation, but would also describe the character of the people. See Gen. 32:28.

to draw other nations together under the leadership of King David. Through God's covenant with David (cf. 2 Sam. 7:5-16), this new conglomerate blossoms into *one holy kingdom* where Israel mediates the divine revelation of God to other nations. This promise of royal dynasty is reflected in 2 Sam. 7:16: "And your house and your kingdom shall be made sure for ever before me; your throne shall be established for ever."

The third promise, *worldwide blessing*, means that God will one day include the whole world in the covenantal family. This promise is upgraded to covenant status when God says to Abraham at the offering of Isaac,

> By myself I have sworn, says the Lord, because you have done this, and have not withheld your son, your only son, I will indeed bless you, and I will multiply your descendants as the stars of heaven . . . and by your descendants shall all the nations of the earth bless themselves, because you have obeyed my voice (Gen. 22:16-18).

All of the Old Testament covenants find their fulfillment in the New Covenant that Jesus Christ made with His Church. The death, burial, and resurrection of Jesus are the climax of the biblical story, for the paschal mystery was God's ultimate deed: "For God so loved the world that he gave his only Son, that whoever believes in him should not perish but have eternal life" (Jn. 3:16). The entire story of the Bible is Christ-centered. The Old Testament prophetically spoke of Jesus' coming, the Gospels describe His life on earth, the Epistles speak of life in light of His coming. This New Covenant certainly is the grandest of all, for it is a worldwide covenant where God rules and reigns as the head of His *one holy Catholic Church*.

The Bible Becomes a Catholic History and Book

To enter into God's story, we need to understand how we have come to participate in it. It is true that the divine history recorded in the Old Testament focused primarily on the nation of Israel, but the history and truth that the Israelites died for and taught to their children would one day become the history of a people they knew not. Even so, throughout the history of the Bible, those who belonged to the covenantal family recognized that the story they were living extended beyond themselves to future generations. Their history, with all its triumphs and disgraces, would one day become our history as twenty-first-century Roman Catholics. With the dawn of the New Covenant, Jesus integrated the nations into His universal kingdom, opening wide the gate to Yahweh's covenantal family. Those who enter through that gate—Jesus Himself (cf. Jn. 10:1-10)—take on a new identity, including a new personal history. Suddenly, all that went before us in that small land of Canaan becomes intimate and important for us today.

Saint Paul describes how Jesus opened the covenantal family to those outside of Israel:

> Therefore remember that at one time you Gentiles in the flesh, called the uncircumcision by what is called the circumcision, which is made in the flesh by hands—remember that you were at that time separated from Christ, alienated from the commonwealth of Israel, and strangers to the covenants of promise, having no hope and without God in the world. But now in Christ Jesus you who once were far off have been brought near in the blood of Christ. For he is our peace, who has made us both one, and has broken down the dividing wall of hostility, by abolishing in his flesh the law of commandments and ordinances (Eph. 2:11-15).

For the sake of continuity between the Old and New Testaments, the point must be made that neither Jesus nor Paul had plans of starting a new religion; rather, all that they taught and did was an extension of what preceded them. As Catholics, we should never read the Old Testament with an attitude that ties the Old Testament strictly to the Jews, and the New Testament to Christians:

> The Church, as early as apostolic times, and then constantly in her Tradition, has illuminated the unity of the divine plan in the two Testaments through typology, which discerns in God's

works of the Old Covenant prefigurations of what he accomplished in the fullness of time in the person of his incarnate Son (Catechism, no. 128).

Christians therefore read the Old Testament in light of Christ crucified and risen. Such typological reading discloses the inexhaustible content of the Old Testament, but it must not make us forget that the Old Testament retains its own intrinsic value as revelation reaffirmed by Our Lord Himself:

> [T]he New Testament has to be read in the light of the Old. Early Christian catechesis made constant use of the Old Testament. As an old saying put it, the New Testament lies hidden in the Old and the Old Testament is unveiled in the New (Catechism, no. 129; cf. DV 14-16).

As Catholics, we should embrace both the Old and New Testaments, not simply because they are a dynamic unity, but because they have been handed down to us as a precious family heirloom through the expansion of God's covenantal family. Most people are not deeply interested in the history of someone else's ethnic or religious group. What captures our imaginations and stirs our interest is reading about our own history.

It is of the utmost importance for the modern Christian to understand what Saint Paul teaches about this integration between Jews and Gentiles—the Old and New Testaments. In Eph. 3:6 he says, "[T]he Gentiles are fellow heirs, members of the same body, and partakers of the promise in Christ Jesus through the gospel." In other words, those who have come into the Catholic family have a new history. Israel's history is now also Catholic history and, as Saint Paul states, Abraham "is the father of us all" (Rom. 4:16). Pope Pius XI once made the striking observation that "spiritually, we are all Semites."[19]

---

[19] As quoted in Marvin Wilson, Our *Father Abraham* (Grand Rapids: Eerdmans, 1989), 19.

Paul elaborates further on this theme when he depicts Gentiles as branches from "a wild olive tree . . . grafted, contrary to nature, into a cultivated olive tree" (Rom. 11:24). As Gentiles, we are allowed to "share the richness of the olive tree" (Rom. 11:17). The "root" of which Paul speaks is the line of heroes, such as Noah, Abraham, Isaac, Jacob, Moses, David, and Solomon, who have participated in the previous covenants.

Mary has a unique role as one who stands between the Testaments. As Cardinal Ratzinger points out, Mary

> binds together, in a living and indissoluble way, the old and the new People of God, Israel and Christianity, synagogue and church. She is, as it were, the connecting link without which the Faith (as is happening today) runs the risk of losing its balance by either forsaking the New Testament for the Old or dispensing with the Old. In her, instead, we can live the unity of sacred Scripture in its entirety.[20]

The Bible is so very exciting to read because we, like Abraham and David, are stepping into the divine drama, we are receiving the baton, we are walking in the New Covenant. Matthew wrote, "Truly, I say to you, many prophets and righteous men longed to see what you see, and did not see it, and to hear what you hear, and did not hear it" (Mt. 13:17). How privileged we are to participate in God's story from the vantage point of the New Covenant!

No longer do we search aimlessly for meaning, trying to find ourselves. The adoption into the Catholic Church, the New Covenant, gives our lives meaning, continuity, and challenge. However, it is one thing to have received the Bible as a family heirloom; it is another to live by it. To do this we must understand it—which brings us to the subject of how to read the Bible.

---

[20] Joseph Cardinal Ratzinger, *The Ratzinger Report* (San Francisco: Ignatius Press, 1985), 107.

Understanding the Big Picture

For many of us, reading the Bible is itself a struggle. For some, the word "Bible" evokes feelings of warmth, stability, authority, and wisdom. But for many Catholics today, it instead evokes fear, because it seems to be Israel's story—mysterious, chronologically confusing, and impenetrable to modern readers. How tragic this is, since Scripture is a letter written by Our Heavenly Father to His children for the purpose of revealing Himself to them.

Those who pick up the Holy Bible for the first time might expect that Genesis through Revelation will read as easily as *Gone With The Wind*. But the novice soon learns that the Bible does not read like a popular novel. In fact, it is not put together as a sequential narrative at all. Instead, the books are grouped by types of literature rather than linear narration. Consequently, the once-excited inquirer puts the untapped treasure back down on the coffee table with a sigh of "What's the use?" How unfortunate, because waiting between the pages of the Bible is the story for which everyone is searching.

The difficulty we face today is how to make this now personal, ancient story of salvation history come alive. Without assistance we may flounder, because the Bible's seventy-three books are grouped by literary style (such as history, poetry, wisdom literature, and prophecy) rather than by strict chronology, as many might expect. Using the literary style as a tool to organize the Bible would not impede an Israeli student, because the history of the Jews is intrinsically tied to their self-identity. Modern western Christians do not enjoy this luxury. Instead, they first have to string the books together so that the critical plot becomes evident and, second, through the guidance of the Church, understand the meaning of the plot so they can make it their own story. Hahn explains it this way: "You have to study salvation history in such a way that you can see yourself standing in that stream."[21]

---

[21] See note 15, *supra*.

The first step to understanding the Bible chronologically is to identify which of the seventy-three books are narrative in nature. The term "narrative" refers simply to those books that keep the story moving from one event to another. The narrative books provide us with continuity, or give us an ordered account of connected events from Genesis to Revelation. Robert W. Jenson calls this "realistic narrative," which

> is a particular way of telling a sequence of events which is distinguished from other possible forms by two characteristics. First, the sequential events are understood jointly to make a certain kind of sense—a dramatic kind of sense. . . . Second, the sequential dramatic coherence is of a sort that could really happen, i.e., happen in a presumed factual world out there, external to the text.[22]

There are twelve narrative books in the Old Testament. Add to that list, for the sake of simplicity, one of the four Gospels (Luke) and the Acts of the Apostles, as illustrated below.

1. Genesis	6. I Samuel	11. Nehemiah
2. Exodus	7. II Samuel	12. I Maccabees
3. Numbers	8. I Kings	13. Luke
4. Joshua	9. II Kings	14. Acts
5. Judges	10. Ezra	

By reading through these fourteen books consecutively, one will have read through the entire Bible with a sense of historical continuity. The remaining fifty-nine books can then be read in the context of the narrative books. For example, the Book of Psalms, which for the most part was written by King David, should be read in the context of 2 Samuel, the narrative book that describes the events in the life of David. The prophet Hosea, who repeatedly tries to bring conviction and repentance, should be read in the context of 2 Kings, which describes the imminent downfall of

---

[22] Robert W. Jenson, "How the World Lost Its Story," *First Things* (October 1993), 20.

14 Chronological Books of Bible History

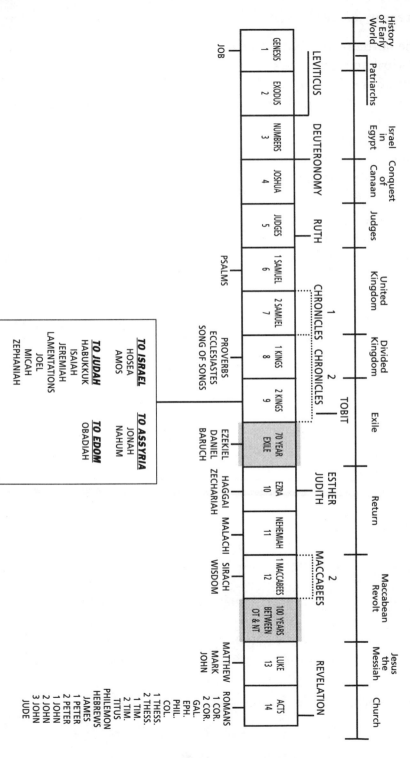

the northern kingdom of Israel. The Book of Ruth is the story of a Moabite woman who leaves the false gods of Moab and clings faithfully to the God of Israel. This beautiful love story takes place during the time of the Book of Judges, which records Israel's spiraling cycle of disobedience as it forsakes the one true God and serves false gods. Refer to the chart on p. 34 to determine the context of the non-narrative books.

People who try to read through the Bible in a year often end up frustrated. The attempt, which usually begins January 1, comes to a disappointing halt around the end of February as the Book of Leviticus is encountered. But the student of the Bible does not have to feel obligated to first read the Bible from cover to cover. Start by reading for continuity and understanding; get the big picture. If one will first restrict his reading to only the fourteen narrative books and read four chapters a day, he will have read the story line in approximately one hundred days, or three months.

After one has read through the narrative books once, he should then go back and read them again, but this time incorporate a few of the non-narrative books in their historical setting.

Reading through the Bible with a copy of the new Catechism is highly recommended, because the sacred Scriptures along with sacred Tradition make up the full deposit of faith. When questions of faith or morality come up, the index of the Catechism is valuable for finding official Church doctrine.

The problem for many students of the Bible is that, while they know many of the individual stories, they fail to grasp "the story." They fall into the trap of studying particulars to the neglect of the total picture; or, put another way, they fail to see the forest for the trees. Studying the minutiae of theology is, of course, important, but studying it against the backdrop of a comprehensive understanding of the biblical drama will yield better fruit. In-depth Bible study presupposes that one is familiar with the story and knows how to read through it.

Catholic apologist Frank Sheed describes how this lack of pedagogical structure is a problem within Catholicism in general. He observes that as children come through school,

they have learnt a great number of things, but there is no
order, no hierarchy, in the things they have learnt about the
faith . . . but they are all there in a kind of heap.[23]

He goes on to say that students "need some framework on which
they can arrange their knowledge, to which all the rest can be
related."[24] I believe the fourteen narrative books provide that
framework for understanding Scripture in its entirety.

Once we have familiarized ourselves with the "big picture,"
we "will have laid the groundwork for a lifelong love for the
Holy Bible, and for a lasting, fruitful familiarity with its master
plan and the details of its pages."[25]

The Bible should be read as a book of divine Revelation. The
Bible illuminates the human mind and imparts knowledge, pro-
viding a story that is "living and active, sharper than any two-
edged sword, piercing to the division of soul and spirit, of joints
and marrow, and discerning the thoughts and intentions of the
heart" (Heb. 4:12). As Saint Thomas Aquinas taught, it casts
"prophetic light"[26] on every area of life. The Bible, under the
guidance of the Magisterium, reveals to us those things we would
not otherwise be able to know by reason or natural revelation
alone, but which "God has revealed to us through the Spirit" (1
Cor. 2:10). The Roman Catholic Church teaches that Christ, the
Word become flesh, is "the sum total of Revelation" (DV 2).

It is important when reading Scripture to remember that the
Church sees the Bible as a basic component of her deposit of
faith, but the Bible alone is not enough for sound interpretation.
The Church does not rely on the Scriptures alone for her certainty about revealed truth. "Hence, both Scripture and Tradition
must be accepted and honored with equal feelings of devotion
and reverence" (DV 9). Vatican II clearly affirms that "sacred
Tradition, sacred Scripture and the Magisterium of the Church

---

[23] Frank J. Sheed, Are We Really Teaching Religion? (New York: Sheed & Ward, 1953), 14.
[24] Ibid.
[25] Eugene Kevane, The Advent of Christ, Divine Providence and Human Progress Series,
vol. II (Washington: Catholic University of America, 1962), 10.
[26] Saint Thomas Aquinas, Summa Theologiae, IIa IIae q. 171, art. 3.

are so connected and associated that one of them cannot stand without the others" (DV 10). Pope Pius XII, in his encyclical *Humani Generis,* declares that Scripture must be explained "according to the mind of the Church which Christ Our Lord has appointed guardian and interpreter of the whole deposit of divinely revealed truth."[27]

A favorite metaphor of mine to understand better the Church's relationship to Bible study is what I call the "train trip." Showing a student how to read through the Bible historically is like laying down the fourteen segments of track. Then as one travels along the historical route of the Bible, the Magisterium of the Church, which is guided by the Holy Spirit, acts as a conductor explaining all that the traveler is seeing. The interpretation of the tour through the Bible is not left to one's own imagination. God has indeed given the pilgrim a sure guide for the journey home.

Jeffery Cavins is a popular conference speaker on Scripture and apologetics, and is the host of "Life on the Rock," a weekly television program produced by the Eternal Word Television Network. He resides in Birmingham, Alabama, with his wife Emily and their two children.

---

[27] Pope Pius XII, Encyclical Letter *Humani Generis* (1950), N.C.W.C. Translation (Boston: St. Paul Books & Media), no. 22.

CHAPTER III

Divine Revelation
How God's Plan Is Known by Us

CURTIS J. MITCH

The topic of divine Revelation is vast and complex. Yet, for the faithful Christian, it is a matter too important to push aside in the hope of moving onto something more "practical." We are considering here how God and His plan are made known to the world. This is surely of some interest to us! Don't we question at times what we are to believe as Catholics? While the specific answers to most questions cannot be answered here, we will benefit from knowing where to look for them, for God expects us to believe what He has revealed.

The Meaning of Divine Revelation

Since the dawn of history, the Creator of the universe has made Himself known to the crown of His material creation–the human race. God introduces Himself and initiates a relationship with men and women whom He has fashioned to know, love, and serve Him forever. The biblical term for Revelation (Gk. *apokalypsis*) means the disclosure or unveiling of something that was previously hidden. Divine Revelation refers to those truths that God has made known to us for our salvation. We could never discover revealed truths on our own; they stand far above human reason and understanding. Were it not for God's decision to reveal Himself, we would never have known clearly God's love or His plan for the world. The purpose of our lives would remain hidden in mystery.

Surely, *some* knowledge about God is possible apart from Revelation. God's existence, in fact, can be known with certainty by reflecting on the world around us. The Old Testament states this clearly: "From the greatness and beauty of created things comes a corresponding perception of their Creator" (Wis. 13:5). Saint Paul echoes the same point in the New Testament: "Ever since the creation of the world his invisible nature, namely, his eternal power and deity, has been clearly perceived in the things that have been made" (Rom. 1:20). Human reason, then, cannot reach fully into the mystery of God, but it can point us in the right direction. Anyone who carefully examines the design of the world can know that a great Designer and Artist is responsible for its existence and beauty. Sometimes this type of knowledge about God is called "natural revelation," because it involves no *super*-natural intervention by God in history. The discovery of God's existence, then, is outside the realm of divine Revelation in the strict sense.

But what great truths of God and His plan are made known to us by divine Revelation? The Church views the content of Revelation as the disclosure of God's *Person(s)* and His *precepts*, His inner life and His laws. God desired to introduce Himself just as He is—Father, Son, and Holy Spirit—and to make known to us His instructions for living. In the words of Vatican II, "God wished to manifest and communicate both himself and the eternal decrees of his will concerning the salvation of mankind" (DV 6). This statement underscores God's purpose for revealing Himself to us in the first place: to welcome us into His family. God made known Himself and His plan for our *salvation*, not just for our information. He wants us to be clear on the meaning of our lives. Without His instructions, we would have little sense of direction in this world.

Having defined the basic meaning of Revelation, it remains for us to consider three of its most distinctive characteristics: (1) God's Revelation is always mediated, (2) God's Revelation was made known gradually, and (3) God's Revelation demands from us a response of faith and obedience. These characteristics of God's self-manifestation run throughout Old Testament history, culminate in Jesus Christ, and carry over into the life of the Church.

God's "Communications Media"

Divine Revelation is always *mediated* to us in one way or another. Throughout salvation history, the one invisible God (cf. Col. 1:15) has used the things of this world as instruments for revealing Himself and His plan for our lives. When we look to the Bible, we find God, at every turn, using such things as fire, persons, audible voices, visions, tablets of stone, written pages, and holy angels as "go-betweens" when communicating something about Himself to His people. In short, the world's Creator used the world itself as His communications media. How appropriate of God to introduce Himself to us by meeting us right where we are. Do we not live every day of our lives in space and in time, in the world and in history? This is exactly *where* God has spoken.

We might look at this from different angles. From God's perspective, He stoops down to our level to reveal Himself. He is a loving Father, reaching to embrace His children and communicate in a way that is understandable and sensitive to their needs. From our perspective, divine Revelation meets us on the ground; God adapts His message to our limitations and communicates with us in tangible ways. Because we depend on our five senses for acquiring knowledge, it is fitting that God should accommodate His saving message to our human nature and speak to us on our own terms. Revelation without any sights or sounds would surely go undetected; we would never know when it arrived. Rather, God gives us Himself and His plan in an earthly package that we are able to receive.

So God bends down to intervene in human history. Simple enough. Yet, it is unlikely that many of us have reflected on this

much or thought it through. By speaking at very *specific* moments
in history, God has done more than we realize. He not only
employs "things" to mediate His presence, but He works within
history itself. For example, God revealed the Ten Commandments
atop Mt. Sinai ages ago (Ex. 20). They were not spoken *directly*
to anyone in the twentieth century, yet they are essential for us to
know God's will clearly. The Ten Commandments have been
mediated to us down through history. Moses heard them
and received them on stone tables (Ex. 24:12). The Levites were
then charged with teaching them to Israel (Lev. 10:11) and parents were commissioned to pass them on to their children (Deut.
6:6-7). Centuries later, Jesus Christ confirmed their ongoing
importance for the Church as part of her faith (Mt. 19:17).

The point is simply this: God's people are not prevented from
knowing His law simply because they were not present *when* and
where the original Revelation was given. None of us was there
at Mt. Sinai, and the stone tablets have since perished. It was
God—standing above and outside time—who ensured that His
law made its way to us. It is He who put in place the mechanism
for transmitting His Revelation from generation to generation. A
chain of many links fills the gap between Mt. Sinai and your local
parish catechist!

All of this boils down to the basic truth that, on this side of
heaven, all interaction between God and man is mediated.
Whether God uses persons, places, objects, or even history to
manifest Himself, it is universally true that no one has direct
access to the Almighty in the absolute sense. Heaven alone is
defined as the unmediated Beatific vision of God. Only there do
the righteous encounter God "face to face" (1 Cor. 13:12) and
"see him as he is" (1 Jn. 3:2).

Stages of Divine Revelation

A second characteristic of divine Revelation is that God chose to manifest Himself *gradually*. In His wisdom, Almighty God chose to reveal Himself to the human race in carefully timed steps, and not all at once. Revelation was given to man in manageable increments, as God intervened in salvation history in stages. This Revelation became ever clearer and more explicit up to the coming of Jesus Christ.

The Bible shows us that God is closely linked with His covenants. God paints a more vivid portrait of Himself each time He makes a covenant with His people. These covenants unite God and His people in a family relationship. God protects and cares for His children as a Father, and His sons and daughters are called to love, obey, and trust Him in return. From covenant to covenant, God steps further into the light, manifesting more of His life and love to His children each step of the way. Moving down the line from Adam, Noah, Abraham, Moses, David, and finally to Jesus Christ, we see God slowly unveiling His plan for Israel and all the nations. The history of salvation recorded in the Bible is a crescendo of divine Revelation. As God moves closer to His people, the more clearly they see Him and desire His love.

The Obedience of Faith

The third characteristic of divine Revelation involves our *response*. When God offers Himself to His people, He expects us to embrace Him and give our full assent to His plan. God wants nothing less from us than the "obedience of faith" (Rom. 1:5; 16:26). After all, God is our Creator and He alone knows what is best for us and what is profitable for leading us to heaven. The New Testament teaches that "without faith it is impossible to please him. For whoever would draw near to God must believe that he exists and that he rewards those who seek him" (Heb. 11:6). A living faith, then, is required of those who receive God's Revelation directly or as it is handed on. We saw above that Revelation was always given to facilitate our salvation. To reject

God and turn our backs on His will is foolishness; we would only endanger our souls and subject ourselves to God's just punishment.

The Bible is full of such warnings about the dangers of rebellion. One example stands out. When God rescued Israel from slavery in Egypt, He brought them safely into the wilderness and wished to give them the Promised Land. To ensure that Israel's gratitude and commitment were sincere, God put the nation to the test. He requested that twelve spies inspect Canaan and bring back a report to the Israelites. As it turned out, Canaan was a dangerous-looking place, and the inhabitants were powerful and numerous. Ten of the twelve spies declined God's offer to enter Canaan. They even convinced the people that God's plan was senseless and dangerous. Only two spies, Joshua and Caleb, stepped out in faith. They alone trusted that God would protect His people in spite of the odds. God, for His part, had to respond to Israel's faithlessness with justice and punishment. He swore an oath that no one of that generation would ever see Canaan, except Joshua and Caleb (cf. Num. 14:20-24). The Israelites were thus condemned to wander aimlessly for forty years in the wilderness and eventually die. The Book of Hebrews recalls this episode to warn the early Christians to steer clear of unbelief and disobedience. The author speaks of the Israelites when he says, "[T]he message which they heard did not benefit them, because it did not meet with faith in the hearers" (Heb. 4:2).

Conversely, God rewards His faithful and obedient children. Like Joshua and Caleb, the righteous will receive God's promises and inherit the eternal homeland, heaven itself. When Abraham trusted that God would bless him with a son, the Lord "reckoned it to him as righteousness" (Gen. 15:6). Zechariah and Elizabeth, the parents of John the Baptist, were also blessed by God for their fidelity to His law. According to Luke, they "were both righteous before God, walking in all the commandments and ordinances of the Lord blameless" (Lk. 1:6). Divine Revelation is a divine invitation: God the Father wants His children to respond to Him with heartfelt love and gratitude.

Revelation Completed in Jesus Christ

We have thus far considered the meaning and characteristics of divine Revelation. God manifested Himself slowly to man as the centuries progressed, so that the content of His Revelation was growing steadily more complete. Yet it was not until the Father sent His Son that His perfect will was shown forth and His inner life as a Trinity was clearly revealed.

The New Testament summarizes the history of Revelation in a single statement: "In many and various ways God spoke of old to our fathers by the prophets; but in these last days he has spoken to us by a Son" (Heb. 1:1-2). This passage encapsulates the entire scope of Revelation and highlights the greatness of God's self-disclosure in Christ. God's numerous interventions in salvation history were only a foretaste of the great things He had in store for us. He had indeed spoken in the Old Testament, but only in a provisional and incomplete way. Jesus, the long-awaited Messiah, fulfilled all the hopes, prophecies, and anticipations of the Old Covenant. Our Lord Himself said, "Think not that I have come to abolish the law and the prophets; I have come not to abolish them but to fulfil them" (Mt. 5:17). It is through Christ that the way, the truth, and the life of God is made known in its fullness and beauty (cf. Jn. 14:6). Jesus, in summary, "completed and perfected Revelation" (DV 4).

Jesus' entire life manifested the Father and His perfect will. Vatican II teaches that Christ revealed the truth and love of God by His "words and works" (DV 4). As a divine Person, Christ is uniquely qualified to make the Trinity known to the world. Through His many signs and miracles, Jesus extended God's mercy to the afflicted. Through His Passion, Jesus demonstrated God's love for sinners (cf. Rom. 5:8). Even His presence among His disciples marked a mysterious encounter with God. As Jesus told Philip, "He who has seen me has seen the Father" (Jn. 14:9).

Since Jesus Christ perfects all that God revealed in the Old Testament, it is not surprising that the characteristics of divine Revelation should apply also to Him. First, Christ is God's perfect *mediator*; He alone unites God and man. He is a perfect bridge of communication spanning the distance between heaven and earth, the Father and fallen sinners. He touches the shore of God's life in His own divinity, and the shore of man's weakness in His humanity. Saint Paul's assertion brings this into focus: "[T]here is one God, and there is one mediator between God and men, the man Christ Jesus" (1 Tim. 2:5).

When Christ became man, He united Himself to the human race in every way except our sinfulness. God did not choose to complete His Revelation through another burning bush (Ex. 3:2) or still small voice (1 Kings 19:12). Rather, God came closer to us than ever before; He became one of us. Christ's humanity is the tangible instrument of His divine life. His own body was sacrificed for our sins, only to be raised again and given to us in the sacraments (cf. Jn. 6:51). Saint John marveled at this inexhaustible mystery that touches even our senses. He recalls that Jesus was "heard . . . seen . . . looked upon . . . touched . . . and was made manifest to us" (1 Jn. 1:1-2). The Incarnate Christ, then, is God's gift to the world, delivered in a package that is tailored to our needs and human limitations.

According to the second characteristic, God's *gradual* Revelation reached its goal and climax in Christ. Jesus' coming is the definitive unveiling of God's will. The greatest of all mysteries—the Blessed Trinity—was finally made known through Christ's life and teaching. Yet, even this final phase is marked by increments and progress. Jesus completed Revelation in general, but He ascended to the Father before giving us all that He needed to say! As He told the disciples at the Last Supper, "I have yet many things to say to you, but you cannot bear them now. When the Spirit of truth comes, he will guide you into all the truth" (Jn. 16:12-13). It is the Holy Spirit who completes Jesus' teaching ministry. In the age of the apostles, the Spirit continued to instruct the young Church regarding Christ and the New Covenant (cf. Jn. 15:26; 1 Cor. 2:9-10; 1 Pet. 1:12). It is He—the third Person of the Trinity—who kept watch over the early Church to guide her practice and preserve her from error.

The fullness of the Gospel is summed up in Jesus' death and Resurrection, while the ongoing guidance of the Spirit gave definitive shape to the saving message in the Church's earliest days.

This needs to be understood clearly. The Catholic Church maintains that God's Revelation was whole and complete with the death of the last apostle (c. 100 A.D.). Jesus Christ *and* the Holy Spirit had by then given us the entire deposit of faith; the Christian Gospel "was once for all delivered" (Jude 3) to the Church (cf. Catechism, nos. 66-67). *Public Revelation*—that which God expects all to receive with faith—was completed by the end of the first century. God will not reveal something new about Himself or His plan until Jesus returns in glory (cf. DV 4).

In line with the third characteristic, God's Revelation in Christ demands a *response* of *faith and obedience* from those who receive it. We see in Jesus not only the final word of divine Revelation, but also the perfect example of fidelity to God's will. Jesus, "the first-born among many brethren" (Rom. 8:29), has cleared a spiritual path for all God's children to follow. Free from sin, He always desired and embraced the Father's plan even in suffering and death. At one point, Jesus stated, "My food is to do the will of him who sent me, and to accomplish his work" (Jn. 4:34). We see this illustrated later as Jesus placed Himself wholly in the Father's hands in the garden of Gethsemane. He said, "[N]ot what I will, but what thou wilt" (Mk. 14:36). Our response to God, then, consists in imitating and obeying Jesus Christ through the power of the Spirit. God is asking us to surrender our entire lives to His all-wise plan. "Take my yoke upon you, and learn from me," Jesus bids us, "for I am gentle and lowly in heart, and you will find rest for your souls" (Mt. 11:29).

Scripture and Tradition:
Revelation Handed on in the Church

In many respects, this final section is the most practical for today's Catholic. If God intends for us to know Him and live according to His will, we surely must know where His Revelation is found. It is not enough to say that God revealed Himself in history and ultimately in His Son. We at the threshold of the twenty-first century live at quite a distance from these events. The concern here is the transmission or handing on of Revelation in the life of the Church. We must be sure that God's truth has reached us intact and has not been lost or corrupted since the end of the first century. To understand this, we will look at Scripture and Tradition as channels of Revelation, and then examine the role of the Church's Magisterium in proclaiming the Gospel authoritatively.

The Written Word of God

God's Revelation is communicated in a unique way in the sacred Scriptures. The word "Bible" (Gk. *biblion)* refers to a book. In a certain sense, however, the Bible is a whole library of books. The Catholic Church accepts a total of seventy-three books as the canon or official list of biblical writings. Yet, there is something—indeed someone—who brings unity to each of the individual books and tells the continuous story of salvation in them from beginning to end, from Genesis through Revelation. That someone is God Himself. The sacred Scriptures are *sacred* precisely because the Holy Spirit has authored each one of them. There can be no doubt that several human authors also played pivotal roles in this great project. But they are secondary or instrumental authors employed by God according to His will.

Saint Paul describes the Bible's divine authorship in terms of its *inspiration.* He writes to Saint Timothy, "All Scripture is inspired by God and profitable for teaching, for reproof, for correction, and for training in righteousness, that the man of God may be complete, equipped for every good work" (2 Tim. 3:16-17; cf. 2 Pet. 1:20-21). The term translated "inspired of God" (Gk. *theopneustos*) means "breathed of God" and is linked with God's Spirit and speech. The Scriptures contain God's own words breathed by the Holy Spirit; they contain instructions He wants His children to hear. Since God is Truth, His words are infallibly true and cannot, when properly understood, be found to assert errors of any kind. God's Word in the Scriptures is as trustworthy and reliable (i.e., inerrant) as God Himself! According to the classic statement of Pope Leo XIII in 1893,

> [I]nspiration not only is essentially incompatible with error, but excludes and rejects it as absolutely and necessarily as it is impossible that God Himself, the supreme Truth, can utter that which is not true. This is the ancient and unchanging faith of the Church.[1]

This is not to say that the inerrant truth and meaning of the Bible are easily discovered by its reader. The Scriptures are full of different types and genres of literature: historical narratives, poetry, prayers, apocalyptic visions, and letters. Each of these present God and His plan in a different manner, and thus different rules apply for interpreting them (cf. DV 12). Moreover, the ancient languages in which the Bible was written (Hebrew, Aramaic, and Greek) are foreign to the vast majority of Christians today. These languages and the many styles of ancient writing require more study and work than most of us are able to give on our own. It is a rare bird who thinks himself enlightened after reading through the Book of Leviticus for the first time! All of this should lead to a profound appreciation for the mystery of biblical inspiration and our own need for a trustworthy interpretation (cf. 2 Pet. 1:20; 3:15-16). As we shall see, it is the duty of the Church's Magisterium to interpret properly and definitively the meaning of God's written Word.

It is thus important for Catholics to realize the profound value of the Bible in the ongoing life of the Church. First and foremost, the Scriptures are used in the liturgy. During the first half of the Mass—the Liturgy of the Word—the Church proclaims God's written Word to evoke from us a response of faith and obedience. To hear God's voice in the readings is so great a

---

[1] Pope Leo XIII, Encyclical Letter On the Study of Sacred Scripture *Providentissimus Deus* (1893), no. 20 (Boston: Daughters of St. Paul), 26.

privilege that we respond, "Thanks be to God" and "Glory to you, O Lord." The Psalms are part of the Church's daily worship in the Liturgy of the Hours. Vatican II, quoting Saint Ambrose, also emphasizes the use of the Bible in personal prayer:

> [P]rayer should accompany the reading of sacred Scripture, so that a dialogue takes place between God and man. For, "we speak to him when we pray; we listen to him when we read the divine oracles" (DV 25).

The faithful transmission of the Bible rests squarely on the shoulders of the Church. Since in the Scriptures we have a treasure of inestimable value, it has been the responsibility of the Church through the ages to preserve the written oracles of God and continuously proclaim them to the world. This fact should in no way be underestimated, especially since the original texts of the Bible (i.e., autographs) have long since perished. It is only because of the assiduous copying of the biblical books by Christian monks and scribes, like the Jewish scribes before them, that we have a Bible in our day. God's Word has been mediated to us not only in human language, but also through history.

Furthermore, it is only because of the Catholic Church and her Tradition that we know what the Bible is! The list of the seventy-three inspired books is not itself found in the pages of Scripture. There were many books considered candidates for the biblical canon that were not ultimately included. There were also several books (no less than seven) just in our New Testament whose authenticity and authority were debated in the early Church. To this day, Catholics and Protestants still disagree about the number of books in the Old Testament. How is one to discern accurately which books were inspired by the Holy Spirit and which were not? Again, the official list of the inspired biblical books, and thus God's written Revelation, has been mediated to us. The Catholic Church, in her official decision (393 A.D., Council of Hippo) and subsequent confirmations (397, 419, 1442, 1546 A.D.), provides us with the sure knowledge of exactly which books are the written and inspired Word of God.

Sacred Tradition

Is all of God's New Covenant Revelation, then, located within the pages of the Bible? The Church answers in the *negative* because she relies also on sacred Tradition. Along with sacred Scripture, Tradition transmits the Revelation of God that was given to the Church by Jesus Christ. Both of these together flow from "the same divine well-spring" (DV 9).

Sacred Tradition may be understood in different ways. In a general sense, Tradition is an overarching term to describe all of Christ's Revelation, both spoken and written, which was entrusted to the Church (cf. 1 Tim. 6:20). Saint Paul has this meaning in mind when he commands the Thessalonians, "So then, brethren, stand firm and hold to the traditions which you were taught by us, either by word of mouth or by letter" (2 Thess. 2:15). This "letter" (probably 1 Thessalonians) has divine authority because it was authored by both Saint Paul and the Holy Spirit.

But what authority stands behind these oral traditions? These too are binding upon the believers because the Gospel *preached* by the apostles is also the Word of God. Earlier, Saint Paul told the Thessalonian Church:

> [W]e also thank God constantly for this, that when you received the word of God which you heard from us, you accepted it not as the word of men but as what it really is, the word of God, which is at work in you believers (1 Thess. 2:13; cf. 1 Pet. 1:25).

This Tradition is itself part of God's Revelation for His Church. Hence, when the New Testament explicitly condemns different traditions (cf. Mt. 15:1-6; Col. 2:8), it is only denouncing those that are merely human in their origin. The Tradition that the apostles committed to the early Churches comes from Christ and the Holy Spirit (cf. 1 Cor. 11:2; 2 Thess. 3:6) and thus is authoritative as Christian teaching. After all, Christ commissioned the apostles to *preach* the Good News (Mt. 28:18-20; Mk. 16:15). The spread of Christianity in the world was accomplished primarily through the living and oral transmission of the Word of God by the apostles and their appointed successors.

The more specific meaning of Tradition, however, consists of the teachings that God Himself delivered to the apostles but were not completely recorded in inspired Scripture. The fullness of the Christian faith cannot be contained in a book, even an inspired one. The ecclesial or "Church" offices of pope, bishop, and priest, the rubrics and celebration of the liturgy, and the seven Christian sacraments are essential elements of the faith. These cannot be confined to a book even though they are part of the Church's life in every age. Indeed, the Church was alive and flourishing before any word of the New Testament had been written (cf. Acts 2:42). In some instances, the writers of the New Testament even preferred to instruct the young communities in person rather than by writing to them (cf. 1 Cor. 11:34; 2 Jn. 12). This is not to undervalue or marginalize the written Word of God; it is only to distinguish it from the fullness of Christianity which encompasses it.

Sacred Tradition is so vast and yet, ironically, many Catholics wonder where to look for it. One might think it more convenient to put it all in a single volume, so that we could place it beside the Holy Bible on our coffee tables. But this is to misunderstand Tradition. When the Church speaks of Tradition, she is referring to her faith found in the creeds and canons of the Church councils, the teachings of the popes, the writings of the early Church Fathers, the teachings of the saints and doctors, and especially the celebration of the liturgy. There are places besides the Bible where the Christian Gospel—God's Revelation—is preserved. This Tradition mediates to us the riches of Christianity, not only in the form of beliefs, but also in the life and worship of the Church. The new and everlasting covenant is made present here and now in the Church. This will help us to see that Tradition is not a collection of secret beliefs whispered from ear to ear down through Church history. The councils, the creeds, the liturgical rites, and the writings of the Church's greatest Fathers and saints all bear witness to the Church's treasury we call *Tradition*.

The faith that the apostles handed on to the early Church is the same faith we hold today. Tradition does not add to what was given before the death of the last apostle, whether handed down orally or in writing. However, our ongoing reflection on God's Revelation can yield a fuller understanding of our faith as the centuries pass. As the Church gradually mines the treasures given her in the first century, she is called to make explicit what Christian believers have always held implicitly. Directed by the Holy Spirit, she is entrusted with God's Revelation and is thereby called to unpack all the many implications that the truth has upon our lives. The *content* of Tradition does not grow throughout history, but the Church's *understanding* of it does expand and mature. The Church always holds to the ancient faith of the apostles, while developing her doctrines more clearly and applying that faith to meet the needs of Christians in every age.

Preserving and Proclaiming the Christian Faith

While Scripture and Tradition comprise God's revealed plan for our lives, it is the duty of the Church's Magisterium, the pope and the bishops united with him, to proclaim this revealed Gospel throughout history and the world. This clearly distinguishes the Church from Revelation itself. The apostles, faithful to the commission of Our Lord, handed over to the Church everything that God had made known for our salvation. But this "handing over" did not stop with a body of teaching. The apostles appointed successors to fill their positions and pass on their teaching offices (cf. 2 Tim. 1:6; 2:2). Jesus Himself established an appropriate teaching authority to guard His Revelation and give a living voice to Scripture and Tradition. Hence, it is the principal duty of the Magisterium, which traces its authority to Christ and the apostles, to proclaim God's Revelation to all men and women and dutifully preserve it for each new generation.

Knowing well the limitations and imperfections of His creatures, God Himself equipped the Church with the provisions necessary for faithfully transmitting His revealed Gospel. In addition to the teaching offices of the apostles and the bishops they appointed, God gave to the Church the Holy Spirit. Jesus told His apostles, "[T]he Counselor, the Holy Spirit, whom the Father will send in my name, he will teach you all things, and bring to your remembrance all that I have said to you" (Jn. 14:26). Later He reassured them, "When the Spirit of truth comes, he will guide you into all the truth" (Jn. 16:13). This was necessary because human persons, despite their good intentions, are prone to error. Had God left His Revelation in the hands of the Church without a sure guarantee of its faithful transmission, it would have been corrupted, misinterpreted, and altered by fallible human teachers.

As it is, however, the Holy Spirit guides the Church and preserves her from falling into error when officially teaching on matters of Christian belief and life. This gift of the Holy Spirit is called *infallibility*, and is given to the Pope individually and as head of the college of bishops (cf. LG 25; Catechism, nos. 888-92). Similar to the way the Holy Spirit inspired human authors to write inerrant Scripture, infallibility means that the same Spirit guides the Magisterium and prevents it from teaching errors about faith and morals. Yet, there is a significant difference. God communicated new Revelation in the first century when He inspired the Bible, but the gift of infallibility involves preserving the Church from misinterpreting the Revelation that was already given in Scripture and Tradition. The post-apostolic Church does not give us new Revelation. Rather, the Spirit guides the Church's Magisterium, protecting her teaching throughout history and leading her to an ever-fuller understanding of the treasures of the New Covenant. In this sense, the Church is "the pillar and bulwark of the truth" (1 Tim. 3:15).

When God set out to reveal Himself and His wonderful plan of salvation, He arranged all things to culminate in His Son. Jesus Christ sums up and brings to perfection all of God's Revelation. He built His Church upon Peter and the apostles (cf. Mt. 16:18; Eph. 2:20) to pass on to us His treasures and His truth. May God's Revelation enkindle within us the fires of faith, hope, and love as we move steadily toward our calling—the glory of heaven.

Curtis Mitch received his master's degree in theology from Franciscan University of Steubenville. He formerly worked as a lay pastoral associate in the Diocese of Pittsburgh, Pennsylvania, and is currently working on a Catholic study Bible that will be published by Ignatius Press. He resides in Steubenville, Ohio, with his wife Stacy and their two children.

CHAPTER IV

The Church as the Family of God

FR. PABLO GADENZ

Growing up in the United States as a son of native Italian parents was the best of two different worlds. On the one hand, I could enjoy as much baseball as I wanted, and on the other, I could enjoy as much pasta as I wanted. There was an area, however, in which the American environment was no match for my Italian heritage—the area of religion. You see, Rome is the capital of Italy, but Rome is also the heart of the *Roman* Catholic Church. Being a Roman Catholic is and has always been a family matter for me. Among other things, my uncle (may he rest in peace) was a priest of the Diocese of Trent, as in the famous Council held between 1545 and 1563. My upbringing included periodic trips to Italy to visit my relatives, my extended family. On one trip in 1973, my family visited Castel Gandolfo, the summer papal residence in the hills surrounding Rome. I distinctly recall standing almost directly underneath the balcony from which Pope Paul VI greeted the pilgrims. I could see the Pope straight above my head, waving his arm in blessing. Spanish-speaking pilgrims nearby shouted out the Italian cheer (with more enthusiasm than grammatical accuracy): *"Viva la Papa!"*

Pope Paul VI was *il Papa*, the Holy Father, and all of us gathered
there were his spiritual children. Being a Roman Catholic is a
family matter.

Nineteen years later, on May 18, 1992, I was once again in
Rome, this time in St. Peter's Square. The occasion was another
family celebration—not of my own natural family, but of the spiritual family (and friends) of Opus Dei, whose founder Msgr.
Josemaría Escrivá had been beatified the previous day. After the
Mass of Thanksgiving celebrated by the Prelate of Opus Dei, the
Holy Father Pope John Paul II rode through the square in his
popemobile, greeting the hundreds of thousands of pilgrims. By
a happy coincidence, the day was also the Pope's birthday, and
the pilgrims from the various countries all sang "Happy
Birthday" to the Pope. It reminded me of a custom in my own
family, in which we celebrate birthdays by singing "Happy
Birthday" first in English, then in Spanish, and then in Italian.
Being a Roman Catholic is a family matter.

The understanding of the Church as a family is not merely my
personal experience, but—as I was to discover through my theological studies in preparation for the priesthood—it is also the
Church's self-understanding. The Second Vatican Council
"described the Church in diverse ways: as the people of God, the
body of Christ, the bride of Christ, the temple of the Holy Spirit,
the family of God."[1] I want to focus this study on the last named
image—the Church as the Family of God. In doing so, it is not at
all my intention to propose the image of the Church as the Family
of God in opposition to or in rivalry with the other images of the
Church mentioned above. All of "[t]hese descriptions of the
Church complete one another and must be understood in the
light of the mystery of Christ or of the Church in Christ."[2] The
image of the Church as "God's household" or family does, however, deserve special attention.

---

[1] Synod of Bishops, "The Final Report of the 1985 Extraordinary Synod of Bishops,"
Origins 15 (1985), 446.
[2] *Ibid.*

As Pope John Paul II says, this image

> is in some way contained in all the others. It figures in the Pauline
> analogy of the body of Christ (cf. 1 Cor. 12:13, 27; Rom. 12:5),
> to which Pope Pius XII referred in his historic encyclical *Mystici*
> *Corporis*. It is also found in the notion of the People of God, to
> which the council made reference.[3]

I highlight the image of the Church as the Family of God
because such an understanding is especially timely given the
recent worldwide discussions on the nature and role of the family
in society. There is a great need—as well as a great opportunity—
at this moment in history to preach the "gospel of the family."[4]
The Family of God image is closely related to the "gospel of the
family" because there is an *analogy* between the natural human
family and the supernatural family of the Church. This analogy is
expressed by referring to the Church as the Family of God; it is
also expressed by referring to the natural family as the "domestic
Church." By striving to understand the truth of the supernatural
family, light is shed on the truth of the natural family. Similarly,
the experiences of natural family life shed light on the truth of
the family of the Church. In order to respond to the "signs of the
times," therefore, let us consider more fully the truth about the
Church as the Family of God.

The Natural Family and the Church Family

The United Nations declared the year 1994 as the
International Year of the Family. For that occasion, Pope John
Paul II issued his *Letter to Families*, which compares the natural
family with the Church:

> The family itself is the great mystery of God. As the "domestic
> church," it is the *bride of Christ*. The universal Church, and every

---

[3] Pope John Paul II, Annual Holy Thursday Letter to Priests, "Priesthood and Pastoral
Care of the Family," *Origins* 23 (1994), 722.

[4] Pope John Paul II, *Letter to Families*, Vatican Translation (Boston: St. Paul Books &
Media, 1994), no. 23.

particular Church in her, is most immediately revealed as the
bride of Christ in the "domestic church" and in its experience of
love: conjugal love, paternal and maternal love, fraternal love,
the love of a community of persons and of generations.[5]

This text echoes passages from an earlier document, the
Apostolic Exhortation On The Role of the Christian Family in the
Modern World (*Familiaris Consortio*), in which the Pope also
speaks of the family as a revelation of the Church: "The Christian
family constitutes a specific revelation and realization of ecclesial
communion, and for this reason too it can and should be called
'the domestic Church.'"[6] The Pope also mentions again the variety of interpersonal relationships that exist in the family, and
which find their counterpart in the Church:

> In matrimony and in the family a complex of interpersonal
> relationships is set up–married life, fatherhood and mother-
> hood, filiation and fraternity–through which each human person
> is introduced into the "human family" and into the "family of
> God," which is the Church.[7]

The loving relationships within the family serve as a model for
relationships within the Church:[8] "Thanks to love within the
family, the Church can and ought to take on a more homelike or

---

[5] *Ibid.*, no. 19, original emphasis.

[6] Pope John Paul II, *Familiaris Consortio*, Vatican Translation (Boston: St. Paul Books &
Media, 1981), no. 21, citing LG 11 and AA 11. The Pope later explains that "we
must examine the many profound bonds linking the Church and the Christian family
and establishing the family as a 'Church in miniature' (*Ecclesia domestica*), in such a
way that in its own way the family is a living image and historical representation of
the mystery of the Church" (no. 49).

[7] *Ibid.*, no. 15. In his annual "Message for World Mission Sunday" given during the
International Year of the Family, the Pope wrote: "Christ himself chose a human fami ly
as the place for his incarnation and preparation for the mission entrusted to him by
the heavenly Father. Furthermore, he founded a new family, the Church, as a prolon
gation of his universal action of service. Church and family, therefore, in view of
Christ's mission, have mutual bonds and converging purposes" (May 22, 1994).

[8] For example, in an Allocution to Roman seminarians (June 24, 1939), Pope Pius XII
expressed the relationship between the pope and seminarians in familial terms: "It is
false to distinguish the juridical Church from the Church of charity. There is no such

family dimension, developing a more human and fraternal style of relationships."[9]

The Catechism links the natural family and the family of the Church through the Holy Family of Jesus, Mary, and Joseph (cf. Catechism, nos. 1655-56).[10] This link between the Holy Family of Nazareth and the family of the Church finds classical expression in the Encyclical On Devotion to St. Joseph (*Quamquam Pluries*) by Pope Leo XIII:

> Now the divine home which Joseph governed as with the authority of a father contained the first fruits of the infant Church. Just as the Most Blessed Virgin is the Mother of Jesus Christ, so she is the Mother of all Christians whom she brought forth on the Mount of Calvary in the midst of the supreme sufferings of the Redeemer. Jesus Christ, too, is, as it were, the first-born among Christians who, by adoption and redemption, are his brothers. Such are the reasons why the Blessed Patriarch regards as being confided to him in a special manner the multitude of Christians who compose the Church, that is to say, this immense family, spread throughout the world, over which, since he is the Spouse of Mary and the Father of Christ, he possesses, as it were, a paternal authority. It is therefore natural and very proper that St. Joseph, just as he once provided for the needs of the family at Nazareth and surrounded it with his holy protection, should now shelter, under his heavenly patronage, the Church of Christ and defend her.[11]

---

distinction; the Church which was founded juridically, whose head is the Pontiff, is also the Church of Christ, the Church of charity, the worldwide family of Christians. Let those sentiments which in a true Christian family closely unite father with sons and sons with father reign between Us and you" *Papal Teachings: The Church,* arranged by the Benedictine Monks of Solesmes, trans. E. O'Gorman, R.S.C.J. (Boston: St. Paul Editions, 1962), no. 952; cf. no. 1338.

[9] *Familiaris Consortio*, no. 64. In his 1994 Holy Thursday Letter, the Pope repeats this call: "The Church, in fidelity to the will of Christ, is striving to become ever more a 'family,' and the Apostolic See is committed to encouraging this growth" *Origins* 23 (1994), 722.

[10] The Catechism also emphasizes that the supernatural family of the Church plays an important role in instructing those preparing to have a natural family, indicating that the Church is indispensable for the passing on of "family values" (cf. Catechism, no. 1632).

[11] Pope Leo XIII, Encyclical Letter On Devotion to St. Joseph *Quamquam Pluries* (1889), quoted in *Papal Teachings: The Church*, no. 503.

The analogy between the Church and the family is not a recent discovery, but can also be found in the early Church. John Zizioulas, an Orthodox theologian, writes that the Christians of the early centuries transferred "to the Church the terminology which is used of the family."[12]

The Church as a Family

The Catechism, in its very first paragraph, speaks of God's plan to unite all mankind into the unity of His family, the Church (Catechism, no. 1; cf. nos. 541-42). This plan unfolds through salvation history: "This 'family of God' is gradually formed and takes shape during the stages of human history, in keeping with the Father's plan" (Catechism, no. 759).[13] The Church develops as "the building of God. . . . This edifice has many names to describe it: the house of God in which his family dwells; the household of God in the Spirit" (LG 6; cf. 1 Cor. 3:9; Eph. 2:19, 22; 1 Tim. 3:15).

The Second Vatican Council is rich in its teaching on the Church as the Family of God.[14] Moral theologian Germain Grisez summarizes the Council's perspective:

> Vatican II speaks often of the Church as the "People of God" (see LG 9-17). This expression, rooted in the Old Testament in which Israel is God's chosen people, can be helpful, but it also suggests the limitation of intimate communion before the fullness of God's revelation in our Lord Jesus. Another expression, which the Council also uses, is more suggestive of intimacy: "family of God." The supreme exemplar of the unity of the

---

[12] John D. Zizioulas, *Being as Communion* (Crestwood, NY: St. Vladimir's Seminary Press, 1993), 56-57.

[13] In the fullness of time, the Church of God became a universal family. "The Church of God, by a wondrous act of Divine Providence, was so fashioned as to become in the fullness of time an immense family which embraces all men" Pope Pius XI, Encyclical Letter On St. Josephat *Ecclesiam Dei* (1923), no. 1, in Claudia Carlen, ed. *The Papal Encyclicals* (1740-1981) (Raleigh, NC: McGrath Publishing Company, 1981).

[14] Augustin Cardinal Bea remarks that an important element of the teaching of Vatican II, drawn from the biblical and liturgical movements, "is the doctrine that God makes men *members of his own family*" James Brand, trans., *The Church and Mankind* (Chicago: Franciscan Herald Press, 1967), 22.

Church is the divine family, the Trinity (see UR 2). Priests "gather God's family together as a brotherhood of living unity, and lead it through Christ and in the Spirit to God the Father" (PO 6). In Jesus, the human family is called to be the family of God (see GS 32, 40, and 92). The unity of the family of God's children strengthens and perfects the unity of the human family (see GS 40, 42, and 43).

Because human persons are not naturally children of God, it requires a second birth of the Holy Spirit for them to become so (see Jn. 3:3-8). Without at all lessening the realism of the relationship, this rebirth can be considered adoptive incorporation into the divine family; by it we share the image of the eternal Son, and he becomes the firstborn of many brothers (see Rom. 8:14-15, 29). God's adopted children share in his Spirit, whose presence is a pledge of all the divine good to which they are heirs (see Rom. 8:14-17; Gal. 4:6-7; Eph. 1:13-14).[15]

Since the day of Pentecost, in these "last days," the time of the Church (cf. Catechism, no. 732), the Church continues Christ's mission of gathering all mankind into one family. Indeed, the Church

travels the same journey as all mankind and shares the same earthly lot with the world: it is to be a leaven and, as it were, the soul of human society in its renewal by Christ and transformation into the family of God (GS 40).

A person who enters the Church by faith and Baptism becomes a disciple of Christ. By doing the will of the Father in heaven, he forms part of Jesus' "true family" (cf. Mt. 12:49). "Becoming a disciple of Jesus means accepting the invitation to belong to *God's family*" (Catechism, no. 2233, original emphasis). If after Baptism the person falls away from the Church, then by repentance and conversion he returns like the prodigal son "to God and to the bosom of his family, which is the Church" (Catechism, no. 1439).

---

[15] Germain Grisez, *Christian Moral Principles*, vol. 1 of *The Way of the Lord Jesus* (Chicago: Franciscan Herald Press, 1983), 463-64.

The Church Family:
From the Small-Scale to the Large-Scale

The Family of God image can be applied to the Church at any level, from the domestic "small-scale Church" to the universal "large-scale Church."[16]

> [T]he great family which is the Church . . . finds concrete expression in the diocesan and the parish family, in ecclesial basic communities and in movements of the apostolate[.] . . . No one is without a family in this world: the Church is a home and family for everyone.[17]

At the parish level, priests, who represent in a certain sense the bishop in each local assembly, "assemble the family of God as a brotherhood fired with a single ideal" (LG 28). "In the name of the bishop they gather the family of God as a brotherhood endowed with the spirit of unity and lead it in Christ through the Spirit to God the Father" (PO 6). Priests should "unite their efforts and combine their resources under the leadership of the bishops and the Supreme Pontiff . . . so that all mankind may be led into the unity of the family of God" (LG 28).

At the diocesan level, the bishop who governs a particular Church—a "diocesan family" (CD 34)—is sent "by the Father to govern his family" and to promote the welfare of his subjects "as of his very own children" (LG 27; cf. CD 16). Family ties also "ought to exist between local Churches, as between sisters" (UR 14).

At the universal level, the Church is a family with the pope as the father figure. The "largest-scale" Church family is even larger than the entire Pilgrim Church on earth, because it includes the Church Suffering and the Church Triumphant. It includes those "brothers who are in the glory of heaven or who are yet being purified after their death," thus embracing all

---

[16] Cf. *Familiaris Consortio*, no. 48.
[17] *Ibid.*, no. 85.

"who are sons of God and form one family in Christ" (LG 51; cf. Heb. 3:6; Catechism, no. 959).

The Family of God in Sacred Scripture

Even a cursory reading of the New Testament reveals a plethora of texts that use familial terminology to describe the relationships of Christians to God and to one another in the Church. "God sent forth his Son . . . so that we might receive adoption as sons" and cry out "Abba! Father" (Gal. 4:4-6; cf. Rom. 8:14-17). Christians are truly "children of God" (Jn. 1:12; 1 Jn. 3:1-2), brothers and sisters and mothers of Christ (cf. Mk. 3:35), who is "the first-born among many brethren" (Rom. 8:29; cf. Heb. 1:6, 2:17). Jesus teaches His followers to call His Father "Our Father" (Mt. 6:9). Christians refer to one another as "the brethren" (e.g., Acts 15:23). The Church herself is described as the Bride of Christ and the mother of Christians (cf. Eph. 5:32; Rev. 12:17; 21:2; Gal. 4:26). Clearly, the New Testament authors, inspired by the Holy Spirit, made much use of familial imagery to describe the new Christian life. A closer look at the New Testament is needed, however, in order to see how to weave together all of the texts that use familial terminology into an image of the Church as the Family of God.

In the words of Saint Jerome, Christ the Son of God came to earth to institute a new family.[18] Jesus transforms Israel, the People of God of the Old Covenant, into the Church, the People of God of the New Covenant. Protestant exegete Joachim Jeremias explains that "Jesus speaks constantly of a new people of God that he is gathering, and with a wealth of pictures."[19] Jeremias concludes that Jesus' favorite image for the new People of God is that of the family:

---

[18] Saint Jerome, *Epistle 22*, no. 21 (*Patrologia Latina*, vol. 22, 408).

[19] Joachim Jeremias, *New Testament Theology* (New York: Charles Scribner's Sons, 1971), 168. Among the "wealth of pictures," Jeremias mentions and gives scriptural citations for the images of the flock, the throng of wedding guests, God's planting, the net, God's building, the city of God, and the members of the New Covenant (168-69).

His favourite of all the images for the new people of God is
the comparison of the community of salvation with the eschatological family of God. It is the substitute for the earthly
family which Jesus himself and the disciples accompanying
him have had to give up (Mk. 10:29 ff). In the eschatological
family God is the father (Mt. 23:9), Jesus the master of the
house, his followers the other occupants (Mt. 10:25). The
older women who hear his word are his mothers, the men and
youths his brothers (cf. Mk. 3:34). And at the same time they
are all the little ones, the children, indeed the νήπιοι of the
family (Mt. 11:25) whom Jesus addresses as children,
although in age they are adult. The family of God appears
above all in table-fellowship, which is an anticipation of the
meal of salvation at the consummation. In another passage,
Jesus extends the framework of the family of God more widely, beyond the circle of his followers: he calls all those who
are in need, oppressed or in desolation his brothers (Mt.
25:40). In so doing he includes them in the family of God.[20]

It is significant that Jeremias notes that the "family of God
appears above all in table-fellowship." In a footnote following
this sentence, Jeremias cites a number of Gospel texts, including
the narrative of the institution of the Eucharist at the Last Supper
(Mk. 14:22-25). The text from Mark and its parallels (Mt. 26:26-
29; Lk. 22:14-20; 1 Cor. 11:23-26) are significant because, in the
institution of the Eucharist, Jesus establishes the (new) covenant
in His blood. The claim proposed here is that the covenant is the
key reality that makes the "family of God [appear] above all in
[Eucharistic] table-fellowship." The covenant is also the key idea
which links the People of God in the Old Testament and the
People of God in the New Testament.[21] The covenant is the con-
necting thread that weaves together the texts that use familial
terminology into the image of the Church as the Family of God.

---

[20] *Ibid.*, 169-70.
[21] For an Old Testament example linking "covenant" with "table-fellowship" and the
People/Family of God, see Ex. 24:8-11.

Understanding the nature of "covenant" is therefore essential for understanding the Church as the Family of God. While "covenant" is a complex idea with many aspects (e.g., legal, juridical, cultic), one aspect of interest here is the *relational* aspect. A covenant between God and man, or between a group of men, establishes a relationship between them analogous to natural kinship relationships. Speaking of the covenant between God and Israel, Yves Congar writes that the "covenant binds the people and God into a kind of mystical kinship."[22] Dennis J. McCarthy, one of the leading covenant scholars of the twentieth century, explains the nature of a covenant as follows:

> There is no doubt that covenants, even treaties, were thought of as establishing a kind of quasi-familial unity. In the technical vocabulary of these documents a superior partner was called "father," his inferior "son," and equal partners were "brothers."[23]

A fuller scriptural understanding of the image of the Church as the Family of God requires an exposition of the series of covenants made in the Old Testament leading up to the new covenant in Christ. Such an exposition is given in the last major section of this chapter, in which a systematic essay is presented that highlights the development of the Church from the perspective of salvation history.

Before moving on, however, let us examine the New Testament text that perhaps most directly presents the Church as the Family of God: "So then you are no longer strangers and sojourners, but you are fellow citizens with the saints and *members of the household of God* (οἰκεῖοι τοῦ θεοῦ) (Eph. 2:19). The phrase "members of the household of God" recalls Old Testament references to the covenants with the People of God,

---

[22] Yves Congar, O.P., *The Mystery of the Church*, trans. A. V. Littledale (Baltimore: Helicon Press, 1965), 16.

[23] Dennis J. McCarthy, S.J., *Old Testament Covenant: A Survey of Current Opinions* (Richmond: John Knox Press, 1972), 33.

the house of Israel (e.g., the Davidic covenant in 2 Sam. 7:8-16; 1 Chron. 17:7-14). J. Goetzmann explains the levels of meaning contained in the Hebrew and Greek words for "house" (Heb. *bayit*, Gk. *oikos*):

> Both words denote the building (the house, and also palace or temple). But because Heb., like Gk., has no word for the small social unit which we call the family, *bayit* (and hence LXX *oikos*) acquired, in addition to its original meaning of dwelling place, that of household (those bound together by sharing the same dwelling place), in a broader sense that of family and clan, and even that of the still bigger tribal unit (e.g., the house of Judah).[24]

Therefore, the New Testament passages that refer to the Church as the "house of God" can be interpreted as supporting the view of the Church as the Family of God (cf. 1 Tim. 3:15; Heb. 3:1-6, 1 Pet. 4:17). In Eph. 2:19, rather than simply "house of God," the text says "members of the household of God" (cf. Gal. 6:10 "those who are of the household of faith"), supporting more clearly the image of the family. Thus, Christians are members of the household of the Family of God.[25]

The Family of God in the History of Salvation

This section follows the Catechism's outline of the revelation of the Church by examining her origin in the Holy Trinity and her gradual unveiling in human history (cf. Catechism, nos. 758-69).

---

[24] J. Goetzmann, "οἶκος" *The New International Dictionary of New Testament Theology*, 3 vols., ed. C. Brown (Grand Rapids: Zondervan Publishing House, 1975-1978), vol. 2, 247. Note that the variety of meanings associated with the Hebrew and Greek words for "house" (e.g., family, temple, and kingdom dynasty) permits the linking of the image of the Church as the Family of God (Eph. 2:19) with the image of the Church as the temple of the Holy Spirit (Eph. 2:21-22) and the Church as the kingdom of God (1 Pet. 2:5, 9).

[25] Cf. O. Michel, "οἰκεῖος," *Theological Dictionary of the New Testament*, 10 vols., eds. G. Kittel and G. Friedrich (Grand Rapids: Eerdmans Publishing Company, 1964-76), vol. 5, 134. Cf. Goetzmann, 251.

The Family of God Rooted in the Trinitarian Communion

The first paragraph of the Catechism states that God is infinitely perfect and blessed in Himself. God is not "alone"; God is the Trinity: one God in three Persons—Father, Son, and Holy Spirit—a communion of persons really distinct from one another, the distinction residing solely in the relationships which relate them to one another (cf. Catechism, nos. 254-55). These relationships are familial relationships: The Father loves the Son, the Son loves the Father, the Holy Spirit is the bond of love between the Father and the Son. These familial terms are not projections of human concepts onto God. Any fatherhood in the created order—by nature or by grace (cf. 1 Cor. 4:15)—is derived from the fatherhood of God: "For this reason I bow my knees before the Father (πατέρα), from whom every family (πατριά)[26] in heaven and on earth is named" (Eph. 3:14-15). Hence, only God can be called Father in the primary sense of the word (cf. Mt. 23:9); all other fathers are called so analogously. These familial terms for God are not gender terms but rather relational terms. They indicate that the being of God is relational; being means communion.

From the communion of love in the Trinity stems God's plan to communicate freely the glory of His blessed life. This plan "unfolds in the work of creation, the whole history of salvation after the fall, and the missions of the Son and the Spirit, which are continued in the mission of the Church" (Catechism, no. 257). The Trinity is thus the source and model for the natural communion of mankind in the family and for the supernatural communion in the Church.[27] Concerning the mystery of the unity of the Church, Vatican II's Decree on Ecumenism explains that the "highest exemplar and source of this mystery is the unity, in the Trinity of Persons, of one God, the Father and the Son in the Holy Spirit" (UR 2). "The universal Church is seen to be 'a people

---

[26] The Greek word πατριά can also be translated as fatherhood or paternity.

[27] Cf. Catechism, no. 2205. *The Letter to Families* says that *"the primordial model of the family is to be sought in God himself,* in the Trinitarian mystery of his life. The divine 'We' is the eternal pattern of the human 'we,' especially of that 'we' formed by the man and the woman created in the divine image and likeness" (no. 6, original emphasis).

brought into unity from the unity of the Father, the Son and the Holy Spirit'" (LG 4, quoting St. Cyprian).

Now it is clear how the communion of Father and Son in the Trinity is the source and exemplar for fatherhood and sonship in the human family and in the Church family. But it is not clear how the Holy Spirit relates to these families. Speculation about this relationship requires caution; it must be remembered that in the analogies between God and creatures, there is always a greater dissimilarity than similarity. Some attempts have been made by orthodox theologians and canonized saints, however, to understand the Holy Spirit in terms of a familial analogy. It may be useful, therefore, to consider cautiously such ideas and see what insight they may provide.

Applying the familial analogy to the Trinity, many theologians compare the Father, Son, and Spirit to a father, mother, and child, respectively.[28] Since this triad does not bring out the Father-Son relationship very well, other theologians compare the Father, Son, and Spirit to a father, child, and mother, respectively. In these models, the Holy Spirit is compared to a mother—in particular, a virginal mother. Fr. Manteau-Bonamy, in explaining the Marian teachings of Saint Maximilian Kolbe, describes the Holy Spirit "as the divine source of all motherhood."[29] Matthias Scheeben, a nineteenth-century German theologian, explains as follows:

> As the mother is the bond of love between father and child, so in God the Holy Spirit is the bond of love between the Father and the Son; and as she brings forth the child in unity of nature with the father by transmitting the nature from the father to the child, so the Holy Spirit manifests the unity of nature between the Father and the Son, not of course by transmitting the divine nature to the Son, but because He Himself is the fruit of their mutual unity and love.[30]

---

[28] Bertrand De Margerie, *The Christian Trinity in History* (Petersham, MA: St. Bede's Publications, 1982), 274-92.

[29] H.M. Manteau-Bonamy, O.P., *Immaculate Conception and the Holy Spirit: The Marian Teachings of St. Maximilian Kolbe* (Libertyville, IL: Prow Books / Franciscan Marytown Press, 1977), 56.

[30] Matthias Scheeben, *The Mysteries of Christianity*, trans. Cyril Vollert, S.J. (St. Louis: B. Herder Book Co., 1946), 183.

Using the concept of virginal motherhood, Scheeben makes an analogical connection between the Holy Spirit, Mary, and the Church.

> [Mary is] the Virgin of virgins, who was made a mother in a supernatural manner by the power of the same Holy Spirit and who, through the Holy Spirit and with Him, is the bond of love between the Father and His Son become man, just as He is between the Father and the Son in the Godhead. And such too, modeled upon her, is the Church which, animated by the Holy Spirit, is in Him and through Him the spiritual, virginal mother of all those whom in the power of the Holy Spirit she presents to God the Father as His children, and incorporates in the incarnate Son as members of His mystical body.[31]

The Church—Prefigured Since the Origin of the World

The communion of love which is the Trinity is manifested in the entire divine plan of creation and salvation. God's wise and loving plan from all eternity was to create man so that he could share in His divine life as a son in the Son (cf. Catechism, no. 356). God created the world "for the sake of communion with his divine life" (Catechism, no. 760). Therefore, the Church herself was "[a]lready present in figure at the beginning of the world" (LG 2; cf. Catechism, no. 759), anticipating the communion with the divine life brought by Christ (cf. Catechism, no. 760).

The high point of God's creation is the creation of man and woman in His image and likeness (Gen. 1:27). God did not create man as a solitary being, but as a social being. The communion of man and woman, who were created for each other, reflects the Trinity (cf. Gen. 2:18-25; Catechism, no. 372). In this regard, Pope John Paul II comments:

> Being a person in the image and likeness of God thus also involves existing in a relationship, in relation to the other "I." This is a prelude to the definitive self-revelation of the Triune God: a living unity in the communion of the Father, Son and Holy Spirit. . . . [M]an and woman, created as a "unity of the two" in their common humanity, are called to live in a commu-

---

[31] *Ibid.*, 188.

nion of love, and in this way to mirror in the world the communion of love that is in God, through which the Three Persons love
each other in the intimate mystery of the one divine life. . . . This
"unity of the two," which is a sign of interpersonal
communion, *shows that the creation of man* is also marked by
a certain likeness to the divine communion (*"communio"*).[32]

The analogy between the communion in the Trinity and in
creation can also be extended to the Church. Scheeben explains:

> Scripture says that God formed the woman out of the rib taken
> from the side of Adam; the Fathers teach that Christ formed
> the Church out of the water and blood streaming from His
> side: in like manner we may say that the Father and the Son
> have taken and formed the Holy Spirit from their side, their
> heart. And as Eve can, in a figurative sense, be called simply
> the rib of Adam, since she was formed from the rib of Adam,
> St. Methodius goes so far as to assert that the Holy Spirit is the
> *costa Verbi* ["rib of the Word"], particularly since He not only
> has His origin from the side of the Logos, but remains there,
> and is thence communicated to creatures in order to form the
> bride of Christ from Him.[33]

The first woman, Eve, is formed from the rib of the first
Adam, the "son of God" (Lk. 3:38). The Church is formed from
the side of Christ, the second Adam, the Son of God (cf.
Catechism, no. 766).

Man and woman are called to live a familial communion,
established in marriage, where "the two become one" (Gen.
2:24). The communion of love between man and woman is life-
giving: Adam and Eve become the parents of the whole human
family (cf. Gen. 3:20; Wis. 10:1; Tob. 8:6). God created the human
family as one united family descending from our first parents. This
means that all men are truly brothers.[34] Through the unity of the

---

[32] Pope John Paul II, Apostolic Letter On the Dignity and Vocation of *Women Mulieris
Dignitatem*, Vatican Translation (Boston: St. Paul Books & Media, 1995), no. 7, original emphasis.
[33] Scheeben, 184-85.

human family, God has thus woven into the very fabric of creation His plan for uniting all people into His family, the Church.

The Church–Prepared in the Old Covenant

Because of the Fall and the subsequent spread of sin, the communion of men with God, and among themselves, was destroyed (cf. Catechism, no. 761). The natural unity of the human race was not destroyed, but the harmony among men that should have resulted from this natural unity was lost. The restoration of "family communion" would come about only by God's plan of salvation in Christ through the Church. "The gathering together of the Church is, as it were, God's reaction to the chaos provoked by sin" (Catechism, no. 761). God's plan for the Church, then, is to restore at a supernatural level the communion of the members of the human family with God and with each other.

This reunion in the Church is prepared through a series of covenants in the Old Testament. The covenant with Noah (Gen. 9:8-17) is God's attempt to "restart" the human family as a unity (cf. Catechism, no. 56). Cardinal Ratzinger comments on this covenant:

> This unity of all men is shown twice: once in the creation account, in which God formed "Adam" (that is, mankind), the root of all the other men to come, in his likeness; and a second time in Noah, with whom a new race of men is started after the catastrophe of the first race. The genealogies of Genesis 10 endeavor to prove in detail that the whole of historical humanity owes its existence to God's saving covenant of grace with Noah and can live only under the constant care of God assured in that covenant.[35]

---

[34] Cf. Catechism, no. 361. Vatican II speaks of the unity of the human race in several texts. For example, "In his fatherly care for all of us, God desired that all men should form one family and deal with each other in a spirit of brotherhood" (GS 24). "All men form but one community. This is so because all stem from the one stock which God created to people the entire earth (cf. Acts 17:26), and also because all share a common destiny, namely God" (NA 1; cf. Catechism, no. 360).

Despite the second attempt at unity through the covenant with
Noah, sin continues to spread, scattering the members of the
human family across the face of the earth (cf. Gen. 11:1-9).

The preparation for the gathering together of the Church
then continues with the covenants with Abraham (Gen. 15:18;
17:1-14), Moses (Ex. 24:8), and David (2 Sam. 7:12-16; 23:5).
The plan of God through these covenants is to father a growing
and expanding family. Abraham is the head of a tribe (Gen.
14:14), though still childless, when God makes a covenant with
him. The covenant made through Moses is with not one but
twelve tribes, forming the nation of Israel. The covenant with
David forms a kingdom, in which Israel rules over other nations.
The mission given to Israel by its divine election can be understood as one of setting the example as the first-born son—and
therefore the priestly nation (cf. Ex. 13:1; 19:6)—for all the
other children-nations (Deut. 32:8-9), to lead them to the Lord
and teach them His ways (cf. Is. 2:2-5; Mic. 4:1-4). Solomon is
given wisdom, so that all people can come to know the name of
the Lord (cf. 1 Kings 8:41-43; 10:24).

Because of its infidelity to the covenant, Israel failed to carry
out its mission. The prophets then announced a new covenant,
unlike the previous covenants (cf. Jer. 31:31-34). But until the
establishment of the New Covenant, the law remained as an
instruction for the heirs of the promise (cf. Gal. 3:19). "[T]he
heir, as long as he is a child, is no better than a slave, though he
is the owner of all the estate; but he is under guardians and
trustees until the date set by the father" (Gal. 4:1-2).

---

[35] Joseph Cardinal Ratzinger, *The Meaning of Christian Brotherhood* (San Francisco:
Ignatius Press, 1993), 9-10.

The Church—Instituted by Jesus Christ

In the fullness of time, the Word of God "became flesh and dwelt among us" (Jn. 1:14) "so that we might receive adoption as sons" crying out "Abba! Father!" (Gal. 4:5-6; cf. Rom. 8:14-17). We become children of God (Jn. 1:12; 1 Jn. 3:1-2), with Christ the "first-born among many brethren" (Rom. 8:29), together in the "household of God" (Eph. 2:19). Christ instituted this New Covenant, establishing an international or universal covenant family: the Church. The New Covenant thus fulfills and transcends the covenants of the Old Testament. All people are called to be in this New Covenant family; it is no longer just for those belonging to a particular tribe, nation, or kingdom. The covenant family has grown to be universal or *catholic*.

In this New Covenant family, "vertical" communion with the Trinity is established through one's incorporation into Christ, by which one shares in His sonship, in His filial relationship to the Father. This process which restores communion with God is called *justification*, which includes the remission of sins, sanctification, and the renewal of the inner man (cf. Catechism, no. 2019). Hence, justification entails the restoration of family standing as a child of God, a true transformation and infusion of grace. The "instrumental cause" through which we receive this infusion of grace is the Sacrament of Baptism.

In His New Covenant, Christ does not save us as isolated individuals (cf. LG 9; GS 32). Rather, He establishes a "horizontal" communion with all of the brothers and sisters in Christ throughout history.

> Whoever becomes the son of this Father no longer stands alone. Entrance into this sonship is entrance into the great family of those who are sons along with us. It creates a relationship. To draw near to Christ means always to draw near to all those of whom he wants to make a single body. The ecclesial dimension of baptism is already apparent, then, in the trinitarian formula. It is not just an afterthought but has been introduced into the

concept of God by Christ. To be born of God means to be born into the whole Christ, Head and members.[36]

Both the "vertical" communion and the "horizontal" communion are expressed in the first two words of the prayer that Jesus taught us to pray: "Our Father."

In the Church instituted by Jesus Christ, there is a visible structure and hierarchical organization that follow from the covenant family model. In each stage of salvation history, God's family has a visible structure, which is God's provision for unity in His family. Jesus transformed the old People of God by choosing twelve apostles (Mk. 3:14-15) as the patriarchs or father figures of the new Israel (Mt. 19:28; cf. Gal. 6:16; Eph. 2:20). While all twelve apostles form twelve foundations for the new Jerusalem (Rev. 21:14), it is on the foundation rock of Peter, the first of the apostles (Mt. 10:2), that Jesus builds His Church (Mt. 16:18), instructing him to tend the sheep of the flock (Jn. 21:15-19), praying specifically for him that *his* faith may not fail, and entrusting him with the task of strengthening the brethren (Lk. 22:32).

The successor to Peter, the pope, is the earthly father figure for the whole Church: He is *il Papa*. Bishops (ἐπίσκοποι) are the "overseers" in God's household, the Church (1 Tim. 3:5, 15), after the model of Christ, the Pastor of souls (1 Pet. 2:25), who "was faithful over God's house as a son" (Heb. 3:6). Priests are the "elders" (πρεσβύτεροι) (Acts 14:23); that is, they are the elder brothers in the supernatural family. As elder brothers (cf. Ex. 13:1), they are also spiritual fathers (cf. Judg. 17:10), after the model of Christ the High Priest (Heb. 3:1), who is both the "first-born among many brethren" (Rom. 8:29) and the New Adam (cf. Rom. 5:14; 1 Cor. 15:45). The structure with which Jesus endowed His community will remain "until the Kingdom is fully achieved" (Catechism, no. 765; cf. GS 40).

---

[36] Joseph Cardinal Ratzinger, *Principles of Catholic Theology*: Building Stones for a *Fundamental Theology*, trans. Mary Frances McCarthy, S.N.D. (San Francisco: Ignatius Press, 1987), 32-33.

The Church—Manifested by the Holy Spirit

The Church, animated by the Holy Spirit toward the fulfillment of her mission, is "called upon to save and renew every creature, so that all things might be restored in Christ, and so that in him men might form one family and one people of God" (AG 1).

Since all men are not yet in full communion with the Church, it is worthwhile at this point to consider the relationship of non-Catholics to the family of the Church, beginning with non-Catholic Christians. The term "separated brethren" indicates that a real but imperfect familial communion exists between Catholics and non-Catholics who have been properly baptized (cf. UR 3; Catechism, no. 838).[37] Non-Catholic Christians and Catholics are "brothers," separated by the fact that they belong to different fraternal communities.[38] "The division among Christians is a serious reality which impedes the very work of Christ."[39] We should therefore all be spurred on to work for the unity Christ desires (Jn. 17:20-21):

> [O]ur thoughts go out to those brothers and communities not yet living in full communion with us; yet we are united by our worship of the Father, the Son, and the Holy Spirit and the bonds of love. We are also mindful that the unity of Christians is today awaited and longed for by many non-believers. For the more this unity is realized in truth and charity under the powerful impulse of the Holy Spirit, the more it will be a harbinger of unity and peace throughout the whole world. Let us, then, join our forces and modify our methods in a way suitable and effective today for achieving this lofty goal, and let us pattern ourselves daily more and more after the spirit of the Gospel and work together in a spirit of brotherhood to serve the human family which has been called to become in Christ Jesus the family of the sons of God (GS 92).

---

[37] Pope John Paul II, in his Encyclical Letter On Commitment to Ecumenism *Ut Unum Sint*, writes that "the very expression *separated brethren* tends to be replaced today by expressions which more readily evoke the deep communion—linked to the baptismal character—which the Spirit fosters in spite of historical and canonical divisions" Vatican Translation (Boston: St. Paul Books & Media, 1995), no. 42, original emphasis.

[38] Cf. Ratzinger, *Brotherhood*, 91.

[39] Pope Paul VI, Apostolic Exhortation On Evangelization in the Modern World *Evangelii Nuntiandi*, Vatican Translation (Boston: St. Paul Books & Media, 1975), no. 77.

We next consider the relationship of non-Christians to the family of the Church. This is an important consideration because it addresses a potential objection to the understanding of the Church as the Family of God. The objection can be expressed as follows: The mission of the Church is to the whole human race; it is a universal mission. An understanding of the Church as the Family of God seems to forfeit this universality since a barrier is established between Christians and non-Christians, between those who are members of the family and those who are not. In reviewing what we have considered concerning the covenants established throughout salvation history, we see that the difficulty between family and universality begins with the covenant with Abraham. This covenant introduces a tension as the children of Abraham are separated "as a special family from the great human family of the children of Adam (or, rather, of Noah)."[40] How is the reunion of the whole human family to occur if some of the children are elected through special covenants while the others are seemingly rejected?

The answer to the objection is found in what Ratzinger calls the biblical "theology of two brothers." "At important points in salvation history there appear pairs of brothers, the election or rejection of each of whom is strangely connected. These are, in particular, Cain and Abel (and Cain and Seth), Ishmael and Isaac, Esau and Jacob."[41] The term "brother" may also refer to a collective entity: The nation of Israel, among all the brother nations, is God's elect—Israel is God's "first-born son" (Ex. 4:22). In the New Covenant established by Christ, the Church becomes the new Israel (cf. Gal. 6:16), the bearer of God's election. There still remains a boundary between Christians and non-Christians, between the brotherly community or family and those "outside" the family. While there is a boundary, there is an openness to

---

[40] Ratzinger, *Brotherhood*, 10.
[41] *Ibid.*, 11.

those "outside." The brotherhood of Christ "*is not yet* universal, but it seeks to become so. Men, in general, *are not yet* brothers in Christ, but they can and must become so."[42] The original, natural unity of the human family allows us to apply the "theology of two brothers" collectively to the Church and to the non-Church. Herein lies the answer to the objection between universality and family:

> In relation to Christian brotherhood this means that, however important it is for the Church to grow into the unity of a single brotherhood, she must always remember that she is only one of two sons, one brother beside another, and that her mission is not to condemn the wayward brother, but to save him. The Church, it is true, must unify herself to form a strong inner brotherhood in order to be truly *one* brother. But she does not seek to be *one* brother in order to finally shut herself off from the other; rather she seeks to be one brother because only in this way can she fulfill her task toward the other, living for whom is the deepest meaning of her existence, which itself is grounded wholly in the vicarious existence of Jesus Christ.[43]

The mission of the Church toward the "other brother" is accomplished, according to Ratzinger, through missionary activity, through works of charity, and through suffering.[44] "The last and highest mission of the Christian in relation to nonbelievers is to suffer for them and in their place as the Master did,"[45] continuing in salvation history the mystery of vicarious election and vicarious rejection.

> It is when [the Church] is called to suffer for others that she achieves her highest mission: the exchange of fate with the wayward brother and thus his secret restoration to full sonship and full brotherhood.[46]

---

[42] *Ibid.*, 33, original emphasis.
[43] *Ibid.*, 80, original emphasis.
[44] Cf. *ibid.*, 75-84.
[45] *Ibid.*, 83.
[46] *Ibid.*, 84.

The Church—Fully Completed in Glory

The Church on earth is on pilgrimage toward her heavenly homeland. At the glorious return of Christ at the end of time, the Church will reach her fulfillment as the new Jerusalem, the Bride of the Lamb (Rev. 21:2). At that moment, "all the just from the time of Adam, 'from Abel, the just one, to the last of the elect' will be gathered together with the Father in the universal Church" (LG 2), that is, in the universal Family of God.

Being a Roman Catholic is a family matter. As I discovered in my own life, however, it is not simply a matter of celebrating one's own natural family, or the national family of one's heritage. Rather, to be Catholic means to be a member of a universal family, a family that transcends borders and generations, space and time. To be a Catholic means to be a member of the Family of God, joined together by bonds of grace that are even stronger than human relationships. To be a Catholic means to desire that all human beings become members of your family and to work for that goal by communicating the Gospel of Jesus Christ—the "gospel of the family"—to the whole human family.

To be a Catholic means to have a Mother named Mary. Mary is the Mother of God, Mother of the Holy Family, and the Mother of the Church. She is the New Eve, the mother of all the living (cf. Gen. 3:20). She is the mother of all beloved disciples (cf. Jn. 19:27), of all who bear testimony to Jesus (cf. Rev. 12:17). Let us pray with the whole Family of God and with Mary, our Mother, for a new Pentecost:

> O Mary, mother of God,
> mother of the church, . . .
> [o]n this eve of a new Pentecost, . . .
> in communion with the Holy Father,
> we unite ourselves to you,
> so that the outpouring of
> the Holy Spirit . . .
> may make of us the
> church family of the Father,
> the brotherhood of the Son,

[and] the image of the Trinity. . . .
Amen!"[47]

Fr. Pablo T. Gadenz is a Roman Catholic priest ordained in 1996 for the Diocese of Trenton, New Jersey. He is currently assigned to Saint Ann's Church in Keansburg. He holds electrical engineering degrees from Princeton University and Columbia University, and worked for Bell Laboratories for three years. He prepared for the priesthood at Franciscan University of Steubenville and Saint Charles Borromeo Seminary in Philadelphia.

---

[47] Synod for Africa, "Final Message of the Synod for Africa," *Origins* 24 (1994), 11.

CHAPTER V

Justification as Divine Sonship

Is "Faith Alone" Justifiable?

RICHARD A. WHITE

Introduction

Hazel Motes, the hero of Flannery O'Connor's novel *Wise Blood*, once stated in a moment of self-reflection, "Nobody with a good car needs to be justified."[1] I'll let the reader judge whether Hazel had a good car:

> It was a high rat-colored machine with large thin wheels and bulging headlights. . . . [O]ne door was tied on with a rope and . . . it had an oval window in the back. . . . Inside it was a dull greenish dust-color. The back seat was missing but it had a two-by-four stretched across the seat frame to sit on. There were dark green fringed window shades on the two side-back windows. . . . The car rode with a high growling noise. . . .[2]

Hazel's car stands as a poignant image of the soul of every sinner who refuses to acknowledge the need for justification. It's not a

---

[1] Flannery O'Connor, *Collected Works* (New York: Library of America, 1988), 64.
[2] *Ibid.*, 38, 40-41.

pretty picture! While some of us may have good cars, we all need to be justified.

But if we need justification, what is it and how do we get it? In this chapter, I am going to focus on how justification is treated in the New Testament. Keep in mind, though, that for many years the meaning of justification has been a major point of controversy between Catholics and Protestants. Indeed, disagreement over justification substantially contributed to the Protestant Reformation of the sixteenth century. Before turning to justification in the Bible, therefore, it will be helpful to review how the two sides have presented it.

Protestants emphasize that justification takes place by *faith alone* (*sola fide*). When we trust in Jesus and have faith that He has died and risen to save us from our sins, then we are justified; this means that, in spite of our sinfulness, God *declares* that we are just. That is, though we deserve condemnation and punishment as sinners, God the judge passes down a "not guilty" verdict and forgives our sins. This verdict is given not because we are righteous, but because the perfect righteousness of Christ is imputed (applied externally) to us and accepted by God on our behalf. Thus, justification is a once-and-for-all legal declaration that we are counted innocent before God the judge and that our sins are forgiven. This declaration is distinct from anything that we do—thus good works are excluded—or become.[3] Protestants often criticize Catholics for not adequately coming to grips with this last point.

According to Catholic teaching, what we *do* is related to our justification, but only because of who we become when we are justified, namely, children of God. According to official Church teaching, justification is our becoming sons and daughters of God. The Council of Trent defined justification as "a transition from that state in which a person is born as a child of the first Adam to the state of grace and of adoption as children of God

---

[3] Protestants affirm the reality of our sanctification (becoming holy), but this is a fruit of justification and is thus distinct from it.

through the agency of the second Adam, Jesus Christ our savior."[4] Or as the Catechism puts it, justification "brings about filial adoption so that men become Christ's brethren" and gain "a real share in the life of the only Son" (no. 654).

There are several corollaries to this teaching. First, the gift of divine sonship which is justification is a real participation in Christ's sonship and the life of the Trinity. Thus, we are not only declared sons and daughters of God, but are actually made such, in our very being. Second, justification is totally gratuitous. We cannot earn God's justifying grace any more than a child can earn his birth. And finally, once the child is born, he is expected to grow in maturity, and what he does actually affects his standing in the family. This holds true for our standing in God's family too. So through grace we not only have faith but do good works in love. This is not "works righteousness" (the idea that we can earn our salvation) or justification by faith alone (the Protestant view), but "faith working in love."

Is this what the Bible teaches? In the pages that follow, we will investigate this question. Is the Catholic Church's teaching on justification reflected in Scripture or not? Or is the Protestant doctrine of justification by faith alone justifiable? Because of limitations of time and space, we will confine our treatment primarily to Saint Paul's Epistle to the Romans and to the Epistle of Saint James.[5] Paul and James are the New Testament authors who devote the most time to this theme.

Justification in Paul and James

To begin with, let's consider the New Testament verb "to justify" (*dikaioo* in the Greek). Not surprisingly, Protestants and Catholics often disagree over its meaning. Protestants insist that

---

[4] *Decrees of the Ecumenical Councils,* vol. 2, ed. Norman P. Tanner (London and Washington, DC: Sheed & Ward and Georgetown University Press, 1990).

[5] For an excellent and more exhaustive study of the biblical basis for the Catholic Church's teaching on justification, see Robert A. Sungenis, *Not by Faith Alone: The Biblical Evidence for the Catholic Doctrine of Justification* (Santa Barbara, CA: Queenship Publishing Co., 1997).

dikaioo means "to declare righteous" but *not* "to make righteous." As one Protestant author put it:

> The verb means in general "to declare a person to be just. . . .
> It is to declare forensically that the demands of the law . . . are
> fully satisfied with regard to a person. . . . "To justify" . . . is
> to effect an objective relation, the state of righteousness by a
> judicial sentence. This can be done . . . by imputing to a per-
> son the righteousness of another, that is, by accounting him
> righteous though he is inwardly unrighteous.[6]

According to this view, justification is a once-and-for-all act in
which God declares that we are just. As was mentioned above,
the image is that of a legal courtroom. God is the righteous judge,
we are the guilty criminals, and Christ is the innocent but willing
substitute. Justification is a kind of legal exchange: We get
Christ's righteousness, which is externally imputed to us, and He
gets our punishment. Justification in this sense is not a "making
righteous" but a "declaring righteous." And since this declarato-
ry act is distinct from any ethical quality within us, it must take
place by faith alone.

There is certainly some truth in this view, but it is not the
whole truth. God is a holy judge who demands satisfaction for
sin. But even more, He is a loving Father who makes us His
children. Jesus dies and rises so that we may share in His sonship.
Justification is God the Father's declaring us to be His sons—
seeing in us what He sees in His Son. His judgment, then, is that
of a Father, and is based solely on what He has done in generat-
ing us anew through grace.

There is another point that follows from this. If by justification God *declares* us to be His children, He also *makes* us His
children. For when God's word goes forth to declare something
to be true, it makes it true (cf. Is. 55:10-11). As John Henry
Newman wrote:

---

[6] L. Berkhof, *Systematic Theology* (Grand Rapids, MI: Eerdmans, 1949), 510-11.

God's word, I say, effects what it announces. This is its characteristic all through Scripture. . . . Thus in the beginning He
said, "Let there be light, and there was light." . . . So again in
His miracles, He called Lazarus from the grave and the dead
arose; He said, "Be thou cleansed," and the leprosy departed;
He rebuked the wind and the waves, and they were still; He
commanded the evil spirits, and they fled away. . . . It would
seem, then, in all cases that God's word is the instrument of
His deed. When, then, He solemnly utters the command, "Let
the soul be just," it becomes inwardly just.[7]

Thus, when God declares the person to be righteous, filial
life is really given (cf. 1 Jn. 3:1). To sum up, then, the verb
dikaioo might mean "to declare righteous," but God's declaration is effective and so it also means "to make righteous." God
simultaneously declares us just and makes us His children, so
that justification involves not only forgiveness of sins, but also
bestowal of supernatural life.[8]

Justification in Romans

In his Epistle to the Romans, Saint Paul addresses the theme
of justification in some detail. He informs us of his aim at the
beginning of the letter: "to bring about the *obedience of faith* for
the sake of his name among all the nations" (Rom. 1:5). The term
"obedience of faith" is instructive, for it shows that obedience
and faith are two sides of the same coin; faith requires obedience
and obedience is grounded in faith. He underscores this point by
mentioning the "obedience of faith" at the very end of the epistle

---

[7] John Henry Newman, *Lectures on the Doctrine of Justification*, third ed. (New York:
Longmans, Green, and Co., 1900), 81-82.
[8] As the great Catholic theologian Matthias Scheeben stated, "If the sinner is to be
freed from God's disfavor, it will not at all suffice for God . . . simply to remit the
guilt[.] . . . To forgive the sin fully, God must again confer on man that favor and
grace which He had bestowed on him before he sinned. God must again draw man up
to His bosom as His child, regenerate him to new divine life, and again clothe him
with the garment of His children, the splendor of His own nature and glory" *The
Mysteries of Christianity* (St. Louis: B. Herder Book Co., 1946), 616.

too (Rom. 16:26). Further, in chapter one we are presented with another major theme of Romans:

> For I am not ashamed of the gospel: it is the power of God for salvation to every one who has faith, to the Jew first and also to the Greek. For in it the righteousness of God is revealed through faith for faith; as it is written, "He who through faith is righteous shall live" (Rom. 1:16-17).

Paul gives us two important pieces of information: First, the Gospel is salvation to everyone who believes, not just Jews but Gentiles too; and second, the righteous shall live by faith.

At this point, it is important to recognize that in Romans Paul is combating a group of Jewish Christians called Judaizers. They claimed that they were righteous because they obeyed certain religious obligations, especially circumcision, and that these rituals were necessary for salvation. Paul calls these ceremonial observances "works of the law." One of his major arguments in Romans is that we are justified by faith apart from the "works of the law"—and that the "righteousness of faith" is a reality for Gentiles too. Paul's opponents do not have a special claim to the covenant promises merely because they are physical descendants of Abraham and are circumcised. On the contrary, "He is a Jew who is one inwardly, and real circumcision is a matter of the heart" (Rom. 2:29). The true sons of Abraham, Jew or Gentile, are those who have faith.

Paul goes on to show that in committing wickedness, the Gentiles are without excuse (Rom. 1:18-32). However, he maintains that the Jews are no better because they had God's law but failed to obey it (Rom. 2:1-4). Paul's conclusion, then, is that God shows no partiality; it is the one who is obedient to God, Jew or Gentile, who is justified. He has some harsh words for his opponents:

> But by your hard and impenitent heart you are storing up wrath for yourself on the day of wrath when God's righteous judgment will be revealed. For *he will render to every man*

according to his works: to those who by patience in *well-doing* seek for glory and honor and immortality, he will give eternal life; but for those who are factious and do not obey the truth, but obey wickedness, there will be wrath and fury. There will be tribulation and distress for every human being who does evil, the Jew first and also the Greek, but glory and honor and peace for every one who *does good*, the Jew first and also the Greek. For God shows no partiality. . . . For *it is not the hearers of the law who are righteous before God, but the doers of the law who will be justified* (Rom. 2:5-11, 13).

Paul stresses "well-doing" and draws a correlation between our obedience to the law and our justification. Indeed, we will be judged according to our deeds, and it is the "doers of the law who will be justified." In short, according to Paul, works are the basis for God's judgment! This is a far cry from justification by faith alone.

Paul continues along the same lines. On the one hand, Gentiles who instinctively obey the law "show that what the law requires is written on their hearts" (Rom. 2:15). On the other hand, Jews who boast in the law, but do not keep it, condemn themselves. "You who boast in the law, do you dishonor God by breaking the law?" (Rom. 2:23). In either case, Paul is insisting on the necessity and importance of obedience. He then continues his argument with the example of circumcision, an issue especially important to his opponents:

So, if a man who is uncircumcised keeps the precepts of the law, will not his uncircumcision be regarded as circumcision? Then those who are physically uncircumcised but keep the law will condemn you who have the written code and circumcision but break the law. For he is not a real Jew who is one outwardly, nor is true circumcision something external and physical. He is a Jew who is one inwardly, and real circumcision is a matter of the heart, spiritual and not literal (Rom. 2:26-29).

Paul turns the argument of his opponents on its head. They do not possess an inside track to God's covenant because they are circumcised. On the contrary, those who keep the law, Jew or Gentile, are the truly circumcised ones because circumcision is a matter of the heart. Paul thus emphasizes that obedience to God's law, written on the heart, is much more important than the observance of any ritual obligations, such as circumcision. The latter are useless without the former.

In chapter three, Paul continues his argument by stressing that the unbelief of the Jews does not nullify God's faithfulness (Rom. 3:1-4). The opposite is true, for in judging unrighteousness God's righteousness is demonstrated (Rom. 3:5-6). But this, of course, is not a reason to be unrighteous (Rom. 3:7-8). The conclusion, then, is that Jews are no better than Gentiles, for both groups are under sin (Rom. 3:9).[9] "For there is no distinction; since all have sinned and fall short of the glory of God, they are justified by his grace as a gift, through the redemption which is in Christ Jesus" (Rom. 3:22-24). Paul's opponents, then, have no reason to boast, and the "works of the law" count for nothing. As Paul concludes,

> Then what becomes of our boasting? It is excluded. On what principle? On the principle of works? No, but on the principle of faith. For we hold that a man is justified by faith apart from works of law. Or is God the God of Jews only? Is he not the God of Gentiles also? Yes, of Gentiles also, since God is one; and he will justify the circumcised on the ground of their faith and the uncircumcised through their faith (Rom. 3:27-30).

Paul's argument is the same as that of Rom. 2: In a nutshell, God does not discriminate. There is no conflict here between faith and good works, but faith and "works of the law." The Judaizers claimed that by keeping the latter—for example,

---

[9] Paul appeals to Ps. 14 to prove his point. There God is with "the generation of the righteous" (Ps. 14:5), who are being persecuted by all men—Jews and Gentiles alike—who are referred to as "evildoers who eat up my people . . ." (Ps. 14:4). Paul quotes Ps. 14: "None is righteous, no, not one; no one understands, no one seeks for God. All have turned aside, together they have gone wrong; no one does good, not even one" (Rom. 3:10-12). In keeping with the context of Ps. 14, the point is clear: Both Jews and Gentiles have turned away from God. This is not to deny of course that every single individual is sinful too. However, that was not the point of Ps. 14. For if the "evildoers" refer to every human being, who is left to be "my people"? Apparently, there are indeed some who do good, that is, the "generation of the righteous" (Ps. 14:5).

circumcision, food laws, and sabbaths—they were righteous. Paul exposes their hypocrisy and answers that, whether circumcised or uncircumcised, we are justified by faith. Or, as he says in his Epistle to the Galatians, "For in Christ Jesus neither circumcision nor uncircumcision is of any avail, but *faith working through love*" (Gal. 5:6).

Paul does *not* say that we are justified by faith alone. Martin Luther added the word "alone" to his translation of Rom. 3:28 because he thought that was the sense of the text. However, such an interpretation makes no sense in the context. After Paul states that we are "justified by faith apart from the works of the law," his conclusion is not "Or is God the God of the one who does good works only?" but rather "Or is God the God of Jews only? Is He not the God of Gentiles also?" (Rom. 3:29). Clearly, his point is that God does not discriminate against Gentiles and that both Jews and Gentiles are justified by faith. Thus, the "boasting" that Paul is combating is, as N.T. Wright observed, "not the boasting of the successful moralist; it is the racial boast of the Jew, as in 2:17-24."[10] And faith is not opposed to good works any more than Rom. 3 ("a man is justified by faith") is opposed to Rom. 2 ("the doers of the law ... will be justified"). Faith and good works go hand in hand, in contrast to the "works of the law," which do not justify.

In Rom. 4, Paul buttresses his argument by appealing to an event in the life of Abraham, the father of the faith. He points out that Abraham was justified (in Gen. 15) before he was circumcised (in Gen. 17), and therefore righteousness comes not through circumcision but through faith, for "Abraham believed God, and it was reckoned to him as righteousness" (Rom. 4:3; cf. Gen. 15:6).[11] This would have dealt a blow to Paul's opponents, who probably appealed to Abraham's circumcision to

---

[10] N.T. Wright, *What St. Paul Really Said* (Ann Arbor, MI: Eerdmans, 1997), 129.

[11] In Rom. 4:2-6, Paul uses the term "works" four times, but then interchanges another term, namely, circumcision. Indeed, in vv. 9-12, the term circumcision replaces the whole sense of "works." It is evident then, that "works" in 4:2-6 does not refer to good works but convey the same sense as "works of the law" in Rom. 3.

prove that it was necessary for salvation. This position is under-mined if, as Paul points out, Abraham was justified by faith without being circumcised.[12]

Paul's argument is also problematic for Protestant interpreta-tions. If justification is a once-and-for-all legal declaration, then how do we explain the fact that Abraham was justified (Gen. 15) *after* he enjoyed a positive relationship with God (Gen. 12-14)? That is, long before he is declared righteous in Gen. 15, Abraham performed great acts of faith and obedience in Gen. 12-14. Indeed, the Letter to the Hebrews points to Abraham's obedience in Gen. 12 as a superlative act of faith: "By faith Abraham obeyed when he was called to go out to a place which he was to receive as an inheritance; and he went out, not knowing where he was to go" (Heb. 11:8). Thus, Gen. 15 could not be Abraham's conver-sion experience, as many Protestants contend, though he was jus-tified then. On the other hand, the passage conforms quite well to the Catholic idea of progressive justification. Justification, though momentary when one first receives it through Baptism, is also progressive. It is the life of the child of God maturing in God's grace. Abraham was in God's favor as far back as Gen. 12, even though he is "declared righteous" in Gen. 15.

In Rom. 4:13 and the following verses, Paul points out that Abraham is the "father of us all" (Rom. 4:16). How? Not through circumcision but through faith: "In hope he believed against hope, that he should become the father of many nations; as he had been told, 'So shall your descendants be'" (Rom. 4:18). The faith of Abraham was an obedient faith, a faith that overcame all earthly obstacles of suffering. As Paul writes:

---

[12] In Rom. 9, Paul adds a related point: "For not all who are descended from Israel belong to Israel, and not all are children of Abraham because they are his descen-dants" (Rom. 9:6-7). His opponents should not trust in circumcision, because that is not how the covenant promise is handed down. Abraham's son Ishmael was circum-cised in Gen. 17 before Isaac was born, and yet God told Abraham that "through Isaac shall your descendants be named" (Gen. 21:12; Rom. 9:7). Paul concludes, "This means that it is not the children of the flesh who are the children of God, but the children of the promise are reckoned as descendants" (Rom. 9:8). The "children of promise" are justified by faith, not circumcision. Paul's opponents are the "children of the flesh." This is one of Paul's major themes in Galatians.

He did not weaken in faith when he considered his own body, which was as good as dead because he was about a hundred years old, or when he considered the barrenness of Sarah's womb. No distrust made him waver concerning the promise of God, but he grew strong in his faith as he gave glory to God, fully convinced that God was able to do what he had promised (Rom. 4:19-21).

Abraham overcame death: his own death, the deadness of Sarah's womb, and Isaac's prospective death. "That is why his faith was 'reckoned to him as righteousness.'" (Rom. 4:22). Paul's point is that we are justified by the same faith as Abraham's and that, like him, we should expect our faith to be tested with obstacles. This is not a cause for despair, however, but hope. As Paul writes,

Therefore, since we are justified by *faith* . . . we rejoice in our sufferings, knowing that suffering produces endurance, and endurance produces character, and character produces *hope*, and hope does not disappoint us, because God's *love* has been poured into our hearts through the Holy Spirit who has been given to us (Rom. 5:1, 3-5).

These are what Catholic theologians call the three theological virtues: faith, hope, and love. They are "poured into our hearts through the Holy Spirit" when we are justified; they dispose us toward God. The idea in this passage is that, when faced with sufferings, faith leads to endurance which in turn evokes hope; for we know that suffering is going to produce glory if we persevere. And what is the ultimate basis of our hope? Paul continues:

Since, therefore, we are now *justified by his blood*, much more shall we be saved by him from the wrath of God. For if while we were enemies we were reconciled to God by the death of his Son, much more, now that we are reconciled, shall we be saved by his life (Rom. 5:9-10).

In short, if Christ died for His enemies, think what He must do for His friends! And indeed, now we are "justified by his blood" (Rom. 5:9). Blood, of course, is the principle of family unity. The human family, broken by original sin, is nonetheless united through Adam's flesh and blood (cf. Gen. 3:20). Paul says that we are now justified by Christ's blood. For Christ, the eternal Son of God, unites Himself to Adam's flesh and blood in the womb of Mary, and that flesh and blood is later crucified on the Cross, and then raised on the third day. It is distributed to us in the Eucharist. That's how Christ starts a new covenant: His body and blood become the body and blood of a new and everlasting family![13] Thus, whereas we are made "non-sons" through the blood of Adam, we are justified, made sons, through the blood of Christ.

This makes a perfect transition to Paul's next topic: the analogy between Adam and Christ (Rom. 5:12-21). His opponents had been boasting that they were children of Abraham because of the "works of the law." Paul countered their argument by showing that Abraham's fatherhood was universal, and that he was justified before he was circumcised. Now Paul pushes it back even further. The Jews and Gentiles are both children of the original father, Adam, and thus both share in the same condition of sinfulness. "Therefore as sin came into the world through one man and death through sin, and so death spread to all men because all men sinned" (Rom. 5:12). Paul's opponents have nothing to boast about because the universal effects of Adam's sin extend to both Jews and Gentiles, for both have sinned (cf. Catechism, no. 404). And yet, the universal effects of Christ are just as extensive:

> And the free gift is not like the effect of that one man's sin. For the judgment following one trespass brought condemnation, but the free gift following many trespasses brings justification. If, because of one man's trespass, death reigned through that one man, much more will those who receive the abundance of grace and the free gift of righteousness reign in life through the one man Jesus Christ (Rom. 5:16-17).

---

[13] When Christ uses the word "blood" at the Last Supper, He uses the word "covenant": "Drink of it, all of you; for this is my blood of the covenant, which is poured out for many for the forgiveness of sins" (Mt. 26:28).

Jews and Gentiles alike are united under sin or grace, depending upon whom they are under, Adam or Christ. We are born with the nature of Adam and are thereby sinners. But Christ is the New Adam. When we are united to Him through grace, we are justified.[14] Paul states, "For as by one man's disobedience many were *made sinners*, so by one man's obedience many will be *made righteous*" (Rom. 5:19). Note that in Adam we are not just declared sinners, we are made sinners. By the same token, in Christ we are not just declared righteous but are made righteous. Our righteousness in Christ is not only legal but real, just as our sinfulness in Adam was not only legal but real.

This, of course, is the Catholic teaching: When we are justified, we are declared to be God's children precisely because God makes us His children. For God's grace transforms us from sinners to brothers and sisters of Christ and sons and daughters of the Father. The reality of our divine filiation is expressed magnificently by Paul in Rom. 8:

> For all who are led by the Spirit of God are sons of God. For you did not receive the spirit of slavery to fall back into fear, but you have received the spirit of sonship. When we cry, "Abba! Father!" it is the Spirit himself bearing witness with our spirit that we are children of God, and if children, then heirs, heirs of God and fellow heirs with Christ, provided we suffer with him in order that we may also be glorified with him (Rom. 8:14-17).

The image that Paul uses here is *adoption* (see also Gal. 4:4-7). It expresses an important aspect of our justification, that, as Saint Augustine wrote, "we were something before we were the sons of God, and we received the benefit of becoming what we were not, just as the one who is adopted, before adoption, was not yet the

---

[14] How do we get out of the old Adam and into the new one? Paul says by dying with Christ in Baptism and thereby crucifying the old self (Rom. 6:3-7). Only then will our sonship be revealed fully, as Christ's sonship was revealed, in resurrection (Rom. 1:4; 8:23).

son of the one who adopts him."[15] When we are justified, we enter into a radically new relationship with God as His children. This is aptly called adoption, though it transcends the way we usually think of that term. As one author put it,

> When God makes us His children, we enter into an incompa-
> rably more intimate union with Him than exists among men
> between adoptive child and parent. We become children of
> God by reason of a regeneration and rebirth in which God
> communicates to us His divine nature and life, filling and ani-
> mating us by His Spirit.[16]

Some Protestants argue that this adoption is merely legal and not a real share in Christ's sonship.[17] Or if it is an internal reality of some kind, then it is distinct from our justification. But does Paul set up such a radical demarcation among our justification, sanctification, and sonship? In fact, they all express the same reality. Note, for example, Paul's close identification of justification and sanctification: "But you were washed, you were sanctified, you were justified in the name of the Lord Jesus Christ and in the Spirit of our God" (1 Cor. 6:11). Or again,

> [H]e saved us, not because of deeds done by us in righteous-
> ness, but in virtue of his own mercy, by the washing of regen-
> eration and renewal in the Holy Spirit, which he poured out
> upon us richly through Jesus Christ our Savior, so that we
> might be justified by his grace and become heirs in hope of
> eternal life (Tit. 3:5-7).

To sum up, Paul shows throughout Romans that his opponents have it all wrong. They do not enjoy an inside track to justification merely because they keep the "works of the law" (for

---

[15] Saint Augustine, *Epistles*, 140, 4. Wilfrid Parsons, trans., *Saint Augustine*: Letters (New York: Fathers of the Church, 1953), vol. III, 64.

[16] Mary Gordiana Ney, "Divine Adoption Through Grace" (unpublished M.A. Thesis) (Milwaukee: Marquette University, 1958), 26.

[17] John Murray, *Redemption Accomplished and Applied* (Grand Rapids, MI: Eerdmans, 1955), 167.

example, circumcision). On the contrary, "real circumcision is a matter of the heart" (Rom. 2:29), and Jews and Gentiles are justified in the same way that Abraham was justified: by faith. This faith is not opposed to good works but includes them, for it is only "the doers of the law who will be justified" (Rom. 2:13).

Justification in the Epistle of James

Saint Paul is not the only New Testament writer to discuss justification. We also find a treatment of the theme in the Epistle of Saint James. James does not have to deal with the problem of the Judaizers, so we do not find him talking about the "works of the law." Rather, he focuses on the importance of doing *good works*: "But be doers of the word, and not hearers only, deceiving yourselves" (Jas. 1:22). Or again: "Religion that is pure and undefiled before God and the Father is this: to visit orphans and widows in their affliction, and to keep oneself unstained from the world" (Jas. 1:27). The Christian who does not perform good works does not possess faith because "faith by itself, if it has no works, is dead" (Jas. 2:17).

To drive this point home, James explains that we are "justified by works." Like Paul, he makes his argument by appealing to the example of Abraham:

> Do you want to be shown, you foolish fellow, that faith apart from works is barren? Was not Abraham our father *justified by works*, when he offered his son Isaac upon the altar? You see that faith was active along with his works, and faith was completed by works, and the scripture was fulfilled which says, "Abraham believed God, and it was reckoned to him as righteousness"; and he was called the friend of God. You see that *a man is justified by works and not by faith alone*. And in the same way was not also Rahab the harlot *justified by works* when she received the messengers and sent them out another way? For as the body apart from the spirit is dead, so faith apart from works is dead (Jas. 2:20-26).

By stating that Abraham was "justified by works," James is not excluding faith, but rather showing that faith is "completed

by works." Does this contradict Paul? Not at all. Again, Paul
states that we are justified by faith apart from the "works of the
law," which are something different from good works. Like
James, Paul affirms the positive role of good works in justification
(Rom. 2:5-14).

James' teaching is in harmony with Paul's, but not with
Protestant doctrine, which insists that we are justified by *faith
alone*. In fact, the principle of faith alone directly contradicts
James, who states that "a man is justified by works and *not by
faith alone*." This passage proved so problematic for Martin
Luther that he referred to the Book of James as an "epistle of
straw" and was prepared to remove it from the canon of the New
Testament. Protestants do not go that far today, but rather
attempt to harmonize James' teaching with justification by faith
alone.[18] They usually argue that James means something different by the term "justification" than Paul, although the Greek
term is the same. But there is no evidence in the text for this.
The reason that it is suggested at all is to salvage an interpretation of Paul that does not square with the clear teaching of
James. Of course, Protestants *do* affirm the importance of doing
good works. However, they deny that good works play any role
in our justification.

But what does Catholic teaching mean when it says that we
are justified by works? It does not mean that we can earn our salvation, any more than it means that in James. Indeed, any good
works that we do are purely the result of God's grace, just as faith
comes from grace. Rather, it is a recognition that there is a correlation between good works done in love and our standing
before God. In this sense, justification is a dynamic process in
which God the Father confers higher standing progressively upon
His children as they grow. That justification is a process is evident
in James: Abraham is justified in Gen. 15 (Jas. 2:23) *and* in Gen.

---

[18] For a recent example, see R.C. Sproul, *Faith Alone: The Evangelical Doctrine of
Justification* (Grand Rapids, MI: Baker Books, 1995), 161-67. For a comprehensive
survey of Protestant interpretations of James with rebuttals, see Sungenis, 117-75.

22 (Jas. 2:21). Protestants have a difficult time explaining this.

To sum up, James maintains that Abraham was justified by works. Good works are not opposed to faith but complete it, just as in Paul faith must be obedient. The conflict here is not between James and Paul, but between James and the doctrine of justification by faith alone.

Conclusion

Our look at justification in Paul and James has been brief, but sufficient enough for us to get a sense of their treatment of that theme. On the one hand, the teaching that justification is by faith alone is contradicted by Paul, who says that it is "the doers of the law who will be justified" (Rom. 2:13) and by James, who states that "a man is justified by works and not by faith alone" (Jas. 2:24). The conclusion is unavoidable that, at least for Paul and James, "faith alone" is not justifiable. On the other hand, the Catholic Church's teaching that justification is *through grace alone by a living faith working in love* is fully supported by Paul and James. God is a merciful Father who, in declaring that our sins are forgiven, actually makes us His sons and daughters. Justification is the process by which God changes us from sinners to His children. In the words of Saint John, "See what love the Father has given us, that we should be called children of God; and so we are" (1 Jn. 3:1).

Richard A. White is an assistant professor of religious studies at Benedictine College in Atchison, Kansas. He earned his Ph.D. in religious studies from Marquette University in 1995. He also holds an M.A. in Christian thought from Trinity Evangelical Divinity School. Dr. White converted to Catholicism in 1991. He is married with two children.

Chapter VI

Born Again
What the Bible Teaches About Baptism

Kimberly Hahn

M y husband Scott and I were talking as we walked through the hallway at Gordon-Conwell Seminary when a good friend overtook us. George, a stalwart Evangelical who was enthusiastic about his recent studies on liturgy, tried to pique our curiosity, "I've got to talk to you about the sacraments. I've been doing some reading and I find it rather exciting."

Scott abruptly ended the conversation, replying, "To be honest, George, sacraments bore me."

I remember thinking at the time that it may not be safe to say that sacraments bore you, but I wasn't very interested either. I shared Scott's concern that sacraments seemed like extraneous rituals and traditions that detracted from a vital life of faith. It seemed people were more interested in sacraments than a personal relationship with the Lord.

Scott altered his perspective, however, once he began pastoring a church. His sermon series on the Gospel of Saint John led him to examine sacraments in a new light. For example, he related Jn. 3—being "born from above" or "born again"—to Baptism.

Never before had I heard a sermon equating being born again with Baptism. So, I cautioned him when we got home from church, "I think you need to be careful—you're crossing some lines here. Today's sermon didn't sound very Presbyterian."

As Scott prepared his sermons, his study raised more questions than it answered; it was difficult for him to see anything but a Catholic interpretation for some passages. Those questions, as well as many other theological concerns, became the impetus for us to return to Grove City, Pennsylvania, where we had gone to college, so Scott could examine these issues more thoroughly.

Without going into the details, Scott read (or should I say consumed) hundreds of books over the next two years. He would enter his study and I would not want him to come out. I didn't want to listen to his new insights. I didn't want to hear about the questions he was probing or what answers he was discovering.

I had completed my master's in theology; now my energies focused on family life. We had one little boy and I was expecting another. I had little time and even less interest to delve deeply into theology. However, Scott hoped I would share his enthusiasm.

One day Scott emerged from his study and declared, "Kimberly, there might be seven sacraments and the two you understand you might not really understand." I could not fathom that. I couldn't believe that I might have to rethink the ABC's of theology after earning my master's! At the time, I was unwilling to consider the possibility.

Scott and I continued down different spiritual paths through our time in Grove City and into our move to Milwaukee, where Scott began his doctoral studies at Marquette University. In 1986, at the Easter Vigil Mass, Scott was received into the Catholic Church. That was my first Mass, and I didn't attend another Mass for two-and-a-half years. I was not interested in or open to his understanding of the sacraments. Needless to say, we experienced much turmoil in our lives and our home.

In the midst of our difficulties, we wondered whether we had conceived our third child. It was Christmas time, we were home for the holidays, and the morning of my birthday—Christmas

Eve—I took a pregnancy test. Three thoughts formed when I saw the answer to the test: "I'm pregnant!" "How is this child going to be baptized?" And, "This child is a child of reconciliation." (I believe this last thought was a gift from the Lord, though its meaning vexed me.)

I didn't reveal the questions on my heart to Scott. On the one hand, I didn't want my child to be baptized Catholic; on the other, since Scott was the spiritual leader of our home, it seemed more appropriate for her to be baptized in his tradition. The Lord was very merciful to me in veiling the reality that there was no choice: As a Catholic, Scott committed all of our children, born and unborn, to the care and keeping of the Church.

I wrestled and prayed for months privately—no doubt, Scott did, too—but we didn't talk about it. About a month before our daughter was born, acting on my sense of resolution with the Lord on the matter, I revealed my heart to him: "Scott, I believe this baby should be baptized Catholic. Can you make the necessary arrangements?"

Surprised, he acknowledged my request and made the preparations. He was thankful for a peaceful discussion of her Baptism without a hurtful confrontation that could only end with one of us feeling like a loser. This set the stage for what became a turning point in our family's journey of faith.

Eight weeks later, we took Hannah to be baptized. I didn't know whether the priest would even acknowledge I was a Christian. I simply needed to respond in obedience to what I thought the Lord wanted us to do. I thought the priest might say, "Mrs. Hahn, I'm glad you came. Please sit down while we baptize your child for you."

Instead, I was pleasantly surprised and pleased when Msgr. Fabian Bruskewitz, now Bishop of Lincoln, Nebraska, fully included me, encouraging me to participate as much as I could. It was the most marvelous baptismal liturgy I ever witnessed. And it proved absolutely life-changing. We started in the back of the church where I made the Sign of the Cross on Hannah's head, along with her father and her godparents. Then we brought her forward and followed the liturgy. I was comfortable with most of the ceremony.

Twice I disagreed with the priest, though I tried not to react in a visible way. First, I struggled with the idea of invoking the saints. I prayed, "Oh God, please forgive him for talking to all of those dead people!" And second, I was bothered by his explanation in front of my sons that Baptism was going to make Hannah a child of God. I thought, "Oh Lord, he just doesn't understand Baptism and he's going to confuse the boys, but he means well."

Though I disagreed, I listened intently as Msgr. Bruskewitz explained Baptism to our little boys. He offered this analogy: A deep-sea diver would not be able to function well in an underwater environment unless he were properly suited and empowered to exist there. Likewise, Hannah needed the supernatural grace of Baptism in order to be properly suited and empowered to live in heaven. Applying Jn. 3 to Baptism, Msgr. Bruskewitz shared that, through her rebirth by water and the Spirit, Hannah would now be able to see and enter heaven. That gave me something to ponder.

Then the priest interceded for Hannah—I could hardly contain my joy. Those prayers were everything I would have prayed for her: that she would hear the Gospel and respond, that her lips would speak the Gospel of peace to others, and that she would live out being a child of the King faithfully. Though I was raised a proper Presbyterian—we never said "Amen" out loud—when the priest prayed over Hannah and said, "Amen and amen," I exclaimed, "AMEN!"

When we left Saint Bernard's Church that day, God had changed my heart. From that time on, I wanted a better understanding of what the Catholic Church taught about Baptism. That, in turn, inspired other areas of study in Catholic theology and eventually led to my reception into the Catholic Church three years later. Let me briefly share the results of my study.

Washing Away Original Sin

Let's begin at the beginning. God created Adam in His own image and endowed him with the grace of sonship. As the father of humanity, Adam represented mankind. When Adam sinned, he forfeited the grace of divine sonship for all of us (cf. Catechism, nos. 402-06). Through Adam we inherit *original* sin, which is the absence of the grace of sonship, and *concupiscence*, which is our disordered inclination toward sin (cf. Catechism, no. 1264).

In contrast to the first Adam, Jesus is the second Adam—the representative of a new humanity, through whom the grace of divine sonship has been restored. In Rom. 5:18-19, Saint Paul declares,

> Then as one man's trespass led to condemnation for all men, so one man's act of righteousness leads to acquittal and life for all men. For as by one man's disobedience many were made sinners, so by one man's obedience many will be made righteous.

Keep in mind that the sacred authors of Scripture did not put in the chapter and verse numbering as they wrote. Consequently, when Saint Paul completed Rom. 5, his thought continued into Rom. 6. Look at the first four verses of chapter 6, remembering the discussion in chapter 5 about the first and second Adams:

> What shall we say then? Are we to continue in sin that grace may abound? By no means! How can we who died to sin still live in it? Do you not know that all of us who have been baptized into Christ Jesus were baptized into his death? We were buried therefore with him by baptism into death, so that as Christ was raised from the dead by the glory of the Father, we too might walk in newness of life.

Saint Paul says we have died to sin. To what sin have we died?

Does Saint Paul mean that once we have been baptized, we never sin again? No. The very next chapter details his continual struggle, as a Christian, with sin: "I do not do what I want, but I do the very thing I hate" (Rom. 7:15).

So what then does Saint Paul mean by "died to sin"? Remember his discussion in the preceding chapter regarding original sin? This is the sin to which we have died through Baptism, according to Rom. 6. This is why the Catholic Church teaches that the stain of the old Adam's original sin is washed away through the waters of Baptism by Jesus, the New Adam.

The Forgiveness of Sins and the Holy Spirit

Through Baptism, not only is the stain of original sin washed away, but all actual sins committed up to that point in time are forgiven (Catechism, no. 1263). When Saint Peter preached his first sermon at Pentecost, recorded in Acts 2, he declared who Jesus was and what He had done. He concluded with a challenge to believe in Jesus:

> Let all the house of Israel therefore know assuredly that God has made him both Lord and Christ, this Jesus whom you crucified. Now when they heard this they were cut to the heart, and they said to Peter and the rest of the apostles, "Brethren, what shall we do?" And Peter said to them, "Repent, and be baptized every one of you in the name of Jesus Christ for the forgiveness of your sins; and you shall receive the gift of the Holy Spirit. For the promise is to you and to your children and to all that are far off, every one whom the Lord our God calls to him (Acts 2:37-39).

Saint Peter's preaching resulted in 3,000 Baptisms that day.

Several key thoughts on Baptism expressed in Saint Peter's sermon are highlighted in the Catechism. First, Baptism is the primary sacrament for the forgiveness of sins (no. 977); through repentance and Baptism, forgiveness of sins and newness of spiritual life come. Second, through Baptism we receive the gift of the Holy Spirit. We are restored as children of God who share the same spirit, the Holy Spirit (no. 1265). And third, the promises of forgiveness and the Holy Spirit were not only for Saint Peter's listeners but also for us. These promises included all future generations (no. 1250).

To be frank, when I was a Presbyterian, I challenged people to repent and believe every time I witnessed about my faith, but I don't ever remember telling someone they needed to be baptized for the forgiveness of sins and reception of the Holy Spirit. It never dawned on me to say it the way Saint Peter said it. Why not, I wondered?

Partakers of the Divine Nature

No doubt I was influenced by Martin Luther, who helped to cause the break from the Catholic Church commonly known as the Protestant Reformation. Luther described people as dunghills. When people expressed their faith in Christ, His righteousness legally covered them and their sins much like snow might cover dunghills, having the appearance of purity but without any internal change. It's not a pretty picture.

Since Luther primarily described salvation in courtroom terminology replete with judge, prosecutor, defendant, crimes, punishment, etc., he narrowly interpreted Jesus' actions as merely a legal transaction: Jesus took our sins and paid the penalty; in exchange we received His righteousness. Luther understood this legal substitution, commonly referred to as "the imputation of righteousness," as the basis for our justification, or right standing, before God (cf. Catechism, no. 1992). Although a glorious part of the explanation of what Christ's redemption provided for us, it misses a very significant part of Christ's work on the Cross on our behalf: More than forgiven sinners, we are now children of God, infused with His own divine life (cf. Catechism, no. 1997).

The Catholic Church teaches that there is a legal transaction with eternal consequences; but much more, the Church proclaims that, in and through Christ, we are profoundly transformed as "new creations" (2 Cor. 5:17; cf. Catechism, no. 1214). Not only does Our Heavenly Father exchange Christ's righteousness for our sins but, even more amazingly, He recreates us so that we become His children, filled with His grace which is His divine life. Our justification, then, means we have been made heirs, according to the promises of the covenant. We will inherit eternal life with Our Heavenly Father, provided we respond as obedient children (cf. Catechism, no. 1996).

Let me illustrate the difference between a purely legal view of salvation and the Church's familial view. Some of you have a dog or a cat or a bird. You may love that pet and you may even share your home and the food off your table with that pet. You may go so far as to rewrite your will in order to provide for your pet after your death.

But do you know what you can't do? You can't go down to the county courthouse and adopt your pet as a son or daughter. Why not? You don't share the same nature. Even if you found a judge willing to declare your pet to be your child, that would still be nothing more than a legal fiction.

Yet God, whose divine nature differs far more radically from ours than our nature differs from that of a dog or a cat, declares us, in Christ, to be His children. This is not a legal fiction. It is reality. The sonship that the first Adam lost has now been restored through the second Adam. The moment we are baptized, we become one with Christ as children of Our Heavenly Father. As Saint Peter writes in 2 Pet. 1:4, we have "become partakers of the divine nature." Now we can be His children because He has made it possible to share His divine nature; now we call God "Father."

In Old Testament times, the people of God did not refer to God as Father, though He was their Father from all eternity. In fact, they did not utter His holy name. In contrast, Jesus taught His disciples to pray, saying, "Our Father who art in heaven . . . " Jesus' Father is now Our Father (Jn. 20:17) because we share His divine Sonship. He is the One who gives us the faith to believe, the hope to endure, and the love to respond to His mercy. And He gives these same gifts of faith, hope, and love to our children when they are baptized, just as He promised in Saint Peter's sermon at Pentecost.

Participation in Christ's Divine Sonship

Since we have the grace of Christ's divine Sonship through Baptism, we share the same spirit, the Holy Spirit. Saint Paul declares:

> For you did not receive the spirit of slavery to fall back into fear, but you have received the spirit of sonship. When we cry, "Abba! Father!" it is the Spirit himself bearing witness with our spirit that we are children of God, and if children, then heirs, heirs of God and fellow heirs with Christ, provided we suffer with him in order that we may also be glorified with him (Rom. 8:15-17).

The Holy Spirit enables us to embrace all that participation in divine Sonship entails—the suffering as well as the glory.

Throughout Israel's history, God chose particular men to lead His people as priests, prophets, or kings. He consecrated them by anointing them with the Holy Spirit for a particular mission in His name. All of this was in preparation for the messiah (literally, the "anointed one"), who was consecrated by the same Spirit for His threefold office of priest, prophet, and king (cf. Catechism, no. 436). Now His Spirit consecrates *us* to be a kingdom of priests with His prophetic voice, proclaiming the kingdom of God to our world.

The Son of God is *high priest* of heaven. He has "made us a kingdom, priests to his God and Father" (Rev. 1:6; cf. Rev. 5:9-10; 1 Pet. 2:5). Through the Sacrament of Holy Orders, some men participate even more fully in the priesthood of Christ; but all of us participate in some measure in Christ's priesthood. Baptism commits us to a vital participation in the liturgy and to bear witness in our lives to our baptismal *priesthood* (cf. Catechism, no. 1273). This means we have been consecrated for worship. Rather than observing Mass as an audience watches a performance, we assist at Mass as active participants. Then we go forth from Mass to bring the kingdom of God to bear in every sphere of life, private and public.

We reflect Christ's role as *prophet* when we proclaim to the world the marvelous deeds of God. Some of us are more public witnesses about the faith, while others quietly share with neighbors and friends. However, we all testify to the truth of the faith so that all hearts may be drawn to the Father through the Son.

And just as Christ is *King of Kings* and Lord of Lords, so we are part of a *royal* priesthood (1 Pet. 2:9), called to reign with Him provided we suffer with Him (cf. Rom. 8:17; 2 Tim. 2:11-12). We are sons and daughters of the King. We are citizens of the kingdom of heaven. We bring His kingship to bear in all areas of life, just as we pray with each Our Father, "Thy kingdom come, Thy will be done, On earth as it is in heaven" (Mt. 6:10).

Just as the Son has been anointed to reign as priest, prophet, and king over the kingdom of God, so He has consecrated us by His Spirit through Baptism to participate in His divine mission. Our faithful service in union with His priesthood, His prophetic ministry, and His kingship helps to extend the kingdom of God on earth.

Must You Be Born Again? A Possible Dialogue

If a Bible Christian knocks on your door and asks, "Have you been born again?" perhaps the best answer would be, "Yes, I've been baptized." (Caution: Your answer may surprise your questioner.) Here's a strategy that may help you share about Baptism when someone's question has opened the door for discussion.

Open your Bible to Jn. 3:5-8 and share Jesus' challenge to Nicodemus: "Truly, truly, I say to you, unless one is born of water and the Spirit, he cannot enter the kingdom of God" (Jn. 3:5). Highlight the context of this passage: In a previous chapter, Jesus' Baptism is recorded, which brings together the images of water and the Spirit (in the form of a dove) along with God the Father's recognition of His Son (Jn. 1:32-33; cf. Mt. 3:16-17). The passage immediately following Jesus' conversation with Nicodemus is the only place in the New Testament that records Jesus' baptizing others (Jn. 3:22). The overall context of the passage where Jesus speaks of the necessity of being "born of water and the spirit" is Baptism.

Without downplaying our need for ongoing conversion, emphasize that this passage in Jn. 3 addresses the objective act of Baptism, rather than a subjective conversion experience. Then ask in all sincerity, "When were *you* born of water and the Spirit? When were *you* baptized?"

The Necessity of Baptism

Since you can't enter the kingdom of God, much less participate in it, unless you are born of water and the Spirit, then Baptism is necessary for salvation. The Catechism (no. 1257), quoting Jn. 3:5, affirms this:

> The Church does not know of any means other than Baptism that assures entry into eternal beatitude; this is why she takes care not to neglect the mission she has received from the Lord to see that all who can be baptized are "reborn of water and the Spirit."

Does this mean that if someone is not baptized, such as the thief on the cross who professed faith in Christ just before he died, he can have no hope of heaven? The Catechism (no. 1257) addresses this question as follows: "God has bound salvation to the sacrament of Baptism, but he himself is not bound by his sacraments." In other words, God has given us the gift of the Sacrament of Baptism and taught us through the Church what graces that sacrament provides for us. However, God is not "required" to save only those persons who are baptized—and the Catechism describes the possibilities of Baptism of desire and Baptism by blood (no. 1258). Our responsibility is to obey God's directives through the Church and leave the rest to God's mercy.

Washing of Regeneration

Until I studied the Catholic understanding of Baptism, I assumed spiritual rebirth occurred when someone came to a conscious desire to accept Jesus Christ as his personal Lord and Savior. However, the Bible rarely uses this term—regeneration—

and when it does, it refers to it as the "washing of regeneration" (cf. Catechism, no. 1215). Let us examine Saint Paul's explanation of this powerful thought in Tit. 3:4-7:

> [B]ut when the goodness and loving kindness of God our Savior appeared, he saved us, not because of deeds done by us in righteousness, but in virtue of his own mercy, by *the washing of regeneration* and renewal in the Holy Spirit, which he *poured out* upon us richly through Jesus Christ our Savior, so that we might *be justified* by his grace and become heirs in hope of eternal life.

This text challenged me to define theological terms with biblical definitions, and specifically to think of regeneration as occurring at Baptism.

In another passage, Saint Paul specifically links Baptism with both being justified and being sanctified or made holy. After listing a number of wicked acts for which people will not inherit the kingdom of God, he writes, "And such were some of you. But you were washed, you were sanctified, you were justified in the name of the Lord Jesus Christ and in the Spirit of our God" (1 Cor. 6:11).

The Gift of the Holy Spirit

According to Saint Peter in his sermon quoted earlier (Acts 2:38), not only do we receive forgiveness for our sins through Baptism, but we also receive the gift of the Holy Spirit. Baptism cleanses us so that we can be a holy place in which the Holy Spirit dwells. Saint Paul writes,

> Do you not know that your body is a temple of the Holy Spirit within you, which you have from God? You are not your own; you were bought with a price. So glorify God in your body (1 Cor. 6:19-20).

The Holy Spirit who dwelt in the tabernacle of the people of God in the Old Testament has been placed in our hearts, to dwell in the *temple of our bodies*. That same Holy Spirit who raised Christ from the dead has been given to us that we might have the power to live the life that we have been called to live (cf. Eph. 1:19-21).

The "Character" of Baptism

One of the changes the Holy Spirit makes within us at Baptism is to give our souls an indelible mark—a permanent stamp that can never be changed. Let me offer an illustration. From birth, you have a unique fingerprint; when you touch something, your fingerprint gives evidence of your presence. When you are baptized, or reborn, it is as if the Lord adds to your fingerprint the scar of the Cross so that everything you touch after Baptism says you, a child of God, were here. And your fingerprints, with that indelible mark, show up on sins as well as on good works.

As the Catechism notes,

> Baptism seals the Christian with the indelible spiritual mark (*character*) of his belonging to Christ. No sin can erase this mark, even if sin prevents Baptism from bearing the fruits of salvation (no. 1272, original emphasis).

The permanence of our mark highlights the fact that Baptism cannot be repeated. By virtue of our Baptism, we have been made children of God. Now we must be faithful children throughout our lives so that we

> will be able to depart this life "marked with the sign of faith," with [our] baptismal faith, in expectation of the blessed vision of God—the consummation of faith—and in the hope of resurrection (Catechism, no. 1274, quoting the Roman Missal, Eucharistic Prayer I [Roman Canon] 97).

Members of Christ's Body, the Church

Through Baptism, the Holy Spirit incorporates us into Christ. He is the Head of His Body, and we are members of His Body. Our union with the Son is so close, Saint Paul says we even smell like the Son to the Father (2 Cor. 2:15).

Since we are members of the Body of Christ and the Body of Christ is the Church, we are therefore members of the Church, God's worldwide family (Catechism, no. 1267). Saint Paul teaches,

> [F]or in Christ Jesus you are all sons of God, through faith. For as many of you as were baptized into Christ have *put on Christ*. There is neither Jew nor Greek, there is neither slave nor free, there is neither male nor female; for you are all one in Christ Jesus (Gal. 3:26-28).

What does it mean for us to "put on Christ" through our Baptism? This phrase conjures up an image of our nakedness being covered with the dazzling white robe of Christ's righteousness, similar to the white garment given to the newly baptized during the baptismal liturgy. Perhaps another image would help us grasp this radical change even more vividly: Putting on Christ is like grafting skin from our brother over terribly burned parts of our body, without which we could not live.

In addition, our union with Christ gives us a union with one another because we are members of the same family. Together, we have obligations and privileges. We are called to "[b]e subject to one another out of reverence for Christ" (Eph. 5:21), and to "obey and submit" to lawful Church authority (Heb. 13:17; cf. LG 25). As members of the Family of God through Baptism, we have a right to be nourished by the Word of God, to receive the sacraments, and to receive the spiritual support of the Church (Catechism, no. 1269). Through Baptism, we belong to Christ and to each other.

The Great Commission Is for All of Us

Just before His ascension to the Father, Jesus commissioned His apostles:

> And Jesus came and said to them, "All authority in heaven and on earth has been given to me. Go therefore and make disciples of all nations, baptizing them in the name of the Father and of the Son and of the Holy Spirit, teaching them to

observe all that I have commanded you; and lo, I am with you always, to the close of the age" (Mt. 28:18-20).

This mission—to make disciples by baptizing them and teaching them Christ's commands—has now been handed down to us. Faithful Christians have baptized us and instructed us in the faith, and we have been called to further this mission by making disciples of all nations today.

Those of us who have been called to the vocation of marriage live out the "Great Commission" first, though not exclusively, in the home. As an expression of our faith, we bring our children before the Church for Baptism; but that's only the beginning. Then we teach them to follow all that Jesus has commanded by preparing them to receive the other sacraments, helping them get to Mass and Confession regularly, and teaching the wonderful truths of our faith in an age-appropriate way. We also pray with them and for them so that they grow in an intimate relationship with the Lord. What a blessing to remember that just as Jesus promised His disciples, He has given parents the power of the Holy Spirit so that we can accomplish His work in our family's life by His strength.

The Mystery of Baptism

Some things are difficult to understand in the Christian faith. I'm reminded of a story in which a priest visited a CCD class to see if the children were learning the faith well. He asked the class, rather expectantly, "Who can tell me who the Trinity is?"

A little girl in the back row raised her hand. Since the priest was hard of hearing, he leaned forward for her response. Quietly, she replied, "The Father, the Son, and the Holy Spirit."

Father bent down near her and said, "I'm sorry, I don't understand."

Quickly she rejoined, "Oh, you're not supposed to. It's a mystery."

This little girl could give the same response to the question of how Baptism works. It is beyond comprehension to understand exactly how Baptism cleanses us from sin and makes us children of God. It's a mystery. The Church calls us to believe God's Word and to live it without necessarily understanding the mechanics of how He does what He does in our lives. A family friend, a convert along with his wife and seven children, shared this thought: "I love to evangelize. But there is nothing more significant I do as a witness to the faith than baptize these children so that they can become children of God and then teach them the faith."

Baptizing Children of the Covenant

Now, is it right to baptize children? After all, they can't express their faith or their own desire for Baptism. This is an important question often raised by some of our non-Catholic brothers and sisters in Christ.

Remember Saint Peter's sermon in Acts 2? He declared that the promise of salvation through repentance and Baptism was "to you and to your children and to all that are far off" (Acts 2:39). We have to hear this with Jewish ears.

If you read through the Old Testament, the male children of the Old Covenant were given the sign of the covenant—circumcision—on the eighth day of life. In other words, a Jewish boy was recognized as a Jew within the covenant as an infant, before he could express any faith of his own. And when he was given the sign of the covenant which made him a Jew, he was expected to live as a Jew, to believe as a Jew, and to be faithful as a Jew. At some point in time—his parents hoped—he would come to demonstrate being circumcised of heart as well. (For obvious reasons, baby girls were excluded from the sign of the covenant, but they were also expected to live and believe as faithful Jewish children.)

In the Old Covenant, children were always included. Can you imagine that Saint Peter would have excluded the children from the promise of the New Covenant and never have mentioned it? And not only that, but would he have applied the promise to children and future generations without explaining that he did not mean children before the age of reason? It's unlikely. In addition, the sign of the New Covenant was something both girls and boys could receive, thereby highlighting another aspect of the New Covenant—in Christ there is neither male nor female (Gal. 3:28).

Besides Saint Peter's powerful sermon at Pentecost, we have examples in Acts of whole households' being baptized. The Philippian jailer is one example. He comes to faith, and his whole family is baptized (Acts 16:33). Is it probable that all those children were old enough to make their own decision for Christ? It's possible, but no indication of this is given.

Furthermore, if the New Covenant surpasses the Old, why would it exclude children of believers when children had formerly been included? The new converts from Judaism would not have seen this as an improvement. In fact, the silence of the New Testament about infant Baptism speaks volumes.

The practice of the early Church was consistent—young children were welcomed at the baptismal font. The Catechism (no. 1252) addresses this point:

> The practice of infant Baptism is an immemorial tradition of the Church. There is explicit testimony to this practice from the second century on, and it is quite possible that, from the beginning of the apostolic preaching, when whole "households" received baptism, infants may also have been baptized.

These household Baptisms, in addition to the Philippian jailer's family, are recorded in Acts 16:15; 18:8; and 1 Cor. 1:16.

Further, there is a unique beauty in the Baptism of an infant or young child: He or she is so helpless, so incapable of initiating a relationship with God, that God has to be the initiator. And that is true of us, regardless of our age when we were baptized. We are that desperate, that in need of God's reaching out, touching our hearts, and changing us. We need Our Heavenly Father to restore us to relationship with Him and make us His children; then we respond. As Saint John says, "We love, because he first loved us" (1 Jn. 4:19).

Is Baptism All We Need to Be Saved?

Does that mean that once we baptize our child, we have finished the task of seeing to his salvation? Is salvation a *fait accompli*—is that child going to heaven regardless of what he does? No. After Baptism, we must carefully teach him how to obey the Lord, so that he lives in a state of grace. Through Baptism, our child has been reborn as a child of God; what follows is the maturation process.

Saint Paul cautions the Corinthians not to fall into the trap of presuming that the grace of God which comes through the sacraments will alone save them. He reminds them of the presumption of the people of God when they journeyed from Egypt to the Promised Land. In 1 Cor. 10:1-6, he issues this warning:

> I want you to know, brethren, that our fathers were all under the cloud, and all passed through the sea, and all were baptized into Moses in the cloud and in the sea, and all ate the same supernatural food, and all drank the same supernatural drink. For they drank from the supernatural Rock which followed them, and the Rock was Christ. Nevertheless with most of them God was not pleased; for they were overthrown in the wilderness. Now these things are warnings for us, not to desire evil as they did.

Their failure should encourage us to respond properly to God's grace.

Saint Peter offers another illustration of the need for the baptized to remain faithful. He draws a parallel between the salvation of Noah and his family and our salvation. They were saved from the flood while they were on the ark; we are saved from the floodwaters of sin through Baptism. After the flood, Noah made a vineyard and became drunk. His youngest son, Ham, decided to expose his father's sinfulness. When Noah realized what Ham had done, he cursed him. Ham had to repent of his evil deeds in order to be saved at the end of his life, despite already being saved from the flood by being on the ark.

Saint Peter says,

> Baptism, which corresponds to this [Noah and the ark], now
> saves you, not as a removal of dirt from the body but as an
> appeal to God for a clear conscience, through the resurrection
> of Jesus Christ (1 Pet. 3:21).

Though Noah and his family experienced salvation through
water during the flood, that did not guarantee salvation at the
end of their lives. Ham's failure to continue to respond to grace
is a word of warning: We are saved through the waters of
Baptism; yet, in order for us to be saved at the end of our lives,
we must keep that channel of grace open. In other words, we
must avoid mortal sin at all costs!

On the one hand, we do not want to have a false confidence
that nothing can change our relationship—or our children's—to
God; on the other, we—and our children—should act like the children of God that we are. Just as the Jews believed their children
were children of the covenant, so we should see our children as
Christians. We treat them as children of God, we respect them as
children of God, and we look for signs of faith and nurture them.

We should not rise each morning and pray fearfully, "Oh
God, I hope my kids are not going to hell," any more than we
should worry daily that they will act in such a way that we will
disown them. While any one of us can lose the grace of Baptism
by committing mortal sin, we can still regain that grace by
approaching our Father through the Sacrament of Penance. We
need to strike a balance—to pray fervently for our children's salvation *and* to express confidence in God as their Father. After all,
"faith is the assurance of things hoped for, the conviction of
things not seen" (Heb. 11:1).

Is "Rebaptism" Valid?

As Catholics, we affirm not only infant Baptism, but also the
Baptism of adult believers. "Believer's Baptism" refers to a previously unbaptized adult who is prepared to profess his faith pub-

licly. The Book of Acts records many conversions of adults who hear the Gospel and respond with a public declaration of their faith before they are baptized. We believe that Baptism effects the same changes in adults as in children—washing away original sin and all sins committed up to that point in time. However, the faith of the Christian community, including the faith of the parents and godparents, is the basis for requesting the Baptism of a child; whereas an adult must declare his or her own faith as a prerequisite for Baptism (cf. Catechism, nos. 1253-54). The ongoing conversion experiences of someone who has been baptized demonstrates the work of baptismal grace in his life.

Some Protestants have misunderstood the purpose of Baptism as primarily a public witness of a person's faith. They focus on some examples in Acts without examining the other biblical texts that we have already examined. This is why some denominations teach "rebaptism" for those who have professed faith in Christ, been baptized, and then have fallen away from practicing their faith. When they undergo a more profound conversion than before and want to give public testimony to their renewed faith, what do they need to do? According to some Protestant denominations, they have to be "rebaptized" because now they *really* believe. They come before their members in all sincerity because they want everyone to know God has worked profoundly in their lives. There are those who have been "rebaptized" one, two, three, or more times because they have had several conversion experiences.

The Catholic Church teaches that there is no need to be rebaptized because God accomplished His work the first time. Assuming the minister intended "to do what Christians do," that is, if water flowed and they were baptized in the name of the Father, Son, and Holy Spirit, it "worked." They received the character of Baptism, the seal of being incorporated into Christ. That they have come to faith at a later time is a fulfillment of that Baptism. And besides, there were no re-circumcisions in the Old Covenant!

Short Questions and Answers

Who can baptize? The ordinary ministers of the sacrament are deacons, priests, and bishops, but anyone can baptize children or adults who desire Baptism if there are unusual circumstances such as imminent death. Even a non-believer can baptize if he believes that he is doing what the Church does—using water and the Trinitarian formula as the Church commands (cf. Catechism, no. 1256). In fact, during her training as a nurse, my Presbyterian sister was encouraged to baptize a child if the child was dying and she was unsure the child had ever been baptized. And on more than one occasion, she has baptized a very sick child.

What is essential for a valid Baptism? A baptismal gown? Not essential. A party with family and friends afterwards? Not essential.

There are two essential features for a valid Baptism: Water must flow through pouring, sprinkling or immersion; and the Trinitarian formula ("in the name of the Father, and of the Son and of the Holy Spirit") must be invoked. Ordinarily, though, the rest of the baptismal liturgy should not be omitted.

If you've been baptized as a non-Catholic, is the Baptism valid? Yes, provided the two essential features listed above occurred. A few Fundamentalist and Pentecostal sects may not have water flowing or not even used water, in which case the baptisms would not be valid. And groups which baptize in the name of Jesus instead of using the Trinitarian formula or substitute "in the name of the Creator, Redeemer, and Sanctifier" do not have valid Baptisms.

Do I have an obligation to baptize my child even if my spouse does not agree? If you were married in the Church, you vowed, with at least the approval of your spouse, if not his/her full agreement, to raise your children in the Catholic faith. This commitment included baptizing them at a young age and teaching them the faith well (cf. Catechism, no. 1635).

The time to discuss differing views of Baptism and how the Christian faith will be imparted to your children is prior to your wedding day. Perhaps both you and your spouse agreed that the children would be raised Catholic but, as time passed, one of you challenged that idea. If your spouse no longer supports you in this decision, pray for him/her to have a change of heart so that the division between you does not wreak havoc on your marriage and family. If you are not being faithful to this vow, realize the seriousness with which God takes vows and ask Him for forgiveness for your neglect. Pray for a better understanding of the Sacrament of Baptism and for tools to teach your children the faith well. Then follow through on their Baptism and instruction in the faith.

As parents, we have an obligation to do everything we can for the well-being of our children. If this is true in the natural sphere in terms of nutrition, exercise, and intellectual development, how much more is this imperative in the supernatural sphere of the health of their souls? Through Baptism, we enable our children to enter into a relationship with God the Father through the Son. Through this relationship, they receive the gifts of forgiveness and the Holy Spirit to live a life of faith. Why would we want to withhold these gifts for any length of time? Let me share one woman's story.

One woman who had temporarily left the Catholic Church with her husband, and who had returned alone, was struggling with the question of Baptism for their newborn son. He had been born with very delicate health, which increased her concern. She wanted to baptize him in the Church and her husband did not. She yielded to her husband's wishes with great regret.

One day, her four-month-old son showed signs of breathing difficulty. The couple quickly took him to the doctor's office to be checked. He seemed to be having less difficulty by the time the doctor saw him, so the doctor sent them home. And, since the mother was in the middle of nursing him in the office, she continued nursing him in the car, rather than putting him in the car seat.

Halfway home, she turned the baby around so he could nurse on the other side. He wasn't breathing! Since her husband knew CPR, he pulled over to the side of the road and switched places with her, working on the baby as best he could while she drove to the emergency room. As he tried to resuscitate the baby, the mother said to her husband, "I'm sorry, but no matter what you think, I'm going to baptize our son."

Since she had no water, she wiped her tears from her face and touched him as she said, "I baptize you in the name of the Father, and of the Son, and of the Holy Spirit. Amen."

When they arrived at the hospital, there was nothing the staff could do to revive this little boy. However, the mother was at peace that she had baptized him, and the father agreed it had been the right thing to do. Today, probably thanks to the prayers of this little one, the whole family has been restored to the Catholic Church.

How can our children grow in their appreciation for Baptism? Include in your family's celebrations the baptismal anniversaries of each family member. These celebrations are opportunities to review what God did for your children at Baptism, as well as all He has done for them since then. Scott and I even called the churches where we were baptized as infants to find out our baptismal dates so that we could celebrate our anniversaries, too. What rich memories these special days create!

We should remind our children of their Baptism throughout the day. Every time we make the Sign of the Cross, we are saying, "God, I belong to you as your child because I was baptized in the name of the Father, and of the Son, and of the Holy Spirit." And every time we use holy water, entering or leaving a church, we remember that holy water was the means by which we were baptized. And every time we pray the "Our Father" or the "Glory Be" or repeat the Creed, we are appealing to Our Heavenly Father as His children.

Our own appreciation of God's work in our lives through Baptism will draw our children's hearts closer to Our Heavenly Father. Through Baptism, God made us His children, partakers of the divine nature, members of His Body, and temples of the Holy Spirit. He calls us to live lives faithful to the grace of our Baptism. Everything we do and say should be an expression of our gratitude and love for God and for His great work of grace in our lives. When we could not help ourselves, He chose us, blessed us, called us to be His own, and made us His children. Thanks be to God!

> [Y]ou are a chosen race, a royal priesthood, a holy nation, God's own people, that you may declare the wonderful deeds of him who called you out of darkness into his marvelous light. Once you were no people but now you are God's people; once you had not received mercy but now you have received mercy (1 Pet. 2:9-10).

Kimberly Hahn is an internationally known speaker and author. Along with her husband Scott, she is co-author of Rome, Sweet Home *(Ignatius Press, 1994), which chronicles their celebrated conversion to the Catholic faith.*

CHAPTER VII

The Family That Learns Together, Yearns Together

The Liturgy as Family Pedagogy

SEAN INNERST

Some Preliminaries

Families have always been the places where not only personal but also corporate identity is developed. In fact, to understand oneself as a member of a family is to have a corporate or group identity. "*We* Smiths have always been a proud people," a patriarch or matriarch of the Smith family would say to the younger Smiths at the beginning of a family story. In that word, "we," are contained both the beginning of a lesson on the Smith history and the conferral of an identity. The word "we" says, "You belong to us; you are one of us."

As children grow, they begin to think of themselves as a Smith or a Jones, or whatever family to which they belong. The character of the family, for good or ill, becomes part of their identity. Children naturally yearn to be like those they look up to, again, for good or ill. If the Smith family is made up of people with impressive accomplishments, young Smiths are likely to strive to reach and even surpass those marks. Over time, the Smith standard becomes their own standard: "We don't do that sort of thing." "We're better than that." If the Smiths are all thieves and murderers, that standard might more likely be: "We Smiths have never amounted to anything."[1]

The Catholic liturgy, which is the official worship of the Church, contains instances of the same kind. The Creed we profess at Mass begins, "*We* believe." The Liturgies of the Word, as celebrated in the sacraments, are family stories of the Church by which we are introduced into the corporate identity of the Church. The aim of all this storytelling in the liturgy is to instill a yearning in young Christians (of whatever age!) to be "one of us," to join us in the Family of God which looks to none other than God Himself—in the Person of Jesus Christ—as our standard of family behavior and accomplishment. The Family of God tells its story over and over again to instill a hunger, a yearning in its members for the holiness of Christ and for eternal beatitude with Him in heaven.

Liturgy is the official prayer of the Church, as distinguished from private devotions and prayers. "Pedagogy" needs a word of explanation too. This term usually refers to the science or art of teaching, the method itself. However, it derives from the Greek word *paidagogos*, who was a person, often a slave, who was given custody of the sons of a household. That function may have included some rudimentary instruction in academics, but primarily would have involved the actual training of a boy in those disciplines and virtues that prepared him to take his proper place in the family and society. The *paidagogos* was not so much a teacher but a moral guide—literally, a child-leader. One of his tasks would be to lead or escort a young boy to school. As an esteemed member of the household, he was charged with the vital task of forming the character of the heirs of that household.

In Galatians, Saint Paul uses *paidagogos* in metaphorical reference to the law of Moses. He says that Christians no longer

---

[1] Stanley Hauerwas, William Kirk Kilpatrick, and William Bennett have all contributed to the growing awareness of the importance of stories in building up and passing on the content of a culture. I am much indebted to their work in coming to recognize the same process at work in the liturgy.

need the law—our *paidagogos*—after the coming of Christ (3:23-26). Saint Paul intends that the Galatians think of themselves as adult heirs, as having attained the inheritance promised but never received under the Mosaic law. But knowing what we do about our need to grow continually in Christian faith, we could extend Paul's metaphor a little. Having arrived at the school of *the* Teacher, the *paidagogos* is no longer needed to get us to school, but we still have much need of the discipline he taught. The pedagogy referred to in the title of this chapter is, of course, that of Christ Himself. In the liturgy, He teaches us the disciplines of our new life of grace and the family history of the People of God.

That family history, the history of Israel, and the lessons it teaches are not voided by Christ's coming. He said specifically that His mission was not to abolish but to fulfill what had come before (Mt. 5:17). Speaking of the perpetual value of the older part of our family story, Pope John Paul II noted in his apostolic letter preparing for the new millennium:

> The economy of the Old Testament, in fact, was essentially ordered to preparing and proclaiming the coming of Christ, the Redeemer of the universe, and of his Messianic Kingdom. The books of the Old Covenant are thus a permanent witness to a careful divine pedagogy. *In Christ* this pedagogy achieves its purpose.[2]

I do not mean to imply that liturgy is *merely* a pedagogy. I would not want to even suggest that the sacraments of the Church, the subset of liturgy under discussion, do no more than teach us what to believe or how to behave. That would be to deny that they are primarily channels of life-changing grace. The Church has always taught that not only is perfect worship offered to God in the sacraments, but God also perfects us by our sacramental worship. He bestows, *ex opere operato*—from the very action of the sacrament itself—the grace to heal, perfect, and elevate our human nature. One of the effects of the sacraments is to instill a yearning for holiness.

---

[2] John Paul II, Apostolic Letter On Preparation for the Jubilee of the Year 2000 *Tertio Millennio Adveniente* (1994), no. 6 (original emphasis).

The Church, however, does want us to learn something from the sacraments. The very form of the liturgical life of the Church, the form of liturgical prayer, is vocal and bodily communication. A very large part of our liturgical prayer consists of petitions in which we voice our needs to God. We do so without any misconception that He does not already know them. In stating our needs we remind ourselves of our dependence on God's providence for everything. And, we may believe, it pleases Him, both that we call this to mind, and that we bring even our smallest concerns to Him, befitting the little children to whom He has promised the kingdom of heaven (cf. Mt. 19:14). Apart from the worship implied by prayers of petition, we also express contrition, thanksgiving, adoration, and all the shades of possible human response to the Divinity. Even Catholics who are familiar with the reasons and rhythms of the Church's liturgical worship learn something new about their God and themselves each time they participate in liturgical prayer.

The reason I am so quick to try to settle any possible misunderstandings about our topic is that some of the prayers we hear voiced in our churches today seem more to be designed to inform only ourselves of our obligations in justice to one another than to offer our worship to God. God seems not to come into the picture at all, unless as a kind of silent witness to our own good intentions. Jesus, so the current mood suggests, is relevant only as an example of "doing justice," not as Savior, as the Source of all saving grace.

There is no arguing that our liturgies today are often conducted as though they were aimed solely at individual or communal fulfillment. I read a parish bulletin some months ago that reminded the parishioners that "the liturgy is for the people, not the people for the liturgy." In many parishes that I've visited around the country, it is clear that we, or "the community," is the focus of the whole liturgical enterprise.

However, the root of the word "liturgy" suggests that it is a work *of* the people, not *for* the people. Worship implies an object and that ought not to be ourselves. With all the talk we hear about justice today, we have forgotten that the virtue of religion is a species of justice. We *owe* God worship; it is His due. As an act of worship, the liturgy is *for* God. Not that He needs it in any necessary sense, but our intent should be to conduct it for Him as a gift, however insufficient it appears to be. The Mass is Christ's own perfect act of worship of the Father and that makes up for all our insufficiency at worship, and superabundantly at that.

This reminder is offered because, if Catholic liturgy is anything other than worship—to the exclusion of true worship—it is, at best, a waste of time or, at worst, idolatrous. If either of these is the case, it would be better to stay home. I apologize to those of you to whom this is obvious, and therefore tiresome. No one ought to have to say that liturgy is for the worship of God, but we live in an age when the self-evident sometimes has to be explained.

Liturgy is truly pedagogical; it teaches us something. But what? In the context of the worship of God and in the midst of the transformation worked by His grace, the sacraments of the liturgy teach us about the God of the covenant and how to keep that covenant with Him. In those two things, really, consist the whole of the catechism. The creed, the sacraments themselves, the moral life, and prayer—the traditional four pillars of the catechism—all express in different modes these two things: the God of the covenant and covenant keeping.

The first part of that description is really the most important. That the liturgy is primarily worship of the God of the covenant, we have already touched upon. That God works a transformation in us by grace is vital to our concern with the liturgy as pedagogy because one cannot simply "learn" to be a saint. One can learn the science of the saints, but to *be* a saint one must will it. To will it effectively one must have one's will transformed by grace. Only by that grace can we live in accord with the covenant outlined by Jesus in the Sermon on the Mount.

Pope John Paul II tells us,

> Catechesis is intrinsically linked with the whole of liturgical and sacramental activity, for it is in the sacraments, especially

in the Eucharist, that Christ Jesus works in fullness for the
transformation of human beings.[3]

He reminds us that the aim of all catechetical pedagogy is

to put people not only in touch but in communion, in intimacy,
with Jesus Christ: only He can lead us to the love of the Father
in the Spirit and make us share in the life of the Holy Trinity.[4]

A loving, intimate communion with Christ not only teaches
but transforms us in a way that no other lesson or teaching
method can. This is what Saint Paul urges upon the Romans in
saying, "[B]e transformed by the renewal of your mind, that you
may prove what is the will of God" (Rom. 12:2). By the grace of
Christ in the liturgy, we are not merely informed but transformed.

What is left to us, then, is to examine the method God uses
in the liturgy to work that transformation. The principle captured
in the Latin phrase *ex opere operato* (from the work itself)
expresses the manner in which grace is imparted through the
sacraments. What we have yet to see is His *modus operandi*, His
way of working in the sacraments, whereby He uses a gradual
process which appeals to the intellect and the will—in fact, all
our human powers. In the liturgy, we do not simply step under
some sort of transformation ray which works a change on us pas-
sively. No, God the Father, through the instrumentality of the
Church which His Son has formed and His Spirit filled, appeals
through the use of human instruments to all the capacities of the
human person, with the intention of making creatures into
covenant sons and daughters.

---

[3] John Paul II, Post-Synodal Apostolic Exhortation On Catechesis in Our Time
Catechesi Tradendae (1979), no. 23.
[4] *Ibid.*, no. 5.

The Family of God

To explain the way that God both informs and transforms us in the liturgy, we first need to consider the adjectival use of the word "family" in the title of this chapter. For those who are accustomed to thinking of the Church and even her liturgy in institutional terms, that word may come as a shock. The experience of the average Sunday Mass-goer is anything but familial. We, especially in America, are a culture of strangers. We hear a tremendous amount of talk about "community" in the Church today. In fact, the word "community" has entirely supplanted "Church" in some circles. But for all the talk about community and all the strained efforts at forming it, perhaps best exemplified by the appearance of the formalized ministry of "greeter," there is a woeful lack of community in our parishes. The mere fact that we must designate people to welcome their fellow parishioners to Mass—whose names they may not know—testifies to the lack of welcome people often feel in their own parish communities. We are strangers to each other, even at our liturgies.

I am not implying that we all ought to be intimate friends in our parish liturgies. Strangely enough, there is something in that impulse that is fundamentally at odds with the Catholic conception of the Church. She is the Hebrew *qahal*, the Greek *ekklesia*, that people called together by God for the purpose of worship. It is a human activity, but one that transcends mere camaraderie, mere community, because it is established for our good by God Himself.

Were every person at a given liturgy a stranger to the others, utterly incapable of communicating with any other person by barrier of language; were each of a different racial and national background; in short, if there were insurmountable obstacles present to the formation of human friendship, all those present would still be bound together in an utterly mysterious way by the common activity of Catholic worship to which they have each been called by God. That such a humanly disparate congregation is a theoretical possibility and even an actuality at certain international events expresses the Catholic character of the Church. In fact, it is at just such events that one is struck by the joyous fact that all our fevered efforts at forming community are as nothing before the mysterious power that makes us not merely friends but brothers and sisters in Christ when we worship together.

It is almost certainly the current failure to understand that liturgy is first and foremost worship that has led to the lack of community. In fact, what we long for and call "community" is actually the communion that comes with the grace of Holy Communion, whereby God unites us as His Mystical Body. If we are not worshipping, but only straining for community, we will have neither communion nor even mere community.

Our worship in the liturgy ought to form bonds that are closer than friendship, closer than community. By God's design the liturgy is a covenantal, familial worship in which the Family of God is simultaneously formed, informed, and transformed. While we are here concerned primarily with the middle term, the pedagogical process of being *informed*, the importance of the formation of the covenant family by grace and the transformation of that family in grace ought to remain at the forefront of our considerations.

As has already been suggested above, that God acts on us in the liturgy is the first consideration, and it is that fact which makes worthwhile our consideration of the *way* in which He acts on us in the liturgy. Grace is at work in all three of the modes of God's action upon us in the liturgy. It is not as though, while He is teaching us, He is also bestowing grace upon us. His manner of informing us is a grace-bestowing action in itself. We are not formed and then informed, and then, at a later moment, transformed. The sacramental liturgy does all of these at once when we are well-disposed. The whole of the Mass imparts grace, although the Liturgy of the Word and the Liturgy of the Eucharist each have their proper moment.

There are many elements in our worship that point to its familial character. So many, in fact, that they have become almost invisible to us. Humans have the remarkable capacity, so operative in our ritual activity, whereby familiarity breeds ignorance! The commonplace rarely excites our interest and so is often overlooked entirely.

Our hearts ought to thrill with thanks when our lips part to speak the words "Our Father," the prayer that Jesus Himself gave to us. Of the many references in the New Testament to the familial character of Christian discipleship, Saint Paul offers perhaps the most precise description in his Epistle to the Romans:

> For all who are led by the Spirit of God are sons of God. For you did not receive the spirit of slavery to fall back into fear, but you have received the spirit of sonship. When we cry, "Abba! Father!" it is the Spirit himself bearing witness with our spirit that we are children of God (Rom. 8:14-16).

If individual Catholics are sometimes dulled to the tremendous condescension on the part of the eternal God of which we are the beneficiaries, the Church always celebrates our filiation for us by a profusion of familial references from her common lexicon. We are always speaking of "Fathers" or "Mothers Superior," of "Brother Francis" or "Sister Clare." Not satisfied with "Bishop of Rome," we call the successor of Saint Peter "*il Papa*." Following the example of the Master Himself, we call Him our "Groom" and ourselves His "Bride." The Church is our "Mother," as is Mary. Our Catholic language is peppered with family references till we do not seem to hear them anymore. But we *are* a family, a covenant family.

The likely culprit in our inattention to the familial character of the liturgy is, again, our loss of the sense of the purpose and transformative character of the sacraments. Lacking a sense that a marvelous grace-wrought transformation is taking place as we worship, it's not surprising that those who attend our liturgies would come to the conclusion that all the familial terms of reference we employ are little more than polite address. Our impoverished conception of liturgy as "for the people" is consistent with a belief that the terms "brother," "sister," and "Father" are not indicative of a metaphysical change in us and in our relationship with each other and God, but are merely affectionate forms of reference. That is, they are viewed only as niceties which express mankind's utopian longings for universal brotherhood.

Our Passover Has Been Sacrificed

Since we really *are* the covenant Family of God by Baptism, it ought not to surprise us that the central act of liturgical worship in the Church should be the action of a family. Jesus inaugurated the Mass in the context of a Passover meal. Cardinal Ratzinger writes, "Israel's Passover was and is a family celebration. It was celebrated in the home and not in the Temple."[5] He reminds us that the signal and foundational event for the people of Israel at the time of the Exodus occurred within the family, establishing it as the bastion against the destructive forces of evil, the place where peace was maintained and order retained against the external chaos unleashed by sin. He goes on to say that by the time of Jesus, the whole of Jerusalem took on this same familial role as the "locus of salvation."[6]

With the apostles, Jesus formed on that Passover night a family unit, a *habhura*, such as was allowed by the custom of the day for those who journeyed on pilgrimage to Jerusalem to observe the feast. In the Eucharist, which He instituted on that night, we are made inheritors of the Passover, the family feast at the heart of post-exilic Israel (see 1 Cor. 5:7-8; cf. Catechism, no. 1364):

> Companions of his pilgrimage, we constitute Christ's house;
> thus, the Church is the new family, the new city, and for us she

[5] Joseph Cardinal Ratzinger, *Behold the Pierced One* (San Francisco: Ignatius Press, 1986), 103.
[6] *Ibid.*, 104. Ratzinger also recalls the startling fact that Jesus was violating a religious ordinance in going beyond the Kedron to face His Passion in the Garden of Gethsemane. Beyond that boundary, the *shalom* of Jerusalem, the peace secured within the collective family gathered there for the Passover, gave way to chaos. In His desire to embrace the Father's saving will for us, Jesus strode straight into the territory of the Angel of Death. In this chapter, which was originally a Holy Thursday homily, Ratzinger challenges his readers to go out from the Eucharist having been strengthened by grace to face evil in the world in imitation of Christ.

signifies all that Jerusalem was–that living home which banishes the powers of chaos and makes an area of peace, which upholds both creation and us.[7]

There is one particular aspect of the Passover that shows that the Eucharist is not only a sacrificial family meal but a family pedagogy. Covenant renewals in the ancient world in general, and in Israel in particular, always included a recitation of the great deeds of the stronger party in the covenant in what has been called the historical prologue.[8] This section of the covenant ceremonial intended "to encourage a feeling of gratitude in the vassal so as to establish firmly the claim of the suzerain on him."[9]

In God's command to Israel to keep the Passover as a perpetual ordinance, He says, "This day shall be for you a memorial day, and you shall keep it as a feast to the Lord" (Ex. 12:14). In regard to this memorial, the Catechism comments:

In the sense of Sacred Scripture the *memorial* is not merely the recollection of past events but the proclamation of the mighty works wrought by God for men. In the liturgical celebration of these events, they become in a certain way present and real. This is how Israel understands its liberation from Egypt: every time Passover is celebrated, the Exodus events are made present to the memory of believers so that they may conform their lives to them (no. 1363, original emphasis).

The Passover, then, is a memorial feast in which Israel, gathered in family units, recalled the first phase of the formation of the Mosaic covenant in which God demonstrated His absolute power over all cosmic forces—indeed, over life itself—and so also the allegiance Israel owed Him. The events of the Passover and Exodus are so basic to Israel's identity that they remain a

---

[7] *Ibid.*, 105.
[8] Here I am drawing from J. Levenson, *Sinai and Zion: An Entry into the Jewish Bible* (San Francisco: Harper, 1985), 26 *et seq.* Levenson summarizes in succinct fashion what scholars have come to call the *covenant formulary*, those elements that were common to covenant making and renewal in the ancient Near East.
[9] *Ibid.*, 27.

constant in the covenant renewals. The God of Israel was dis-
tinctively the One who had delivered His people out of bondage
in Egypt.

The Passover *haggadah*, the memorial recitation of the history
of Israel with special attention given to the events of the Exodus,
represented a way of mystically incorporating each new generation into the covenant with Yahweh.[10] As we see the Passover
seder still celebrated among the Jewish people today, the
youngest child asks questions of his elders about the character
and significance of this night (cf. Ex. 12:26-27). "This night" is
not merely the night on which this particular instance of the feast
is celebrated but, ritually, the very night on which the angel of
death passed over those families of Israel whom God had preserved from harm by the blood of the Passover Lamb.

The *haggadah*, then, like the standard historical prologue of
the covenant renewal ceremony, is a recitation of—and also a
participation in—the saving history of Israel. Every year, by the
direct mandate of God, the Jewish people remind themselves of
the covenant obligation they owe to Him. More than that, in the
seder each generation is introduced into the covenant. The family

---

[10] The character of this mystical incorporation effected by covenant renewal is described
by Levenson with particular reference to the recitation of Ps. 81, which he identifies
as a prayer for regular liturgical renewal of the covenant. "The goal of this speech, as
of the covenant renewal in which it probably originated, is to induce Israel to step into
the position of the generation of Sinai, in other words, to actualize the past so that
this new generation will become the Israel of the classic covenant relationship (cf. Deut.
30:19-20). Thus life in covenant is not something merely granted, but something won
anew, rekindled and reconsecrated in the heart of each Israelite in every generation"
(*ibid.*, 81).

While Levenson would not necessarily see in the modern celebration of the Passover
seder a covenant renewal, arguing as he does that covenant renewal liturgies of the
kind suggested by Ps. 81 did not survive into the rabbinic era of Judaism, that does
not necessarily mean that such a view was not held in the first century. In fact, that
Jesus precisely enjoins His followers to keep this ritual meal as a memorial, and that
He makes reference to the "new covenant" in His blood which His sacrifice on
Calvary effects, would argue in favor of just such an appreciation of the Passover as a
covenant renewal. This would certainly be in keeping with Jesus' inclination not to
abolish, but rather to fulfill the Old Law (Mt. 5:17).

I should also mention that Levenson does argue that liturgical renewal of the covenant
did survive into the rabbinic era in the form of the daily recital of the *Shma* prayer.

participates in the covenant of Israel, within the context of the recital or memorial of the saving history of Israel. The children do not merely hear the history of Israel, they are incorporated into Israel by covenant renewal; they do not merely hear the recitation of the saving works of God, they are liberated from slavery and death in Egypt to which they are heirs by blood, not only their own, but that of the covenant. Each child in the family, in effect, becomes a little Israel by incorporation into the covenant with Yahweh and this happens through the instrumentality of what we could call a ritual memorial pedagogy.

As we know, the Passover of the Old Law prefigured and so, in a sense, itself passed over into the Eucharist of the New Law. That transition was effected by Jesus Himself on the night before He died. As Saint Paul affirms, the Christ we receive in holy Communion is "our paschal lamb" (1 Cor. 5:7). As we also know, He instituted the Eucharist at a Passover celebration. What then, we might ask, is our Christian passover *haggadah*? What in our Passover of the New Covenant corresponds to the ritual memorial pedagogy of the great saving works of God? While it is true that the institution narrative of the Mass is itself a "mini *haggadah*," in a fuller sense, it is the whole Liturgy of the Word that we celebrate in anticipation of the Liturgy of the Eucharist which constitutes the new *haggadah*.

Some Scripture scholars have advanced the thesis that the Gospels, at least in their earliest forms, were intended to fulfill the function of the Passover *haggadah* within the context of Christian initiation, as it would have occurred at the Easter Vigil. Bruno Barnhart cites the earlier work of Daube, Bowman, and Standaert as pointing to the conclusion that the Gospel of Mark was just such a "Christian Passover *Haggadah*." He then advances his own case that the Gospel of John is also, if not specifically a "paschal *haggadah*," at least "structured as the basis of a sacramental catechesis."[11] The implication is that the very matter, the

---

[11] Bruno Barnhart, *The Good Wine* (Mahwah, NJ: Paulist Press, 1993), 334 *et seq.*

scriptural matter, at the heart of the Liturgy of the Word, the Gospels themselves, are *haggadah* material.

In fact, the structure of the Liturgy of the Word at the Easter Vigil *today* is obviously arranged to lead the gathered Church through the great saving works of God in salvation history. This is done with the intention of explaining the biblical precedent for the sacraments that will be received by the elect on that very night. After each of the seven possible Old Testament readings in that richest of the Liturgies of the Word during the Church year, a Responsorial Psalm is sung which places the events recounted in the previous reading directly on the lips of the congregation. Just as happens at the Jewish Passover *haggadah*, a past event is made present through its ritual recollection and, as is the case generally with the Responsorial Psalms, the event is then celebrated, not in the third person, but in the first person. To put it succinctly, the congregation is not an audience during the Liturgy of the Word of the Mass, but a body of participants.[12]

Anglicans call their liturgical readings "lessons," and I think that begins to capture the sense of the Liturgy of the Word in the Mass as a pedagogy. But to get the fullest sense of the way in which God teaches us in the Eucharist, we need to recover the Jewish sense of covenantal renewal through a ritual memorial pedagogy that we have inherited in the new Passover instituted by Christ.

A last word about our new Passover. As Saint Paul indicates in 1 Cor. 5:7, by Christ's becoming the "paschal lamb," the sacrificial victim, He shows us, and effects for us, not merely a

---

[12] For a wonderful analysis and meditation on the liturgy as participational and conversional, with particular application to the rites of the RCIA, see Pamela Jackson, *Journeybread for the Shadowlands* (Collegeville, MN: The Liturgical Press, 1993). It should also be noted that this understanding of the liturgy bears heavily on the question, so vital today, of what constitutes "active participation" on the part of the congregation at Mass as called for in SC 14. Without discounting the importance of the bodily and subjective elements of liturgical participation, this understanding suggests that it is the very character of the liturgy itself which, by God's grace, makes us participants in it. It is interesting to note that this passage from Vatican II does say that such "active participation (*participatio actuosa*) . . . is demanded by the very nature of the liturgy." That could just as likely mean that liturgy, by its nature, makes us participants, as that it requires that we (actively) participate.

political passover from slavery into freedom, but an eschatological passover into eternal life. If a yearning to be with Him in eternity is to be instilled in our ritual memorial pedagogy, it must first be clear that this is a sacrifice which leads to death. Without His death there is no passing over to life. This has sometimes been obscured in our liturgies. Second, it must be clear that as the new Passover and the act of a divine Person, the Mass is an eternal event which is constantly present before the Father with the angels and saints in attendance (cf. Rev. 5:6). All the pageantry of the Church's Eucharistic liturgy ought to aim at expressing the sacrificial and eschatological or heavenly character of the new Passover, so as to instill in the congregation a longing to be numbered among the elect (cf. Catechism, no. 1402).

Mnemosyne, the Mother of the Muses

There is an old maxim to the effect that lack of reflection is the enemy of the spiritual life. To state it even more strongly, one could say that to some degree reflection *is* the spiritual life. Our Lady's example of pondering in her heart all the events that surrounded her divine Son's childhood is the model for all Christians who wish to advance in the life of prayer. The act of prayerful and loving remembrance of God's saving work in our lives is the engine of the virtue of hope and the food upon which faith feeds.

To the Greeks, *Mnemosyne* (memory) was the mother of the nine muses, those sacred goddesses who presided over the arts and the sciences of astronomy and history. This myth vividly points to the truth that memory is essential to our human nature. Man is defined as a rational animal. When we say that we are rational, we mean that we are able to make judgments about things, a capacity that other animals do not demonstrate. Yet, without at least the rudiments of memory, rational thought is impossible.

Judgment, the act of asserting something about something, such as, "The ball is red," depends upon our memory. If you cannot remember what a ball is or what red corresponds to, you cannot pair ball and red together in a meaningful way. Without memory, you could not make so simple a statement as, "The ball is red." In fact, the whole process of human training, or what I have called pedagogy, consists in slowly building the store of memory so that we can make more and more sophisticated judgments. "The ball is red" is the first educational step toward "God is one."

The things that Mary pondered over about Jesus probably included her emotions of awe, joy, and sadness, as well as her judgments about what had happened to the Holy Family and why. That is probably what the Bible means by saying that Our Lady "pondered all these things in her heart" (Lk. 2:19, 51). She thought about the experiences and felt again the emotions that those experiences generated in her. All this was made possible by that wonderful human capacity that we share with her: our memory.

In *De Trinitate*, Saint Augustine's great treatise on the Trinity, he looks into the human soul to examine whether there might be some insight found there about the inner life of God.[13] Augustine had considerable warrant in doing so in the phrase from Genesis: "[I]n the image of God he created him; male and female he created them" (Gen. 1:27). If we are created in God's image, Augustine reasoned, then perhaps the geography of the human soul might tell us something about the life of the Trinity whose image it bears.

Augustine reflected on the three powers of the human soul—memory, intellect, and will—and suggested that these three powers are, in a very limited way, like the three Persons of the Holy Trinity: our memory being like the Father, our intellect like the Son, and our will like the Holy Spirit. Again, the likeness is faint. After all, nothing in the world is really "like" God. He is different in kind from everything He has created; He is the perfect

---

[13] Saint Augustine, *De Trinitate*, Bk. VIII, ch. 6. Augustine loved these sorts of analogies suggesting the Trinitarian nature of God. In chapter 10 of the same Book VIII, he reflects that love is threefold in that it requires a lover, a beloved, and the love between them. In *De Civitate Dei* (*The City of God*), Book XI, chapters 21, 23, 24, and 25, he plays with these traces of the Trinity in creation, in the heavenly city, and in the division of sciences.

uncreated Being. So in this very limited way, when we love with our will, we express the image of God as the Spirit who is the eternal love between the Father and the Son. When we think, we express in ourselves the image of God as the eternal Son who is the Father's thought of Himself. When we remember, we express in our souls the image of God the Father who is the eternal Principle in the eternal processions of the Son and the Spirit. Just as there are three Persons in the one God, so also there are three powers—memory, intellect, and will—in the one soul.

So, to draw us back to our considerations of memory where we began, when we ponder or remember God's gifts to us, we do so in an act of homage to the Father, who has saved us in the Son and sanctified us through the Holy Spirit. This pondering of the events of our salvation in homage to the Father is what the Church teaches us to do in the Liturgy of the Word and in the re-presentation of Christ's saving death on Calvary in the Liturgy of the Eucharist.

The precedent for this kind of liturgical remembering is the long, time-honored one we considered above. The ancient Jewish feasts of Passover, Unleavened Bread, Tabernacles (or Booths), and the feast of Weeks were all commemorations or memorials of the events of the Exodus from Egypt, in which the people of Israel gave thanks to God and symbolically relived the tribulations and victories of their forefathers. These feasts, instituted by Yahweh's command, were celebrated by Israel to renew in each generation the national memory of Yahweh's powerful saving acts in the Exodus. Again, the Jews believed that they actually participated, in a ritual fashion, in these defining events from the nation's history over and over again, year after year.

This ritual remembering was considered by the Jews to be a vital part of remaining faithful to their covenant with God. The importance of remembering for the people of Israel is largely responsible for the preservation of the literature of the Old Testament. The Scriptures were memory aids that God had inspired Moses, the prophets, and Jewish historians to commit to writing, so that the great works of God might not be forgotten.

Sacred history was not an academic exercise for Israel, but a vital part of her religious practice.[14]

When Jesus, in the context of a Passover seder meal, said to His apostles, "Do this in memory of Me," He was calling for a familiar practice on the part of His Jewish disciples. The *in meam commemorationem* ("in memory of me") of the Mass, which begins with a sacrificial meal and ends with Jesus' "it is finished" at His death on Calvary, is *the* great saving event of all of human history.[15] It is for this reason that the Mass, the Holy Eucharist, is the daily remembrance—and thanksgiving for that which is remembered—of the Catholic world. We believe, as did the Jews, that we actually participate in that saving event which we celebrate. It is vital to our faithfulness to the New Covenant that we do so. In the Eucharist, all the past saving events of God are summed up and fulfilled in the perfect offering of the Son to the Father. When we remember all that the Father has done for us in the offering of His Son, we honor the Father in the profoundest way possible because it is the Son's own way of honoring the Father.

Memory is the wellspring of all thought and, when we fill our memories with the memories of the heavenly Father and all He has done for us, we are renewed in mind and heart (cf. Rom. 12:2). The memory is an awesome faculty; its sanctification can sanctify us and its degradation can degrade us. If we fill our memory with pornography, then it will act as a tempter and a tool of the Tempter. But if we fill our memory with the memories of the heavenly Father, then it will serve His loving will for us, drawing us into ever greater faith, hope, and charity.

The liturgy of the Church is not only the place where we recall God's love for us, but the premier place where God pours out His love upon us. As such, the liturgy is the best place for us

---

[14] Mircea Eliade, the renowned historian of religions, argues in *The Myth of the Eternal Return* (Princeton, NJ: Princeton University Press, 1954) that Judaism represented a marked departure in the history of mankind with its conception of time as linear. For Eliade, it is primarily the revelation of God in history, as active in human history, which enables man to conceive of time as something other than an ongoing cycle of destruction and rebirth.

[15] See Scott Hahn, "The Fourth Cup," *This Rock*, Sept. 1997, 7-12.

to learn our lessons about who God is and the best place for God to make us who He wants us to be. The liturgy is the Father's universal plan for our mental health. There He seeks to heal all our memories by giving us His memories, the family memories of an infinitely loving Father.

In the first apostolic exhortation of his pontificate, John Paul II wrote, "The blossoms, if we may call them that, of faith and piety do not grow in the desert places of a memory-less catechesis."[16] I would suggest that it is not merely a lack of memorization of doctrinal formulas that has created the spiritual desert in which we find ourselves today. Without memories, minds, and hearts full of the whole family history of the People of God contained in the Scriptures and "stored in the depths of the Church's memory,"[17] we condemn ourselves to an amnesia of the soul. Lacking those memories, we have no individual or corporate identity. Those who attend Mass regularly do hear the family story retold, but not necessarily with the conscious reflection needed to enable them to become what they hear. If we are unfamiliar with the sacred Scriptures, we do not know how they fit into the liturgies we attend.

The liturgy of the Church is the catechetical center of Catholic life, because there God Himself not only teaches us our family history, but also incorporates us into that same family by His transforming grace. That does not mean, of course, that a systematic and comprehensive dogmatic catechesis outside of the liturgy is unnecessary. On the vital connection between memory, catechesis, and liturgical celebration, the Holy Father asks,

> [S]hould we not attempt to put this faculty back into use in an intelligent and even original way in catechesis, all the more since the celebration or "memorial" of the great events of the history of salvation require a precise knowledge of them?[18]

---

[16] *Catechesi Tradendae*, no. 55.

[17] *Ibid.*, no. 22.

[18] *Ibid.*, no. 55.

Proper catechesis prepares us to offer the conscious and active participation in the liturgy that the Second Vatican Council envisioned for the faithful. Therefore, all catechesis ought to aim at making us better worshippers, better adorers, of the Holy Trinity. Our religious education ought to aid in this process of filling the memory with all the events of our Catholic family history so that we will be equipped to offer perfect honor, glory, and praise to the eternal Father in the assembly of the Family of God. Just as young Smiths yearn to become what they hear in the tales of those Smiths who have gone before them, we Christians learn in the liturgy to yearn for that fullness of the stature of Christ which God the Father intends His children to attain (cf. Eph. 4:11-16).

Sean Innerst is the director of the Office of Religious Education and Evangelization in the Diocese of Rapid City, South Dakota. A convert to the Catholic faith from the Society of Friends or Quakers, he edits and writes for a variety of Catholic publications, is a contributor to the Encyclopedia of Catholic Doctrine *(Our Sunday Visitor, 1997), and is preparing a catechetical commentary on the Sunday Lectionary based on the Catechism.*

CHAPTER VIII

The Heart of the Home
Jesus in the Eucharist

EDWARD P. SRI

In writing about the Eucharist and the Bible, I'm reminded of a true story about a young Protestant man who, while flipping through the television stations, came across a strange sight on his TV screen: a Catholic priest talking about the Mass. Struck by the oddity of finding this on television, the young man decided to stop and listen to what the priest had to say. In those few moments his life began to change.

The next morning, he rushed into the office to find a coworker whom he knew to be a Catholic. Awestruck by what the priest on TV had said about the Eucharist, the young Protestant needed to share his excitement with somebody who might understand. So with great enthusiasm he told his Catholic friend all he had learned about the Mass.

"I had no idea you Catholics believe Jesus is really present in the Eucharist!"

The Catholic responded, "Yeah, we do."

"That's amazing! So when there's a Mass, you Catholics believe God really becomes present on the altar, that the bread and wine really become Jesus' body and blood, and that you actually receive Him in Communion?"

"Yeah . . . I think that sounds right."

"So how often does this happen? Once a year? Easter? Christmas?"

The Catholic answered matter-of-factly, "Actually, I think there are Masses every day of the week at most churches, but we only have to go once a week, on Sunday."

"*Have* to go?! What do you mean *have* to go? If I were Catholic, I'd want to go and receive as often as I could!!!"

• • •

I don't think I'd be exaggerating if I said many of us Catholics often do not fully appreciate the great gifts that we have inherited as children in the Family of God, the Church. This is especially true of the greatest gift of all, the Eucharist. A recent survey shows the great confusion Catholics have about this central mystery of our faith: About two-thirds of American Catholic adults think the Eucharist is only a "symbolic reminder" of Jesus–an important religious sign, but not Jesus' body and blood.[1] Yet for 2,000 years the Catholic Church—from the voices of the early Christians to the recent teachings of Vatican II and the Catechism—has consistently taught Jesus' Real Presence in the Eucharist and the centrality of the Eucharist in the Christian life. Indeed, the Eucharist is the very heart of our Catholic home.

Let's return to our family roots and rekindle our love for this great gift Christ has left the Church by taking a fresh look at Jesus' words and actions at the Last Supper, when He instituted the Eucharist.

By entering into the biblical world, the Jewish worldview of Jesus' day, we learn that *practically every detail of the Last Supper account is charged with great meaning*—a meaning, however, which often is lost to modern readers who may not be too familiar with the Old Testament. Sometimes we miss subtle yet important

---

[1] See G. Grisez and R. Shaw, "Has the sacrament become just a symbolic reminder?" Our *Sunday Visitor* (August 28, 1994), 5.

details of the New Testament because we do not fully appreciate the great story that went before—God's preparation for Jesus in the Old Testament. In fact, many of the Gospel narratives about Jesus assume the reader knows the key elements of that Old Testament background, which provide a frame of reference for understanding what Jesus said and did throughout His life on earth.

One biblical scholar recently used the following example to make a similar point.[2] Take the statement, "It's going to rain." On one level, the sentence seems quite clear. However, it may have different meanings depending on its context. For a family that is planning a picnic, this statement is bad news. For a weatherman who predicted today's rain five days ago, it would mean confirmation of his meteorological abilities. But for an East African society suffering from drought and fearing another season of crop failure, it could mean the climactic movement from dwindling hope and sorrow to fulfillment and jubilation.

It is a similar situation with Jesus' words at the Last Supper: "This is my body," "This is the blood of the new covenant," "forgiveness of sins," and "Do this in memory of me." For many contemporary Christians, such talk of body, blood, Passover, and memorial probably would not have a lot of meaning in our day-to-day life. But for a devout, first-century Jew, these words—recited during a Passover meal—would have summed up many of the hopes and expectations of the people of Jesus' day. These simple words could have signaled the movement from expectation to fulfillment, from tragedy to exuberant rejoicing.

A New Passover
"and they prepared the passover"
(Mt. 26:19; cf. Mk. 14:16; Lk. 22:13)

That Jesus began His Passion and celebrated the Last Supper in the context of the Passover would have been of great significance to the Jews of His day. This annual celebration was the feast of

---

[2] The following example is adapted from N.T. Wright, *Jesus and the Victory of God* (Minneapolis: Fortress Press, 1996), 198-99.

all feasts. It summed up Israel's history and identity as the chosen people of God, and fueled their hopes for a new era that
would bring redemption from foreign oppression and forgiveness of sins.

Why was the Passover so important? Because it recalled the
fateful night when God freed Israel from slavery in Egypt during
the time of Moses. Despite several plagues which Yahweh inflict-
ed on the Egyptians, Pharaoh repeatedly refused to let the
Israelites go. But on the night of that first Passover, God instructed the Israelites to slay a lamb, eat its flesh, and then mark their
doorposts with the lamb's blood. All the first-born sons in Egypt
were struck down that night, but the first-born Israelites were
spared because Yahweh "passed over" the homes that had the
mark of the lamb's blood (Ex. 12). After this tenth and most
severe plague, Pharaoh finally released the Israelites from slavery,
and the people fled from Egypt in the night. Thus, the Passover
night marked Israel's redemption from slavery and established
their national identity as God's chosen people. The Passover feast
would commemorate this event forever.

Subsequent generations of Israelites participated in this pivotal event by celebrating the Passover feast. Yahweh instructed
them to keep the Passover as "a memorial" (Ex. 12:14). It is
important to note that, for the Jews, such a memorial feast
involved much more than a simple remembrance or calling to
mind of a past event. It was quite different from modern memorial holidays such as the American celebration of the Fourth of
July. Every year on July 4, Americans recall the signing of the
Declaration of Independence and the founding of their nation.
However, in the biblical understanding of "memorial," the past is
not only remembered, but also *relived*. Mysteriously, the past
event actually was made present here and now in the celebration.
This is why Jews celebrating Passover at the time of Jesus thought
of themselves as one with their ancestors—as though they themselves had fled from Egypt. As one ancient Jewish commentator
explained, "In every generation a man must so regard himself as

if he came forth himself out of Egypt."[3] As such, the Passover memorial forged solidarity across the many generations of Israelites: All Israelites of all generations were delivered from Egypt. All shared in this foundational event. All were truly united in God's covenant family.

The Passover not only looked to the past, but also turned to the future, as participants would plea for Yahweh to vindicate His people once again. Especially in the time of Jesus, the Passover was associated with great messianic expectation and hope for a *new* exodus. Indeed, the whole drama of the exodus became a model of future liberation, and expressed the hope that God would act again and bring salvation to His people. In fact, the prophets had long foretold of another exodus, a great covenant renewal and the arrival of the messianic king who would bring forgiveness of sins and vindicate His faithful people. This message gave great comfort to the Jews, who had been oppressed by foreign rulers for over 500 years and were hoping for Yahweh to redeem them again, liberating His people as He had done many years before in Egypt.

Longing for the Messiah and the new exodus was the heart and soul of first-century Judaism, and the Passover above all other feasts summed up these hopes. In fact, an ancient Passover poem, used in synagogue liturgy, depicts four great events in salvation history occurring on the same calendar day as Passover: the creation of the universe, the covenant with Abraham, and Israel's deliverance from Egypt all occurred on the night of the Passover. And it was on this night that the future messianic king

---

[3] From the *Mishnah* (Pesahim, X, 5), translated by Herbert Danby (Oxford: Oxford University Press, 1933), 151. The text goes on to read: "[F]or it is written [Ex. 13:8], And thou shalt tell thy son in that day saying, It is because of that which the Lord did for me when I came forth out of Egypt." This understanding of memorial is also seen in the modern Haggadah for the Passover ritual: "It was not only our ancestors whom he delivered, but when he delivered them he delivered us with them, because it was not one enemy alone who rose up against us to crush us. The Holy One—blessed be he—rescues us from their hand" T. Maertens, *A Feast in Honor of Yahweh* (Notre Dame: Fides Publishers, 1965), 109.

was expected to bring redemption.[4]

This is the setting in which Jesus chose to celebrate the Last Supper, institute the Eucharist, and begin His Passion. Jesus could not have chosen another night more packed with meaning and expectation than the Passover. Here we will see that Jesus enters the drama of the Passover, brings the Old Testament hopes to fulfillment, and establishes the foundational event for the New Covenant People of God: the Eucharist as the new Passover.

Why is the Mass Called a Sacrifice?

Most Catholics are quite familiar with Jesus' words from the Last Supper, which are repeated by the priest at every Mass:

> This is my body which will be given up for you.
> This is the cup of my blood, the blood of the new and ever-lasting covenant. It will be shed for you and for all so that sins may be forgiven. Do this in memory of me.[5]

While these words might seem like ordinary, humdrum ritual for some, the disciples at the Last Supper would have understood immediately that each phrase and action of Jesus was charged with the language and symbolism of ritual *sacrifice*.

First, since the Passover itself was a sacrifice (Ex. 12:27), the simple fact that the Last Supper was a Passover meal demonstrates its sacrificial character.

Second, Jesus' language of "body" and "blood" also points to sacrifice. In Hebrew thinking, these were the two primary elements that made up an animal sacrifice: The blood of the animal was separated from the body. Hence, Jesus applied to Himself the language of sacrifice. Especially in the context of a Passover meal, His speaking of "body" and "blood" would bring to mind the

---

[4] This poem, called the "Poem of the Four Nights," is found in the targum *Neophyti*, an Aramaic paraphrase of the Hebrew Bible used for synagogue worship. See *Neophyti* I, vol. 2 (Madrid-Barcelona, 1970), 312-13, as cited in Lucien Deiss, *It's the Lord's Supper* (London: Collins, 1975), 35.

[5] See 1 Cor. 11:23-26; Mt. 26:26-29; Mk. 14:22-25; Lk. 22:17-20.

sacrificial body and blood of the sacrificial Passover lamb.

Third, Christ's language of His body being "offered up" and His blood being "poured out" also comes from Jewish sacrificial rites. In the Temple sacrifice, the animal was considered *an offering* of a gift to God and the blood was *poured out* on the altar.

Fourth, Jesus' words "this is the blood of the covenant" probably had the greatest meaning. These were the same words used by Moses in the climactic sacrificial ceremony at Mount Sinai, which sealed God's covenant with Israel and constituted her as God's chosen people (Ex. 24:1-17). Thus the disciples, upon hearing these words, could not help but recall the great sacrifice on Sinai and see Jesus entering into the meaning of that event, forming a new covenant with some type of sacrifice.

The profound meaning of all these sacrificial themes— Passover meal, body being offered up, blood being poured out, blood of the Sinai covenant—cannot be emphasized enough. With all this Old Testament and Temple ritual background in mind, Jesus' words and actions at the Last Supper would have been shouting out "Sacrifice!"

To *what* sacrifice was Jesus referring? Clearly, Jesus said it was *His* body being offered, and it was *His* blood being poured out, the blood of the covenant. The sacrifice of the Last Supper is the sacrifice of Jesus. There in the upper room, Christ offered His body and blood for the forgiveness of sins. In fact, Jesus uses a present participle to depict His blood as being poured out now at the Last Supper. Thus, the Last Supper mysteriously anticipated Christ's sacrifice on Calvary. In this Passover meal, Jesus willingly offered His body and blood—His whole life—as a sacrifice for the forgiveness of sins. All that was left for Him to do was to carry out that offering in the subsequent events of the Passion. In this sense, we can say that Calvary begins in the upper room at the Last Supper.

Once we understand the link between the Last Supper and the Cross, between the upper room and Calvary, we can begin to see the connection between our celebration of the Eucharist today and Christ's sacrifice on Calvary 2,000 years ago.

Christ instructed the apostles, "Do this in remembrance of me" (Lk. 22:19; cf. 1 Cor. 11:24-25). Do what? Celebrate this Last Supper, this new Passover of His body and blood, this sacrificial offering. And how? As a *memorial*. Here again, we must emphasize that the Jewish understanding of memorial was not simply to bring to mind a past event. As we saw above, biblical memorials involved actually *making present* that past event. Thus, participants in a Passover meal believed that they themselves were participating in that first Passover and liberation from Egypt, because memorial means making present.

And so, when Jesus said, "Do this in remembrance of me," He did not instruct the apostles to celebrate a simple meal to help remember Him. Rather, He commanded His followers to celebrate a memorial of the Last Supper. All that was involved in the Last Supper would be made present to worshippers throughout the centuries to follow. Thus, all that is caught up in the Last Supper—including the sacrificial offering of Christ's body and blood—is made present in the celebration of the Eucharist. In this way, each Mass is a bridging of two periods of time. The events of the upper room and Calvary are made present before us. Just as the Jews really participated in their ancestors' exodus through the Passover feast, Christians participate in the new exodus, Christ's victorious death on the Cross, through the new Passover, the Eucharist.

Therefore, the Mass *is* a sacrifice. But it is not about offering a new sacrifice. Nor does it have anything to do with sacrificing Christ all over again. Rather, the Eucharist makes really present to believers throughout history Christ's one, eternal sacrifice on Calvary (cf. Catechism, nos. 1362-67). As the Catechism explains, Christ instituted the Eucharist at the Last Supper so that

> the bloody sacrifice which he was to accomplish once for all on the cross would be re-presented, its memory perpetuated until the end of the world, and its salutary power be applied to the forgiveness of the sins we daily commit (no. 1366).

Through the celebration of the new Eucharistic Passover, Christians have the opportunity to participate in Christ's sacrifice by offering their lives in union with Him at every Mass (cf. Rom. 12:1; Col. 1:24; Catechism, no. 1368).

Holy Communion: "We Are What We Eat"

Thus far, we have seen that the sacrificial dimension of the Eucharist makes present Christ's sacrifice on the Cross to Christians who celebrate this new Passover. Now we will consider how Christ's Eucharistic sacrifice sheds light on the Eucharist as Communion and the Eucharist as His Real Presence. To do this, we first must understand the intimate connection between sacrifice and communion in the Bible.

Admittedly, the whole idea of animal sacrifice in the Old Testament at first seems quite puzzling: Did God really want all that animal blood, guts, torn flesh, and smoke? In reality, the ritual of animal sacrifice was not an end in itself, but a means for expressing interior conversion of heart and a desire for a deepening union with God: The animal offered in sacrifice symbolized a person's giving of himself to God and thus strengthened his relationship with Yahweh.

This communion with God is seen especially in the many Israelite sacrifices that required worshippers to eat part of the offered animal. Here we must emphasize the profound biblical meaning of sharing meals. In modern society, we can sit down and have a meal with complete strangers at a fast-food restaurant and not think much about it. But the ancient Israelites considered eating a meal with others a serious affair. Generally, they would do so only with family members and fellow Israelites in the covenant community. Why? Because shared meals forged covenant bonds and were interpreted as establishing familial relationships—so much so that two enemies could seal a peace agreement by sharing a meal and then, afterwards, even refer to each other as brothers! (cf. Gen. 26:26-31; 31:54-55). This sacred symbolism of meal fellowship explains why the Pharisees were so scandalized when Jesus ate with sinners, tax collectors, and prostitutes. Simply by sharing meals with these outcasts of society, Jesus boldly expressed personal solidarity and covenant communion with those who were excluded from the worshipping community.

This covenant-forging power of meals took on even greater meaning when linked with ritual sacrifice because *God* was involved in sacrificial meals: Part of the animal was offered to God and part of the animal was consumed by the worshipper. Hence, God and man were viewed as sharing this sacrificial meal together, thereby strengthening communion between the two. The communion meal was the climax and completion of these types of sacrifices. *Eating* the animal, and not just sacrificing it, sealed communion (cf. Ex. 24:1-11).

The Passover sacrifice also required a communion meal; eating the sacrificial lamb was an essential part of the Passover from the very beginning in Egypt (cf. Ex. 12:8-12).

This is important, because in the New Testament Jesus is the new Passover lamb offered on the Cross (cf. 1 Cor. 5:7; 1 Pet. 1:19; Rev. 5:6). Saint John's Gospel portrays Christ's crucifixion with profound Passover imagery. Jesus was sentenced to be crucified at "the sixth hour" on the Day of Preparation for the Passover—which was the same hour the Passover lambs would have been sacrificed in the Temple. John also mentions that Jesus was stripped of a seamless linen tunic (Jn. 19:23-24). The same word for this "garment" was used to describe the official tunic worn by the high priest during Temple sacrifices (Ex. 28:4; Lev. 16:4). Moreover, just as the Jewish Passover lamb had no broken bones, so also Jesus' bones were never broken (Jn. 19:33, 36; Ex. 12:46). Finally, just before His death, Jesus said, "I thirst" and was given sour wine raised up to Him on a hyssop branch—the same type of branch used in that first Passover in Egypt for sprinkling the blood of the lamb on the Israelite doorposts (cf. Jn. 19:29; Ex. 12:22). Christ is the new Passover lamb offered on Calvary to bring about the new exodus of true liberation, not from physical slavery in Egypt, but from the spiritual bondage of sin and death.

This is crucial for understanding the Eucharist. Remember, at Passover it was not enough for the lamb to be sacrificed. Partaking in the lamb was what sealed communion. Hence, if Jesus is the true Passover lamb *sacrificed* on Calvary, it would not be surprising to find a *communion* meal accompanying the sacrifice on the Cross. And that is exactly what we find in the Eucharist. Just as God commanded the Jews to eat the sacrificial lamb in the Passover of the Old Covenant, Jesus at the Last Supper commanded us to eat the true lamb—His body and blood—in the New Covenant Passover of the Eucharist. Therefore, we see how Eucharistic communion is not merely an option, but the fullest application of Christ's sacrifice to our lives.

This is why Saint Paul says, "Christ, our paschal lamb, has been sacrificed. Let us, therefore, celebrate the festival" (1 Cor. 5:7-8). Again, the sacrifice finds completion in the festive meal, and it is this meal which deepens communion with God. As Saint Paul later goes on to say,

> The cup of blessing which we bless, is it not a communion in the blood of Christ? The bread which we break, is it not a communion in the body of Christ? (1 Cor. 10:16-17).[6]

In harmony with this biblical logic of sacrifice and communion, the Catechism teaches that the Eucharist brings Christians into deeper union with Jesus (nos. 1382-1401). In Holy Communion, Christ's redemptive work on the Cross is most fully applied to our lives, and we experience the most profound union with our God. By feeding on the Eucharistic Body of Christ, we are transformed by His very life in us. He conforms us to Himself. In this sense, we really become what we eat. "What material food produces in our bodily life, Holy Communion wonderfully achieves in our spiritual life" (Catechism, no. 1392).

The transforming power of Eucharistic communion is a theme expounded upon by some of the earliest leaders of

---

[6] Alternative translation provided in footnote q of the RSVCE.

Christianity. For example, Saint Leo writes, "Nothing else is aimed at in our partaking of the body and blood of Christ, than that *we change into what we consume*, and ever bear in spirit and flesh Him in whom we have died, been buried, and have risen."[7] Similarly, Saint Augustine showed how Christians become more fully members of the Body of Christ, the Church, by partaking in the Eucharistic Body of Christ in Holy Communion:

> If you are the body and members of Christ, then it is your sacrament that is placed on the table of the Lord; it is your sacrament that you receive. To that which you are you respond "Amen" ("yes, it is true!") and by responding to it you assent to it. For you hear the words, "the Body of Christ" and respond "Amen." Be then a member of the Body of Christ that your *Amen* may be true.[8]

Real Presence

Before we go on, it will be helpful to understand what the Catholic Church teaches about Jesus' Real Presence in the Eucharist. That Jesus is really present in the Eucharist does not mean He is not present anywhere else. In fact, the Church teaches that Jesus is present in many ways to His people: in the Scriptures, in Christian prayer (cf. Mt. 18:20), in the poor, sick, and imprisoned (cf. Mt. 25:31-46), in the sacraments, etc. But He is present most especially, in a unique way, in the Eucharist (cf. Catechism, nos. 1373-81; SC 7).

What makes Christ's presence in the Eucharist unique? After the priest's words of consecration at Mass, the bread and wine on the altar really change into Jesus' body and blood. Under the appearances of bread and wine, Jesus' very body and blood are present sacramentally. This is not a chemical change. If we looked at the Eucharist under a microscope, we would not find "Jesus cells" floating around. We would not see messianic membranes or divine arteries. We still would have what looks, tastes, smells,

---

[7] Saint Leo the Great, *Sermo* 63, as translated in Matthias Scheeben, *The Mysteries of Christianity* (St. Louis: B. Herder Book Co., 1964), 486-87, emphasis added.

[8] *Sermo* 272, as quoted in Catechism, no. 1396.

and feels like bread and wine. *But underneath those outward appearances of bread and wine, Jesus' body, blood, soul, and divinity are present substantially in the Eucharist* (cf. Catechism, nos. 1374-76).

But some may object, "Isn't this going a little too far? True, the Eucharist may be an important sacred ritual that we should celebrate to recall Christ's death and resurrection, but He wasn't speaking *literally* when He said, 'This is my body . . . This is my blood.' Jesus was speaking metaphorically here. The Eucharist is only a symbol of Jesus."

It is true that Jesus often used parables and symbols to explain mysteries of the kingdom of God. For example, He said, "I am the vine," and Christians are the branches (Jn. 15:5). Clearly, Jesus did not mean He really is a vine, but He used the vine and branches as good natural symbols for describing the organic life of Christians' sharing in the life of Christ, like branches flowing from the one source of life, the true vine. Whenever Jesus used such symbols—"good shepherd," the "door," the "light of the world," etc.—He often proceeded to offer a brief explanation of the metaphor. He clearly was using figurative language—usually in the form of a parable—to teach a deeper truth.

But there is no indication that Jesus was intending to tell a parable at the Last Supper. He offered no explanation of a metaphor. And note how He did not say "*I am* bread and wine" as He would when using other symbols to describe Himself. Rather, He made a different type of connection altogether. He took bread and said, "This is my body," and took the cup and said, "This is my blood."[9] Here, Jesus identified bread *with His body* and wine *with His blood*. In addition, bread and wine hardly serve as natural symbols for a person's body and blood. Thus, Jesus seems to have been doing something more than speaking symbolically. He was making a real identification between the bread and His body, between the wine and His blood.

This Eucharistic realism becomes even clearer when we

---

[9] See note 5, *supra*.

consider what Jesus said in the famous "Bread of Life" discourse in Saint John's Gospel.

Chapter six of Saint John's Gospel begins with the dramatic scene of Jesus' multiplying the loaves and fishes for the crowd of five thousand along the Sea of Galilee. No doubt, this was His greatest miracle to date, and the crowds of people were so moved that they acknowledged Him as the great prophet. In fact, they were ready to carry Him off and make Him their king! (Jn. 6:14-15). At this great moment, Jesus reached a new height in His career and the peak of His popularity among the people. He won their hearts and had them in His hands.

But then He performed what some might consider the greatest public relations blunder that sent His ratings plummeting: the Bread of Life discourse.

On the very day after the multiplication of the loaves and fishes, Jesus gave one of His most difficult teachings for people to accept—a teaching that made crowds angry and frustrated. He began His discourse by saying, "I am the bread of life; he who comes to me shall not hunger, and he who believes in me shall never thirst" (Jn. 6:35). The Jews began quarreling among themselves, taking offense that Jesus associated Himself with bread coming down from heaven. But instead of backpedaling on this bread imagery, which was not going over well, Jesus upped the ante with even tougher language:

> I am the living bread which came down from heaven; if anyone eats of this bread, he will live for ever; and the bread which I shall give for the life of the world *is my flesh* (Jn. 6:51).

Jesus associated the bread of life with His very flesh which we are to eat! This only provoked the people to anger all the more: "How can this man give us his flesh to eat?" (Jn. 6:52). Notice how the crowd understood that Christ was speaking literally. And notice how Jesus did not correct them. Instead, He became only more explicit:

> Truly, truly, I say to you, unless you eat the flesh of the Son of man and drink his blood, you have no life in you; he who eats my flesh and drinks my blood has eternal life, and I will raise him up at the last day. For my flesh is food indeed, and my blood is drink indeed. He who eats my flesh and drinks my blood abides in me, and I in him. As the living Father sent me, and I live because of the Father, so he who eats me will live because of me. This is the bread which came down from heaven, not such as the fathers ate and died; he who eats this bread will live for ever (Jn. 6:52-58).

When Jesus spoke of eating His flesh, the word used in v. 53 for "eat" in the Greek text could be taken literally or symbolically—it could go either way. But in vv. 54-58, His language becomes quite clear—it must be taken literally. The Greek word used for the verb "to eat" in these verses actually means "to gnaw, to chew"—graphic language which Jesus would not have used metaphorically here. He meant *really* eating His flesh.

At this point, not just the crowds, but a number of Jesus' own followers refused to take any more. Many of His own disciples said, "This is a hard saying; who can listen to it?" (Jn. 6:60). It was too difficult for them to believe: "After this many of his disciples drew back and no longer went about with him" (Jn. 6:66). The day before, the crowd of five thousand was ready to make Jesus king. Now, even His own disciples left Him over this difficult teaching.

Notice how Jesus did not do anything to stop them. His silence is quite loud. He did not say "Wait! You misunderstood! I was only speaking figuratively here!" Jesus was accustomed to clarifying His difficult figures of speech when the apostles did not understand (cf. Mk. 4:34), but He did not do so here. The many who left understood Jesus quite well. They left precisely because they understood that He was speaking literally. Jesus let them go in their disbelief and turned to the twelve apostles to ask them, "Will you also go away?" (Jn. 6:67).

It is clear that Jesus intended for us to have a real communion with His very body and blood: "He who eats my flesh and drinks my blood abides in me, and I in him" (Jn. 6:56; cf. 1 Cor. 10:16).

This is the realism of Eucharistic Communion. Again, this realism fits in well with the biblical and Jewish understanding of the Passover, sacrifice, and communion. The idea of eating only a symbol of the sacrificed lamb would not fit into the Jewish mind-set or the Passover framework. You wouldn't eat a lamb-shaped cracker or a lamb-shaped cookie as a sign of the sacrificial lamb. You really had to eat the lamb to share in the communion with God that was forged by the sacrifice. Similarly, in the new Passover of the Eucharist, Christians do not partake in a mere symbol of Jesus, but really partake in the Lamb of God who takes away the sins of the world—Jesus, really present in the Eucharist.[10]

The Flesh of Christ

Some Protestant Christians have used Jn. 6:63 to argue against the Real Presence of Jesus in the Eucharist in favor of a metaphorical interpretation of the "Bread of Life" discourse in Jn. 6. Verse 63 reads: "It is the spirit that gives life, the flesh is of no avail; the words that I have spoken to you are spirit and life." Thus, some conclude that the "Bread of Life" cannot be understood as really Jesus' flesh. Since the flesh is of no avail and the spirit gives life, the references to eating Jesus' flesh in Jn. 6 must be understood metaphorically, in a spiritual sense.

However, such an interpretation is difficult to maintain after the heavy emphasis Jesus Himself gave to the absolute necessity of eating His flesh in the preceding verses (Jn. 6:51-58, especially v. 53: "[U]nless you eat the flesh of the Son of man . . . you have no life in you"). Further, if someone interprets v. 63 as in any way downplaying the importance of Jesus' flesh, he ends up contradicting what the Scriptures tell us about the importance of Jesus' flesh for our salvation (cf. Jn. 1:14; Eph. 2:15; Col. 1:22). It does not make sense to interpret "the flesh is of no avail" as denigrating the God-Man's flesh, through which the world was redeemed.

---

[10] For further discussion, see Joseph Cardinal Ratzinger, *The Feast of Faith* (San Francisco: Ignatius Press, 1986), 33-60.

On the contrary, in v. 63, Jesus is not speaking of His own flesh. Instead, He is speaking of human flesh in general, in the sense in which He spoke of it to Nicodemus in Jn. 3:6—"flesh" as the aspect of human nature that cannot give eternal life. Only the Spirit from above can give eternal life (cf. Jn. 1:12-13). Similarly, Saint Paul describes how Christians are to "walk not according to the flesh but according to the Spirit" (Rom. 8:4). Thus, in Jn. 6:63, Jesus is not denigrating *His* flesh, the Eucharistic flesh which He gives for the life of the world, as described in 6:51-59. Rather, Jesus is emphasizing the futility of "the flesh" in general—the futility of human nature to attain eternal life on its own. We need Jesus' words, which are spirit and life: "[T]he flesh is of no avail; the words that I have spoken to you are spirit and life" (Jn. 6:63). And what do Jesus' words tell us? Jesus' very life-giving words in the preceding discourse tell us that we must eat His flesh and drink His blood!

Others, in interpreting v. 63, argue that the bread of life is only a symbol of the wise teaching of Jesus, upon which we are to feed ourselves spiritually: *"the words that I have spoken to you are spirit and life."* While the "bread of life" may have a secondary reference to His teaching, Christ's explicit, literal connection of the living bread with His very flesh which we are to eat (cf. Jn. 6:51-58) shows that the primary meaning must be Eucharistic realism. Jesus Himself directly links the bread of life not with His words, but with His actual flesh (cf. Jn. 6:51). And again, while in v. 63 Jesus says it is His *words* that give life, when we look at His actual words in Jn. 6, they tell us "he who eats my flesh and drinks my blood has eternal life" (Jn. 6:54).

Eucharistic Miracles?

From the beginning, God has desired to be with His people, to be close to us, in communion with us. However, because of sin, humanity has distanced itself from God's presence—a point made in the Genesis account of the Fall. Immediately after that first sin in the Garden of Eden, Adam and Eve "hid themselves from *the presence* of the LORD God" (Gen. 3:8). The rest of salvation history can be seen as God's plan of restoring His presence among His people, of reestablishing full covenant communion.

We can see God's presence among humanity gradually becoming more intimate throughout the Old Testament. From the distant voice of God speaking to Noah, to the call of Moses through the burning bush, to the pillar of cloud by day and pillar of fire by night guiding the Israelites in the desert, to the awesome glory cloud of God's presence filling the Holy of Holies in the Temple of Jerusalem, God's presence becomes progressively more intimate throughout salvation history. His closeness to man reaches a climax in the New Testament, in the first chapter of Matthew's Gospel in which Jesus is identified as "Emmanu-el (which means, *God with us*)" (Mt. 1:23). Jesus, who is the Word of God made flesh, is the fullness of God dwelling among humanity. God is truly with His people again.

Jesus consistently transformed the lives of people who drew near to His presence with faith. For example, a woman suffering from a hemorrhage for twelve years reached out and touched just the fringe of His garment in the midst of a large crowd. In an instant, she was cured because she came near to Jesus in faith. He told her, "Take heart, daughter; *your faith* has made you well" (Mt. 9:22). Similarly, two blind men approached Jesus and cried out, "'Have mercy on us, Son of David!' Jesus said to them, 'Do you believe that I am able to do this?' They said to him, 'Yes, Lord.' Then he touched their eyes, saying, 'According to *your faith* be it done to you'" (Mt. 9:27-30). On another occasion, some people brought a paralytic to Jesus who, upon seeing *their faith*, cured the man and forgave His sins (Mt. 9:2-8).

That same Jesus who walked the streets of Palestine—curing the sick, converting the sinners, healing the brokenhearted, and working miracles in peoples' lives—is really present today in the Eucharist at every Mass and in every tabernacle around the world. And He wants to perform great works in our lives. But we have to draw near. And we have to believe.

In a modern secularized culture hungering for religion, searching for God, and longing for the love only Christ can give, this gift of God's very presence in the Eucharist must be proclaimed! At every Mass, we have the opportunity to meet Jesus in this unique way. In Holy Communion, the God of the universe enters us in the most intimate way possible. In those moments after receiving the Eucharist, we have the most profound union with our God, our Creator, dwelling in us. Let us not allow those precious moments to pass by without ardently speaking to Our Lord, bringing to Him our petitions, our thanks, our joys and sorrows, and our heart's deepest desires.

Christ really can work miracles in our lives. He continues to convert sinners, heal the brokenhearted, and call us to follow Him ever more closely. Whether helping us overcome weaknesses and recurring sins or healing personal wounds and sufferings, Christ wants to transform us with His very life, most particularly in the Eucharist. Here He strengthens our souls for this pilgrimage on earth and conforms us to Himself. Indeed, these are the great miracles that Jesus works in ordinary lives all the time.

And we must not forget that His presence in the Eucharist continues while reserved in the tabernacle. There in the parish church, in the tabernacle next to the flickering red candle, He lovingly waits for us to visit Him, adore Him, and bring our lives to Him.[11] Therefore, in the Eucharist—not only at Mass, but also in the tabernacle—Jesus wants to do great works in our lives. But we have to draw near, and we have to believe. There in the Eucharist, Jesus stands before us today just as He stood before the two blind men 2,000 years ago, saying, "Do you believe that I am able to do this?" (Mt. 9:28).

---

[11] "The Church and the world have a great need of eucharistic worship. Jesus waits for us in this sacrament of love. Let us be generous with our time in going to meet Him in adoration and in contemplation that is full of faith and ready to make reparation for the great faults and crimes of the world. May our adoration never cease" Pope John Paul II, The Mystery and Worship of the Eucharist *Dominicae Cenae*, Vatican Translation (1980), no. 3.

Edward P. Sri is assistant professor of religious studies at Benedictine College in Atchison, Kansas. He holds a license in sacred theology (S.T.L.) from the Pontifical University of St. Thomas Aquinas in Rome, where he is currently a doctoral candidate. He also has a master's degree in theology from Franciscan University of Steubenville. He has spoken at various conferences and parishes throughout the Midwest on Scripture, catechesis, and apologetics.

CHAPTER IX

Scripture's Revelation of Mary

TIMOTHY GRAY

The Catholic vision of history is that it is the story of God's relation to man, which is otherwise known as *salvation history*. But salvation history *is* history, and it is the dramatic story of God's calling and reaching out to restore the rebellious family of Adam (humanity) to the Trinitarian Family of God. The climax of "His story" comes when God the Father sends His own Son into the midst of history for the salvation of the world. According to Saint Paul, "when the time had fully come, God sent forth his Son, born of a woman" (Gal. 4:4). Mary is the means by which Jesus comes into the story, into history. Mary's motherhood marks the "fullness of time," the maturity of the Father's plan for salvation. Mary's motherhood defines her role, the part that God has chosen for her to play in the dramatic story of salvation history. This role not only comes at the fullness of time, but affects all time. Mary's role is so central to the story that it is foreshadowed in the past and continually active and celebrated in the present and future.

Even before the liturgy celebrated—and the Church dogmatically proclaimed—the singular and glorious role that Mary plays in salvation history, the Scriptures, both the Old and New Testaments, foretold and revealed the role of the Mother of God. Yet we do not need to begin frantically searching the hundreds of pages of Scripture to discover what it says regarding Mary's role in salvation history. Saint John, the beloved disciple of Our Lord, has already distilled from Scripture the foremost aspects of Mary's role. With the keen eye of a photographer, John captures in a powerful vision the essence of Mary's place in God's providential plan. Chapter twelve of Revelation provides a "word-picture" of John's heavenly vision of Mary. If a picture says a thousand words, then an apocalyptic picture speaks in the tens of thousands. To examine this literally revealing picture is to understand better why all generations call her blessed.[1]

Mother of the Living

John's dazzling vision of heaven in chapter twelve of Revelation reveals "a woman clothed with the sun, with the moon under her feet, and on her head a crown of twelve stars" (Rev. 12:1). Then another astounding sight appears in the heavens, "a great red dragon, with seven heads and ten horns, and seven diadems upon his heads" (Rev. 12:3). The chapter goes on to portray the ensuing war between the woman and the dragon, between the woman's offspring and the dragon's evil minions. But who are the woman and the dragon, and what is this cosmic conflict all about?

---

[1] I have found from experience that people are often apprehensive or nervous about the Book of Revelation. To some, opening the Book of Revelation and reading it instills the anxious feeling of trespassing. Revelation seems like a magician's black hat out of which innumerable interpretive rabbits may be pulled at any time. Too many see this book as an esoteric mystery not to be read. Undoubtedly, many have misread Revelation because they have tried to interpret it in terms of modern-day history rather than within the symbolic language of Israel's prophetic tradition. Although Revelation may be difficult to understand, we should not feel that we should not read it; otherwise, why would God have given it to the Church? Indeed, He gives a special blessing to those who read and hear it: "Blessed is he who reads aloud the words of the prophecy, and blessed are those who hear, and who keep what is written therein" (Rev. 1:3). This blessing is bestowed on those who would read this during the liturgy, as well as on those who would listen. No other book of Scripture contains a special blessing for those who hear it.

We know the woman by the fruit she bears. "[S]he brought forth a male child, one who is to rule *all the nations with a rod of iron*" (Rev. 12:5). For those who have ears to hear (cf. Mt. 13:9), this description clearly discloses the child's identity. This is an unmistakable allusion to Ps. 2:8-9, where the Lord tells the promised messiah that He will rule all the nations:

> Ask of me, and I will make *the nations your heritage*, and the ends of the earth your possession. You shall break them with a *rod of iron*, and dash them in pieces like a potter's vessel.

Undoubtedly, the woman's child is the long-awaited messiah. Since Jesus is the Messiah, the woman is none other than Mary.

But if the woman is Mary, the Mother of Jesus, why does Saint John simply refer to her as "the woman"? We could ask this same question regarding his reference to the child simply as the "one who is to rule all the nations with a rod of iron" (Rev. 12:5). Rather than giving us Jesus' name, John employs the rich symbolic language of Israel's prophetic tradition. This symbolism is not esoteric or confusing. Rather, it imbues John's description of the events of salvation history with their rich theological significance. Only the deeply symbolic language of Scripture can do justice to the profound meaning wrapped in the events of salvation history. Just as the description of the child "subduing the nations with an iron rod" draws on salvation history in order to reveal Jesus as the long-awaited Messiah, so the theological significance of the title "woman" is revealed by its allusion to an earlier biblical prophecy.

By calling Mary "woman," John echoes an important prophecy of the Old Testament—the very first prophecy ever made! In the third chapter of Genesis, immediately after the fall of Adam and Eve, God curses the serpent by saying, "I will put enmity between you and *the woman*, and between your seed and her seed," thus describing the perpetual opposition and conflict between the forces of Satan and the descendants of the woman. The Lord continues speaking to the serpent, foretelling that the woman and her seed would conquer the serpent: "[H]e shall bruise your head, and you shall bruise his heel" (Gen. 3:15). This last line can be a bit confusing, but once it is remembered that the "you" is the serpent, it becomes clear that the "he" who strikes the serpent's head is the male seed of the woman. The serpent in turn can only strike at his heel, thereby signifying the ultimate victory of the woman's seed over the devil. Christian tradition has always seen this passage as the first prophetic promise that a messiah would arise and defeat the demonic enemy. This prophecy has been called the *proto-evangelium*; this Latin phrase taken from the Greek means the "first gospel," the first announcement of the good news.

Thus Scripture begins by describing the drama of salvation history as the struggle between the serpent and the woman, between his followers (human and angelic) and her descendants. Is John comparing the woman of Gen. 3 (Eve) with the woman of Rev. 12 (Mary)? Yes. His comparison becomes even more obvious once a few of the similarities between Gen. 3 and Rev. 12 are brought into sharp focus. In addition to God, there are three main protagonists in Gen. 3: the serpent, Adam, and the woman. In Rev. 12, there are three main protagonists: the dragon (who in Rev. 12:9 is identified as "that *ancient serpent*, who is called the Devil and Satan, the deceiver of the whole world"); the messianic child, Jesus (who is the "New Adam" [cf. Rom. 5:14; 1 Cor. 15:45]); and the woman. The correspondence is striking. Other details linking the two scenes are the conflict between the woman and the ancient serpent, and the pain of childbirth for both women (cf. Gen. 3:16; Rev. 12:2). John's point is that Mary is "the woman" and that her seed, Jesus, brings about the defeat of the ancient serpent. For John, there is no other way to describe such world-shattering events—the fulfillment of the *proto-evangelium* and the identification of the long-awaited "woman" and her messianic offspring—than by using the theologically rich symbolic language of Israel's prophetic tradition.

Saint John gives Mary the title "woman" in order to show us that Mary is the *New Eve*, the woman prophetically foretold who would bear a child who would defeat the dreaded dragon. The early Church Fathers, following the lead of Saints John and Paul, also perceived that since Christ was the New Adam, Mary was the New Eve. Saint Irenaeus wrote, "[T]he knot of Eve's disobedience was loosed by the obedience of Mary: What the virgin Eve had bound in unbelief, the Virgin Mary loosed through faith."[2] It is worth noting that Saint Irenaeus was a disciple of Saint Polycarp, who in turn was a disciple of Saint John, the beloved disciple. This patristic teaching of Mary as the New Eve traces back to Saint John himself. Thus Mary is the true Eve, the true "mother of the living" (cf. Gen. 3:20).

Eve is the biological mother of us all, but Mary's spiritual maternity surpasses Eve's physical maternity. Eve's glory is eclipsed by her disobedience, whereas Mary's glory rests on her obedience. One is the mother of our fallen nature, the other the mother full of grace. Eve comes at the beginning of creation, and her fall along with Adam's sets the tragic trajectory of the Old Covenant. Mary comes at the dawn of the new era, described in Is. 66:22 as "the new heavens and the new earth," and her obedience, in harmony with the obedience of the New Adam, sets in motion the triumph of the New Covenant. Thus the ancient motto, "Death through Eve, life through Mary."

In the contrast made between the Old and New Eve, it must be noted that Mary's faith and obedience are the cause of her fame. Mary is primarily honored for her faith, a faithful obedience through which she became the Mother of the Word. This perspective is important, as is demonstrated in the brief story often mistakenly used to downplay the significance of Mary. Some who misunderstand or are opposed to the dignity and honor paid to Mary cite the following passage as testimony that the role of Mary's motherhood of God is inconsequential to the plan of salvation:

---

[2] Saint Irenaeus, *Adversus Haereses* (Against the Heresies), 3, 22, 4, as translated in W.A. Jurgens, ed., *The Faith of the Early Fathers* (Collegeville, MN: The Liturgical Press, 1970), vol. I, 93.

> While he was still speaking to the people, behold, his mother and his brethren stood outside, asking to speak to him. But he replied to the man who told him, "Who is my mother, and who are my brethren?" And stretching out his hand toward his disciples, he said, "Here are my mother and my brethren! For whoever does the will of my Father in heaven is my brother, and sister, and mother" (Mt. 12:46-50).

Some argue that Jesus is minimizing family blood ties (including motherhood) in favor of the call to obedience to the Father's will. This is true, but the conclusion that Mary is therefore insignificant or no greater than any other disciple of Christ is unwarranted and mistaken. The fact that merit is measured not by blood but by obedience to the Father actually *affirms* Mary's merit. Mary fulfilled the will of the Father perfectly in her life. Her fiat echoes this: "Behold, I am the handmaid of the Lord; let it be to me according to your word" (Lk. 1:38). Elizabeth testifies to this when she greets Mary and says, "[B]lessed is she who believed that there would be a fulfillment of what was spoken to her from the Lord" (Lk. 1:45). If Noah, Abraham, David, and many others were chosen to serve God in special ways because of their righteousness, is it not ridiculous to think that God chose His mother at random? Surely Gabriel singles Mary out when he greets her as "full of grace" and then tells her that he was sent because she has "found favor with God" (Lk. 1:28, 30).

It must also be remembered that Jesus said many things that seemed to downplay family ties. But Jesus was not anti-family. He was loosening the natural family blood ties to incorporate people into the true and ultimate family, His Father's family. Next to the Family of God, all other natural family bonds are of relative worth. This is illustrated by the following incident:

> Another of his disciples said to him, "Lord, let me first go and bury my father." But Jesus said to him, "Follow me, and leave the dead to bury their own dead" (Mt. 8:21-22).

Behind this seemingly outrageous command of Jesus is a radical revisioning of true family commitments. "The only explanation for Jesus' astonishing command is that He envisioned loyalty to Himself and His kingdom-movement as creating an alternative family."[3] Jesus was tearing down so as to build up. The old family of Adam was being reconstituted into the family of Christ. Far from being left behind in this new family, Mary is to be found at its forefront.

Through Baptism and the Eucharist, Jesus establishes His New Covenant family. In Baptism, we are spiritually born into the Family of God and, through the Eucharist, we partake of the body and blood of Jesus. Therefore all the faithful share the same blood. Christian brotherhood is not just a pious sentiment, but a true kinship bond in the blood of Christ. And since Jesus took His flesh and blood from the Virgin Mary, we who partake of the divine mysteries share a blood tie with Mary. We are truly her children. If we take Jesus as our brother, then we must have Mary as our mother. One of the very last acts of Our Lord was to give His mother Mary to us as our mother.

> When Jesus saw his mother, and the disciple whom he loved standing near, he said to his mother, "Woman, behold, your son!" Then he said to the disciple, "Behold, your mother!" (Jn. 19:26-27).

The Church has always understood this to signify that Mary was given to all of Christ's disciples, those whom He loves, and that Mary is therefore the mother of all Christians.

Some Protestants have argued against this view. They assert that Jesus is only giving Mary into John's protection and care because He is dying. Of course, Jesus is entrusting Mary into John's care, and vice versa. It is worth noting that this incident confirms the early Fathers' view that Mary did not have any other children, since Jesus would not have entrusted Mary into the care of John if He had other siblings.

But there is a strong case for showing that more is going on than the conscientious care of a widow. First, Jesus was a

---

[3] N. T. Wright, *Jesus and the Victory of God* (Minneapolis: Fortress Press, 1996), 401.

prophet, and prophets were known for making symbolic actions. "Isaiah's nakedness, Jeremiah's smashed pot, and Ezekiel's brick come to mind as obvious examples,"[4] as well as John the Baptist's living in the wilderness in sparse dress and baptizing in the Jordan. Jesus followed this prophetic tradition in many ways, such as in turning over the money-changers' tables and cursing the barren fig tree—both of which symbolized the forthcoming destruction of the Temple—and in choosing twelve apostles.

In light of these, we must be prepared to see that Jesus' handing over of His mother to His beloved disciple would have symbolic import. In fact, one must wonder why, in recording the greatest event in history, John included his own new relationship to Mary, unless he knew that it had important significance as such for the readers of his Gospel. John's careful description of the Passion of Our Lord puts great significance in every detail. If Jesus' action were not symbolic, why did He not use Mary's and John's names? The title "woman," as we have already seen, has strong prophetic connotations. Jesus' action only makes sense when understood as the symbolic-prophetic sign that Mary is the mother of all Christians. Mary becomes the spiritual mother of the Body of Christ (the Church) at the Cross. This is clearly how John interprets Jesus' intention. In the last verse in chapter twelve of Revelation, he explicitly states who Mary's children are:

> Then the dragon was angry with the *woman*, and went off to make war on the *rest of her offspring*, on those who keep the commandments of God and bear testimony to Jesus.

It is noteworthy that John is the only one of the twelve who follows Christ all the way to Calvary. Could it be accidental that the disciple closest to Mary was the one who had the courage to stand under the Cross? John was the first to take Mary as his spiritual mother. John therefore stands as a witness and sign that the fruit of Marian devotion is a love for Christ that is as strong as

---

[4] *Ibid.*, 415.

death. John shows that the disciple who takes Mary by the hand is able to follow Our Lord all the way to Calvary. As the Body of Christ goes through its corporate crucifixion, one may well wonder if the only disciples who will not flee in cowardice will be those who, like John, are children of Mary. We must beseech Mary that she will inflame our hearts with the same love and courage that John had on Good Friday.

> We ceaselessly recall that nothing must ever make us forget the reality and the consciousness that we are, all of us, sons of the same Mother Mary, who lives in heaven, who is the bond of union for the Mystical Body of Christ, and who as the new Eve, and the new Mother of the living, desires to lead all men to the truth and the grace of her divine Son.[5]

Royal Motherhood

As the New Eve, Mary is the new "mother of the living." How is Mary's motherhood a royal motherhood? The woman in chapter twelve of Revelation appears with a "crown of twelve stars" (Rev. 12:1) on her head. What is the significance of the royal crown of stars? It obviously denotes queenship for the woman. But why does John depict Mary as a queen? And what is the nature of this queenship?

That the crown is made up of twelve stars is an important clue. The number twelve in Scripture connotes the twelve sons of Jacob, and later the twelve tribes that constituted the nation and kingdom of Israel. The twelve stars also echo the story concerning the dreams of Jacob's favorite son, Joseph. One of Joseph's dreams prophetically predicts, through the symbols of the sun, moon, and stars, that Joseph will rule over his brothers and even his parents: "Behold, I have dreamed another dream; and behold, the sun, the moon, and eleven stars were bowing down to me"

---

[5] Pope Pius XII, Address, "Fruits of the Definition," (November 1, 1950), as reprinted in Benedictine Monks of Solemnes, *Papal Teachings: Our Lady*, Daughters of St. Paul, trans. (Boston: Daughters of St. Paul, 1961), 323.

(Gen. 37:9). The meaning of the prediction is so obvious that Joseph's father rebukes him and says, "Shall I and your mother and your brothers indeed come to bow ourselves to the ground before you?" (Gen. 37:10). In the dream, the stars represent the sons of Jacob, and therefore a woman described as wearing a crown of twelve stars would be seen as having authority over the twelve tribes of Jacob, Israel. This woman could be none other than the Queen Mother of Israel.

Yet there is another dimension to the number twelve. When Jesus chose twelve apostles, He was reestablishing the twelve tribes around Himself, the new Israel. For those who have ears to hear (cf. Mt. 13:9), the number twelve signifies the new kingdom of God established by the new and eternal king, Jesus Christ. The twelve stars are no ordinary crown. The vision of Mary crowned with twelve stars reveals Mary as the queen of the kingdom of God!

If the idea of Mary's queenship strikes us as an innovation, it is because we are ignorant of the tradition of queenship in Israel's history. An examination of the important office of queen during the Davidic kingdom will shed much light on Mary's queenship.

In fulfillment of biblical prophecy, Jesus came to restore the Davidic kingdom, albeit in a way that surpassed all expectations. The messiah was to be a descendant of David, who would reestablish the kingdom of God and reign forever (cf. 2 Sam. 7; Ps. 2; 72; 89). That Jesus is a descendant of David, and therefore the heir to the kingdom, is a point often stressed in the Gospels. For example, at the Annunciation Gabriel tells Mary that her child

> will be great, and will be called the Son of the Most High; and the Lord God will give to him the *throne of his father David*, and he will reign over the *house of Jacob* for ever; and of his *kingdom* there will be no end (Lk. 1:32-33).

Jesus is king in the line of David, and His kingdom is the prophesied renewal and expansion of the Davidic kingdom. To understand the biblical nature of Mary's queenship, it must be seen in light of the Davidic kingdom.

When we think of a queen, we most often think of the wife of the king. How then can we give Mary the title of Queen? Mary is the mother of Jesus, not His wife. To some it seems that such a title has no justification whatsoever and is simply given to Mary in an overly zealous and misguided devotion. This apparent problem stems from thinking of queenship and kingship in light of the European monarchical tradition. Queenship in the ancient Near East, particularly for Israel, was quite different.

In the ancient Near East, in sharp contrast to the Western tradition, the wife of the king normally did not reign as queen. Kings often had many wives. King Solomon himself had 700 wives and 300 concubines (cf. 1 Kings 11:3). What is a king to do with so many wives but with only one queenship to bestow? Since the queen receives her authority from an intimate and unique familial relation to the king, and because kings in the ancient Near East had innumerable wives but only one mother, the common practice was that the mother of the king took the office of queen.

This was true for the Davidic kingdom. The mother of the king held an extremely important and influential office known as the *Giberah*, or Queen Mother. In Hebrew, *giberah* literally means "great lady." Since the Hebrew does not have a feminine equivalent to *adon*, lord, the word *giberah* came to signify female nobility and queenship. Thus "great lady" in Hebrew would be analogous to "my lord" and "my lady" in the English titles of nobility. Bathsheba is an excellent example of a queen mother, or *giberah*. When Solomon reigned as king, his mother Bathsheba reigned as queen and, as already noted, it was not for lack of a wife that Solomon's mother reigned. The second chapter of 1 Kings describes the royal ceremony given to the *giberah* as she entered the royal court:

> So Bathsheba went to King Solomon, to speak to him on behalf of Adonijah. And the king rose to meet her, and bowed down to her; then he sat on his throne, and had a seat brought for the king's mother; and she sat on his right (1 Kings 2:19).

Adonijah's request for her intercession to the king testifies to the peoples' recognition of the queen mother's intercessory power.[6] What is important for us is not the specific occasion of the queen mother's intercession, but the formalized ritual that reveals the significance of the queen mother's office. The ritual that surrounds Bathsheba's intercession suggests that it was a common courtly event. Clearly, intercession was a fundamental part of the *giberah's* office.

The royal court functioned as the supreme court of the land. In such a court setting, the *giberah*'s intercession for the poor and needy gave her the role of advocate. Prov. 31 relates the counsel that King Lemuel (who some say is Solomon) receives from his mother. There are several verses that highlight how the queen mother interceded for the weak and needy of the kingdom to the king. She tells the king, "Open your mouth for the dumb, for the rights of all who are left desolate. Open your mouth, judge righteously, maintain the rights of the poor and needy" (Prov. 31:8-9). The queen mother is speaking to the king on behalf of those in the kingdom who need his protection and help. The advice of Lemuel's mother exhibits the powerful role of advocacy and counsel held by the *giberah*.

The seating of the *giberah* at the right hand of the king signifies the importance of her position in the kingdom. To sit at the right hand of the king denotes that one's position is second only to the king. Ps. 110:1 illustrates this ancient symbolism when the Lord says to the messiah, "Sit at my right hand, till I make your enemies your footstool." In the Letter to the Hebrews, this very verse is cited to demonstrate that Christ is above all the angels and creatures, since He sits at the right hand of the Father. Likewise, since the queen is seated at the right hand of the king, she has the most important office in the kingdom, after the king. One queen mother, Athaliah, became the sole ruler of Israel for seven years after the death of her son Ahaziah.

---

[6] Cf. Timothy Gray, "God's Word and Mary's Royal Office," *Miles Immaculatae* 13 (1995), 372-88.

The office of queen mother was also important in the Davidic kingdom because the queen mother guaranteed the legitimacy of a king's succession. Throughout the Books of Kings, when a king takes the throne, both the king and the queen mother are named (e.g., 1 Kings 15:2; 2 Kings 12:1; 14:1-2). The *giberah* is listed with the king in order to prove the king's legitimacy as the rightful heir of David. This role held untold value for Israel, since the promises of God and the covenant with David (cf. 2 Sam. 7) included the promise that the messiah had to come from the Davidic line. When Isaiah prophesies that "a virgin shall conceive and bear a son, and shall call his name Immanu-el" (Is. 7:14),[7] and that this child is to sit "upon the throne of David, and over his kingdom, to establish it, and to uphold it with justice and with righteousness from this time forth and for evermore" (Is. 9:7), he not only identifies the heir to the line of David, but also the queen mother as well. The virgin *giberah* "legitimizes" and identifies the long-awaited heir to the line of David.

Does the New Testament give any witness to a renewal of the institution of the *giberah* in Jesus' kingdom reform? Pope Pius XII claimed that Mary's queenship is revealed in Saint Luke's description of the Annunciation: "[T]he heavenly voice of the Archangel Gabriel was the first to proclaim Mary's royal office."[8] Everyone knows that Gabriel announced Mary's divine motherhood of the messiah, but where does the angel give any detail concerning a royal office for Mary? All the angel speaks of is the royal office and kingdom that Mary's son will have. What does that have to do with Mary's queenship? Everything. The connection with Mary is so simple that it is usually passed over. As we have seen, in the Davidic kingdom one was queen by virtue of her motherhood. The royal office of *giberah* was given to the king's mother. Therefore, when the angel announces that Mary's son is of the

---

[7] Alternative translation provided in footnote i of the RSVCE.

[8] Pope Pius XII, Encyclical Letter On Proclaiming the Queenship of Mary *Ad Caeli Reginam* (1954), no. 34, as quoted in C. Carlen, I.H.M., ed., *The Papal Encyclicals 1939-1958* (Raleigh, NC: Pierian Press, 1990), 274.

line of David and will inherit his throne forever, he is announcing Mary's queenship as well as Christ's kingship.

If the evidence for Mary's queenship is implicit in Luke's Annunciation scene, it is explicit in the scene of the Visitation. After hearing of her older cousin's miraculous pregnancy, Mary goes to visit and assist Elizabeth. Elizabeth greets Mary not by calling out her name, or referring to their family ties, but by humbling herself and saying, "Why is this granted me, that *the mother of my Lord* should come to me?" (Lk. 1:43). The title "mother of my Lord" might seem to express pious humility and nothing more. But, if we are aware of the *giberah* tradition, we can see that Elizabeth is declaring her amazement that the *giberah* and queen of Israel should come and be her midwife. For any Jew, the mother of the lord, that is, the mother of the king, would be the queen mother. Thus Elizabeth announces Mary's queenship by her greeting. Just as later John would announce Jesus with a title that spoke of His mission, "Behold the Lamb of God," so Elizabeth announced Mary's mission with the title "mother of my Lord," or *giberah*.

In the New Testament, Mary's queenship was alluded to by Gabriel, and announced by Elizabeth. In the account of the wedding at Cana, Mary's queenship is manifested by her intercession with the king. Cana is known as the place where Jesus performed His first miracle and began His public ministry. It is also the first place where we see Mary publicly performing the *giberah*'s intercessory role. The young married couple ran out of wine and, in compassion, Mary interceded with Jesus for them. As we have seen, one of the *giberah*'s fundamental roles was to intercede for the people of the kingdom. This is exactly what Mary does at Cana. Mary's intercessory role began at Cana and extends to all those who are in need within her Son's kingdom.

In Baptism, we enter into Christ's kingdom. In that kingdom, we have at Christ's right hand a holy queen mother who is an advocate for us before Christ's throne. We should take courage that, just as Jesus turned the water into wine at Cana because of His mother's intercession, He will grant her petitions on our behalf as well:

With your prayers, invoke the Kingdom of Christ to which your most beloved Mother urges you with her example, and for which her maternal intercession procures for you all the necessary means; does she not in fact hold a privileged post because of the function which Providence wished to give her in the life of the Church and in that of each of its members?[9]

Theotokos: the God-bearing Ark

We have seen how Mary, as the New Eve, is the new "mother of the living," and how her motherhood is one of royalty. Mary's motherhood, however, is even more than royal; it is holy. It is holy because she bore the Son of God Himself. In the Old Covenant, God's presence or glory had dwelt in the tabernacle made at Moses' direction. But access to God's tabernacle was prohibited to the people with the exception of the high priest, who could approach it only on the day of atonement, after many sin offerings. Because of Israel's sin, the tabernacle was lost and God's concrete dwelling among His people was taken away in the exile, which continued up to Jesus' day. But with Mary's *fiat* at the Annunciation, God reestablished, in a greater and more intimate way, His dwelling among Israel.

Rather than dwelling in a tabernacle made of gold and lined with precious gems, God dwelt within the flesh and blood of a human person, Mary. Mary is the ultimate tabernacle, gilded not with gold but by the grace of God. Instead of gems, she is adorned with the virtues, particularly humility and love. The Catechism notes that in Mary, God the Father finally found a proper dwelling place among men for His presence: "For the first time in the plan of salvation and because his Spirit had prepared her, the Father found the *dwelling place* where his Son and his Spirit could dwell among men" (no. 721, original emphasis). Since Eden, God had desired to dwell among His people, and now "[i]n Mary, the Holy Spirit *fulfills* the plan of the Father's loving goodness" (*ibid.*, no. 723, original emphasis).

---

[9] Pope Pius XII, Address, "Restoration of the Kingdom of Christ through Mary," (September 17, 1958), as reprinted in *Papal Teachings: Our Lady*, 462-63.

At the end of chapter eleven of Revelation, just before Saint John sees the vision of the woman crowned with twelve stars, the heavens open up and in God's temple the ark of the covenant is revealed. This scene is continued in Rev. 12, but standing in the place of the ark is the woman crowned with stars. (It is helpful to remember that the Scriptures originally contained no chapter or verse divisions. These were added hundreds of years later. What we see as chapter twelve should be read, as originally written, right on the heels of chapter eleven.) The woman and the ark of the covenant are revealed as one and the same.

In the Old Testament, the ark of the covenant held three things: (1) the stone tablets upon which the finger of God had written the Ten Commandments on Mt. Sinai; (2) a jar containing some of the manna which God had miraculously provided as food for the Israelites during their forty years in the desert; and (3) the staff of Aaron, the first high priest of the Old Law. The ark of the covenant was holy because of what was held inside of it, and its presence became synonymous with the presence of God among the Israelites. Where the ark of the covenant was, there also was the presence of Yahweh. Thus, this holy vessel of God's presence was made and handled with special care. Ex. 39 tells us that the ark was hand-carved of acacia wood and overlaid with pure gold, both within and without. Only the Levites, members of the tribe which had been set aside for service of the tabernacle, were supposed to carry the ark, and then only with poles, themselves being overlaid with gold, which were fed through rings of gold attached to the sides of the ark.

That the early Christians understood Mary as the new ark of the covenant is evident in Saint Luke's crafting of his account of the Visitation (cf. Lk. 1:39-56). Luke subtly parallels Mary's carrying Jesus (in her womb) to visit Elizabeth with the ark's bearing the presence of God to Jerusalem. In 2 Sam. 6, we hear how David, aware of both his unworthiness that the ark should come to him (v. 9) and of the immeasurable blessing that the presence of the ark brings (v. 12), goes to bring the ark of the covenant up to Jerusalem. After David offers sacrifices (v. 13), he leaps and dances (v. 16) before the ark as the procession progresses to Jerusalem amid shouting and the sound of the horn (v. 15).

In Saint Luke's account of the Visitation (cf. Lk. 1:39-56), it is clear that Mary is the new ark of the covenant. Mary, like David, heads to the hill country of Judah. As Mary, bearing Christ in her womb, approaches the home of Elizabeth, Saint John "leaps" in Elizabeth's womb and she exclaims with a "loud cry," reminding us of David's leaping before the ark of the covenant and the shouts of the people of Israel. Elizabeth greets Mary with words similar to those of David, "[W]hy is this granted me, that the mother of my Lord [who is the new ark of the covenant] should come to me?" (v. 43). The following chart summarizes this strong correlation between 2 Sam. 6 and Lk. 1:

2 Sam. 6	Lk. 1
David arose and went (v. 2) back to Judah	Mary arose and went to the hill country of Judah (v. 39)
How can the ark of the Lord come to me? (v. 9)	Who am I that the mother of my Lord should come to me? (v. 43)
house of Obed-edom (v. 10)	house of Zechariah (v. 40)
ark there three months (v. 11)	Mary stays three months with Elizabeth (v. 56)
people rejoice (v. 12)	Mary rejoices (v. 47)
shouting (v. 15)	loud cry (v. 42)
leaping and dancing (v. 16)	the babe leaps in Elizabeth's womb (v. 41)

The quantitative poverty of biblical narratives specifically concerning Mary is compensated by the qualitative wealth of meaning in those narratives. The few words that Luke gives us about Mary are like gems, rare but rich in beauty. One facet of this gem shows Mary's mediating role in salvation history. In the Old Testament the Spirit of God, the *Shekina*, would overshadow and rest on the ark (cf. Ex. 40:34 *et seq.*), thus showing to the people the presence of God. In the Gospel, the angel Gabriel tells Mary that the Holy Spirit will come upon her and overshadow her (cf. Lk. 1:35). The primary role of the ark in the Old Covenant was to mediate the presence of God to Israel, and the role of Mary is to bear Christ to the world. If in the Old Testament cult the ark, which was simply made of precious gold and wood, held such a place of honor due to its mediating the presence of God, we are not surprised that Mary holds a place of surpassing honor in New Testament worship. The ark bore the presence of God and, after the Annunciation, Mary bears God in her womb. Just as the ark contained the tablets of the Old Law, the manna, and the staff of Aaron, Mary holds in her womb Jesus Christ the Messiah who is the New Law, the true bread from heaven, and the true high priest who offers His own life for us.

This role of bearing Christ to the world is a role that all Christians are to share with Mary. We too are called to imitate Jesus' most faithful disciple in bearing the presence of God to the world. Saint Paul reminds us and the Corinthians that our bodies are temples of the Holy Spirit (cf. 1 Cor. 6:19). When we receive the Eucharist, we receive into our bodies the true body and blood, soul and divinity of Jesus Christ. We become like Mary, who held the flesh and blood of the Christ Child in her body through the Incarnation. We should approach this most Holy Sacrament with the fear and rejoicing of David as he brought the first ark of the covenant into Jerusalem. When we receive this most precious gift, Mary's words should be our own: "My soul magnifies the Lord, and my spirit rejoices in God my Savior, for he has regarded the low estate of his handmaiden" (Lk. 1:46-48).

In the Old Testament, the ark also served as a mighty weapon in Israel's holy wars. Israel's holy warfare was fought in conquering and maintaining the Promised Land. The Book of Numbers tells us that "whenever the ark set out, Moses said, 'Arise, O Lord, and let thy enemies be scattered; and let them that hate thee flee before thee" (Num. 10:35). Two significant details about the ark are revealed in this passage. First, as we saw above, the ark is associated with God's presence, demonstrated by the words "before thee." Second, the ark is closely associated with battle. In fact, chapter ten of Numbers describes only two things, the ark and the army of Israel. This relationship between the ark and warfare is found throughout the Old Testament, such as in Ps. 68, which was sung in commemoration of the ark.

The victory at Jericho (cf. Josh. 6) illustrates the power of the ark in battle. The Israelites, led by the Levites carrying the ark, circle the city for seven days. On the last day, at the sound of the horns of the Levites and with the triumphant shouts of the Israelites, the city of Jericho falls without a human battle. In this account, the ark, which leads the procession of the Israelites, signifies that the Promised Land is to be conquered more by liturgical and spiritual warfare than by catapults and swords. The power and presence of God mediated by the ark provide Israel's victory.

Just as the ark played a significant role in Israel's warfare, Mary has a decisive role in the Church's spiritual battles. The Promised Land is a figure of heaven; the ark is a figure of Mary, who is central to the spiritual combat we must fight in order to gain heaven. In fact, the role of the ark in warfare appears to be alluded to in Saint John's description of Mary in Rev. 12. As we saw at the end of chapter eleven of Revelation, John witnesses the heavens open up the ark of the covenant revealed in God's temple. Standing in the place of the ark in Rev. 12 is the woman crowned with stars. Upon the revelation of the new ark of the covenant, the great battle in the heavens begins. The Church, which is the New Israel, understands that the role of the ark of the covenant has been transferred to Mary. She bore Christ's presence to the world and is the spiritual mother of all Christians (cf. Rev. 12:17). She is granted power and protection over the dreaded dragon, who cannot prevail against her (Rev. 12:13-16).

> We believe finally that in the glory where you reign, clothed with the sun and crowned with stars, you are, after Jesus, the joy and gladness of all the angels and the saints, and from this earth, over which we tread as pilgrims, comforted by our faith in the future resurrection, we look to you our life, our

sweetness, our hope; draw us onward with the sweetness of
your voice, so that one day, after our exile, you may show us
Jesus, the blessed fruit of your womb. O clement, O loving, O
sweet Virgin Mary. Amen.[10]

Conclusion

John's apocalyptic picture unveils the heavenly glory and
providential importance of Mary's role in salvation history.
Mary's motherhood is the cornerstone of her crucial role. Three
facets of this cornerstone revealed in John's vision have been
briefly examined. First, Mary is the spiritual mother of all
Christians. Like Eve, Mary's motherhood is *universal* in scope.
But unlike Eve, Mary is faithful to the Father, and thus becomes
a channel of God's grace and life. Mary's faith and faithfulness,
preceded by the action of the Holy Spirit, bring about the fullness
of the Father's plan for mankind. Through Mary, the Father
sends His Son in the Holy Spirit to dwell among Israel. The fruit
of her womb ripens on the tree of life, the Cross. Mary becomes
the means by which the life-giving fruit is made available to all,
to counteract the fruit taken by Eve from the forbidden tree.

Second, Mary's motherhood is a *royal* one. In the tradition of
the Davidic kingdom, where the mother of the king reigns as
queen mother, Mary is the queen mother of God's New
Covenant kingdom. Thus, John sees Mary as the woman
crowned with twelve stars. Therefore, we can pray to her and ask
for her intercession for us with great confidence. We know that
she is the mother of Christ our King and that He has made her
queen so that she may intercede for us.

Finally, Mary's motherhood is not only universal and royal,
but *holy*. By the overshadowing of the Holy Spirit, Mary becomes
the new and paramount ark. Just as the ark of the covenant was
made holy by its precious contents, so Mary is made holy by the
Son of God made flesh within her womb and the indwelling of
the Holy Spirit. If the ark of the covenant was rightfully revered

---

[10] Pope Pius XII, "Fruits of the Definition," *ibid.*, 324.

in Israel's liturgy, it should be no surprise that the ark of the New Covenant, Mary, has a place of great honor in the liturgy and life of the new Israel, the Church. After all, God has placed her in the midst of His heavenly temple and adorned her with a crown of twelve stars. In John's vision, a third of the angels, along with their leader, the great dragon, are thrown down from the heaven, whereas the woman is raised up on the wings of eagles. Clearly God has thrown down "the mighty from their thrones, and exalted those of low degree" (Lk. 1:52). Therefore, the Catechism declares that "Mary, the all-holy ever-virgin Mother of God, is the masterwork of the mission of the Son and the Spirit in the fullness of time" (no. 721). Because she is God's masterwork, it is no wonder that all generations call her blessed.

Timothy Gray is adjunct professor of Scripture and catechetics at the Notre Dame Graduate School of Christendom College in Alexandria, Virginia. He holds a Th.M. degree in Scripture from Duke University and a master's degree in theology from Franciscan University of Steubenville. In addition, he has studied Hebrew at the Hebrew University of Jerusalem. He was formerly the director of education for schools for the Diocese of Rapid City, South Dakota. He frequently writes and speaks on Scripture and the Catholic faith.

Chapter X

The Priest as Spiritual Father

Fr. Pablo Gadenz

"When you become a priest, are you going to encourage people to call you *father?*"

As the words of the question rang in my ears, I could feel myself slipping into a biblical trap, a trap into which many a Catholic has fallen. The person asking the question was a colleague of mine at work. Being an Evangelical Christian, he was committed to the truth revealed by God in the Bible. On several previous occasions we had discussed over lunch various issues dividing Catholics and Evangelicals—for example, the nature of justification and the authority of the Church and Church tradition. I had struggled mightily to show him that the Catholic Church *is* a Bible-believing Church. Now, shortly after I had announced that I was quitting my electrical engineering job to enter the seminary in the hope of becoming a priest, he came to my office and immediately challenged me with the above question.

Having done a little Bible reading myself, I knew that my friend was referring to Mt. 23:9, where Jesus says, "[C]all no man your father on earth, for you have one Father, who is in heaven." Here I was faced with a dilemma like those the Pharisees presented to Jesus. Unlike Jesus, however, I did not have the wisdom to disarm my adversary with a simple, yet profound, answer. If I said "Yes" to his question, citing Church tradition as the authority for calling a priest "father," he would immediately accuse me and the Church of contradicting Scripture, and all my efforts to show him that the Catholic Church takes the Bible seriously would be in vain. If I responded "No" (mainly out of convenience, saying that I would not *encourage* people to call me "father"), he would accuse me of being a hypocrite—wishing to become a Catholic priest and yet at the same time not really believing in what that Church teaches. Faced with this dilemma, I created a diversion so as to avoid answering the question directly: "What Jesus really means in that passage is . . ." Not having on the tip of my tongue other key scriptural passages with which to respond, I tried as best I could to give the typical answer to my friend's question.

The typical answer to the question about the prohibition in Mt. 23:9 is that Jesus is exaggerating. He is using Semitic hyperbole to bring out his point that ultimately God in heaven is Our Father. There are many examples of hyperbole in the Gospel, such as when Jesus says, "[I]f your right eye causes you to sin, pluck it out and throw it away" (Mt. 5:29), and "when you give alms, do not let your left hand know what your right hand is doing" (Mt. 6:3). Clearly, Jesus must be exaggerating in Mt. 23:9 as well, because His statement, if taken in a strict sense, would prohibit a child from calling his male parent "father."

While such a response is generally good enough in the company of Catholics, it does not suffice when among Evangelicals. (It certainly did not suffice for my colleague.) One needs to be more apologetically astute by citing other related Scripture passages. The point of Jesus' teaching—that God the Father is ultimately the reference and source of all fatherhood—is corroborated by Saint Paul in Eph. 3:14-15: "For this reason I bow my knees before the Father, from whom every family in heaven and on earth is named." The latter part of this phrase could also be translated "from whom all *fatherhood* in heaven and on earth is named," meaning that all fatherhood on earth—both natural, physical, and biological fatherhood on the one hand and supernatural, metaphysical, and spiritual fatherhood on the other—comes from God our Father.

That there is such a thing as spiritual fatherhood is also confirmed by Saint Paul. In the First Letter to the Corinthians, he refers to the relationship between himself and the Christians to whom he is writing as one between a father and his children: "For though you have countless guides in Christ, you do not have many fathers. For I became your father in Christ Jesus through the gospel" (1 Cor. 4:15; cf. 2 Cor. 12:14). Two verses later, Paul refers to Timothy, whose biological parents are known from Acts 16:1, as "my beloved and faithful child in the Lord" (1 Cor. 4:17). There are several passages, in fact, where the relationship between Paul and Timothy is described as a spiritual, father-son relationship: "[A]s a son with a father he has served with me in the gospel" (Phil. 2:22; cf. 1 Tim. 1:2; 1:18; 2 Tim. 1:2). Saint Paul also considers himself the spiritual father of Titus (Tit. 1:4) and Onesimus (Philem. 10). Paul's spiritual fatherhood is associated with his mission as an apostle, "a minister of Christ Jesus to the Gentiles in the *priestly* service of the gospel of God" (Rom. 15:16).

The foregoing apologetic may go a little further in convincing an Evangelical friend. With the help of Saint Paul, new light is shed on the saying of Jesus in Mt. 23:9, giving scriptural support for the Catholic practice of calling priests "father." Even the well-developed apologetic, however, only scratches the surface of the issue. It *defends* the Catholic practice, but it does not *explain* why a priest is a spiritual father. An explanation is needed because the practice of calling priests "father" is not merely a custom but is a teaching of the Church. By reason of the Sacrament of Holy Orders, priests "fulfill the preeminent and essential function of father and teacher among the People of God" (PO 9; cf. LG 28). To discover the explanation for this practice, we need to dig a little deeper in the Scriptures to see that spiritual fatherhood is at the core of the priest's very identity. As Pope John Paul II says in his 1986 Holy Thursday letter to priests, the priest "finds the source of his identity in Christ the Priest." Therefore, whatever we say about the relationship between priesthood and spiritual fatherhood will have to be true in a preeminent way about Jesus Christ. In order to understand the priest's identity as a spiritual father, we will have to understand how Christ our great High Priest is a spiritual father.

Before plunging into a discussion of spiritual fatherhood, however, it is useful to consider a related and more familiar concept, namely, that of spiritual brotherhood. Here, the Protestant and the Catholic are on common ground. Protestants will readily identify with the biblical idea of spiritual brotherhood expressed in such phrases as the "brotherhood of believers" and "brothers and sisters in Christ." In fact, the Protestant response to the apologetic on spiritual fatherhood given above might be to emphasize spiritual brotherhood instead of spiritual fatherhood. After all, Jesus says that "you are all brethren" (Mt. 23:8). And Paul, while he may call Timothy his son in some places, also calls him his brother in other places (e.g., 2 Cor. 1:1; Col. 1:1). I am reminded of the Evangelical minister who referred to a priest friend of mine, with whom he worked in campus ministry, as "Brother Dave" rather than "Father Dave." The Catholic position is not, however, brotherhood *or* fatherhood, but rather brotherhood *and* fatherhood. In fact, a consideration of spiritual brotherhood will help us discover spiritual fatherhood and its link to the priesthood.

There does seem to be some connection between brotherhood and priesthood. For example, the Letter to the Hebrews says that brotherhood with the human race was a necessary condition for Christ to become a priest. Christ "had to be made like his brethren in every respect, so that he might become a merciful and faithful high priest in the service of God" (Heb. 2:17). The relationship of brotherhood is necessary but not sufficient, however, for Christ to become our priest. In addition, the Letter to the Hebrews indicates another necessary qualification for Christ to be a priest: His relationship with God.

> For every high priest chosen from among men is appointed to act on behalf of men *in relation to God*... Christ did not exalt himself to be made a high priest, but was appointed by him who said to him, *"Thou art my Son*, today I have begotten thee" (Heb. 5:1, 5).[1]

Jesus is the Son of God. In particular, He is the "first-born" son (Heb. 1:6; cf. Col. 1:15), the "first-born among many brethren" (Rom. 8:29). As the first-born son among many brothers and sisters, Jesus can be a "merciful and faithful" priest who brings "many sons to glory" (Heb. 2:10, 17). Jesus our High Priest, who is Son of God by nature, enables us to become sons and daughters of God through grace (cf. Jn. 1:12; 1 Jn. 3:1-2; Rom. 8:14-17; Gal. 4:4-6).

With so much "family language" in our discussion—father, brother and sister, son and daughter—it becomes clear that the context for our study of priesthood and fatherhood is the image of the Church as the Family of God.[2] A person enters this supernatural family through Baptism, through which one is reborn as a child of God the Father. All those reborn in Baptism are brothers and sisters of one another, with Christ Jesus, the Son of God, as the "first-born" or elder brother. What is the connection in this family picture, however, between Christ our elder brother and Christ our high priest? How does fatherhood fit into the picture,

---

[1] In his presentation of the priesthood of Christ in the Letter to the Hebrews, Albert Vanhoye, *Old Testament Priests and the New Priest* (Petersham, MA: Saint Bede's Publications, 1986), invites us to consider in Christ "the twofold relationship on which all priesthood is based: the priest must be accredited before God . . . and bound to human beings by a real solidarity" (p. 66). "The glory of the high priest is defined by the present and permanent position of Christ in relation to God and to mankind" (p. 73). "[I]f Christ's death resulted in his glorification as high priest, it was because it was an act of filial obedience toward God and of fraternal solidarity with mankind. These two aspects are inseparable, the first governing the second" (p. 80).

[2] The Church is described as the Family of God in several documents of the Second Vatican Council (e.g., LG 6, 28, 32, and 51; UR 2; AG 1; PO 6; GS 32, 40, and 92) and in various paragraphs of the Catechism (e.g., nos. 1, 542, 759, 1439, 1632, and 1655).

not just for Christ but also for Christian priests? To answer these questions, we turn to the pages of the Old Testament for a discussion of the priesthood.

Priesthood in the Old Testament

Careful study of the Old Testament priesthood is needed, because most scholars who consider this topic focus almost exclusively on the Levitical priesthood associated with Aaron and his descendants. As a result, the priesthood of the Old Testament is viewed as being only remotely helpful in understanding the Christian priesthood.[3] However, there is another priesthood in the Old Testament, one that precedes the Levitical priesthood. This pre-Levitical priesthood is associated with the family.

During the age of the patriarchs such as Abraham, Isaac, and Jacob, the priestly functions (such as offering sacrifice) were carried out by the father of a family. In the case of an extended family or clan, the priest was the patriarch or head of the clan. In his classic work *Ancient Israel*, Roland de Vaux writes that "[t]here was no official priesthood in the time of the Patriarchs; acts of public worship (especially sacrifice, the central act) were performed by the head of the family (Gen. 22; 31:54; 46:1)."[4] Priesthood was therefore associated with fatherhood. Even after the patriarchal period, following the establishment of the Levitical priesthood, the association of priesthood with fatherhood is still found. One good example is in Judg. 17:10, in which a traveling young Levite is welcomed into the house of Micah: "And Micah said to him, 'Stay with me, and be to me a father and a priest.'" The significance of this remark, according to De Vaux, is that "the priest had inherited those religious prerogatives which, in the patriarchal period, had belonged to the head of the family."[5]

---

[3] See for example, Vanhoye, 1-59, and Jean Galot, *Theology of the Priesthood* (San Francisco: Ignatius Press, 1984), 21-23.

[4] Roland de Vaux, *Ancient Israel* (New York: McGraw-Hill Book Co., 1961), 345.

[5] *Ibid.*, 348.

In the patriarchal period, the priesthood exercised by the head of the family was passed on from father to son,[6] especially to the "first-born" son, who became the head of the family after his father's death.[7] In the Book of Genesis, patriarchal authority—and therefore the priesthood—is handed on from the father to the "first-born" son through the blessing (cf. Gen. 27). Yet Isaac gave his blessing to his younger son Jacob rather than his older son Esau. This is one of many examples that reveal an element of divine (and human) election in the determination of who is to receive the status of priest and father by being designated the "first-born" son.[8]

A number of Old Testament texts clarify the concept of the pre-Levitical priesthood of first-born sons. Ex. 13:1-2 states: "The LORD said to Moses, 'Consecrate to me all the first-born; whatever is the first to open the womb among the people of Israel, both of man and of beast, is mine." This consecration of the first-born refers to priesthood, as is made clear by comparison with Num. 3:12, in which God tells Moses: "Behold, I have taken the Levites from among the people of Israel instead of every first-born that opens the womb among the people of Israel" (cf. Num. 8:16, 18). Jewish scholar Nahum Sarna explains Ex. 13:1-2 as follows:

> It is explicitly related in Num. 3:12 and 8:16, 18, that in the course of the wilderness wanderings the Levites supplanted the first-born in assuming priestly and ritual functions. It may

---

[6] *Ibid.*, 359.

[7] *Ibid.*, 41.

[8] De Vaux comments that "the displacing of the elder son by a younger one is a theme which often recurs in the Old Testament. Apart from Jacob and Esau, Peres and Zerah, many other examples could be quoted. Isaac inherits, not Ishmael; Joseph is his father's favourite, then Benjamin; Ephraim is preferred to Manasseh; David, the youngest in his family, is chosen from among all his brothers and leaves his kingdom to Solomon, his youngest son. Some would treat these instances as signs of a custom opposed to the right of the first-born. . . . But the examples quoted from Israelite history are exceptions to the ordinary law. . . . Moreover, the Bible states explicitly that these stories stress the fact that God's choice is absolutely unmerited and quite gratuitous" (*ibid.*, 42).

therefore be safely inferred that Moses is here instructed to install the first-born to fulfill priestly duties. Mishnah Zevahim 14:4 expresses the developments this way: "Before the creation of the Tabernacle, shrines (Heb. *bamot*) were permitted, and the worship was performed by the first-born; once the Tabernacle was erected, the shrines were prohibited, and the worship was performed by the priests [of the tribe of Levi]."[9]

The priesthood of first-born sons is implicitly referred to in Ex. 19:22: "And also let the priests who come near to the LORD consecrate themselves, lest the LORD break out upon them." Sarna explains that "Jewish commentators understood 'priests' here as referring to first-born males, in that the latter functioned as priests until they were replaced by the Aaronites, as recounted in Num. 3:11-13 and 8:16-18."[10] Another passage that refers to the priesthood of first-born sons is Ex. 24:5: "And [Moses] sent young men of the people of Israel, who offered burnt offerings and sacrificed peace offerings of oxen to the LORD." "Rabbinic tradition identified the 'young men' as the first-born males upon whom devolved cultic duties prior to the establishment of the priesthood in Israel."[11]

Christian exegetes of patristic and medieval times also recognized the priesthood of first-born sons, which preceded that of Aaron and the Levites. For example, Saint Jerome, in commenting on the passage, "Then Rebekah took the best garments of Esau her older son, which were with her in the house, and put them on Jacob her younger son" (Gen. 27:15), writes as follows:

> On this passage the Hebrews say that the first-born discharged the office of priests and had the priestly vestment, clothed in

[9] Nahum M. Sarna, *The JPS Torah Commentary*: Exodus (Philadelphia: The Jewish Publication Society, 1991), 65.

[10] *Ibid.*, 108.

[11] *Ibid.*, 151-52. In footnote 15 on p. 255, Sarna lists the Mishnah Zevahim, the Targums, and various rabbis as sources.

which they offered sacrifices to God, before Aaron was chosen for the priesthood.[12]

In the *Summa Theologiae*, Saint Thomas Aquinas also refers to the priesthood of first-born sons. In his "Treatise on Law," he writes that the "priesthood also existed before the Law among the worshippers of God in virtue of human institution, for that dignity was allotted to the first-born."[13]

A treatment of the pre-Levitical priesthood of first-born sons would not be complete, however, without a discussion of *Melchizedek*, who is the first man in Scripture to be called a priest (*kohen*; Gen. 14:18). Does the priesthood of Melchizedek have anything to do with fatherhood and first-born sonship? Through recourse to Jewish traditions of interpretation, we discover that Melchizedek is identified in the Jewish Targums and midrashic sources as Shem, the first-born son of Noah.[14] In this interpretation, the blessing by Noah of Shem-Melchizedek in Gen. 9:26 is understood as the patriarchal priestly blessing, which is then passed on by Shem-Melchizedek to Abraham in Gen. 14:19. Hence, Shem-Melchizedek, the first-born son of Noah, is the chief priest and patriarch (father figure) over his house, that is, over all of his extended family which through ten generations

---

[12] Saint Jerome, *Liber quaestionum hebraicorum in Genesim (Corpus Christianorum:* Series Latina, vol. 72, 34): "*Et in hoc loco tradunt Hebraei primogenitos functos officio sacerdotum et habuisse uestimentum sacerdotale, quo induti deo uictimas offerebant, antequam Aaron in sacerdotium eligeretur.*"

[13] Saint Thomas Aquinas, *Summa Theologiae* Ia-IIae, q. 103, a. 1, ad 3 in the Blackfriars Edition, vol. 29 (New York: McGraw-Hill Book Company, 1969). See also IIa-IIae, q. 87, a. 1, ad 3.

[14] Joseph Fitzmyer cites the Targum Neofiti I, the Fragmentary Targums, and the Targum Pseudo-Jonathan, all of which identify Melchizedek as Shem; see his article "'Now This Melchizedek . . .' (Heb. 7, 1)" *Catholic Biblical Quarterly* 25 (1963), 312, fn. 32. In the same footnote, Fitzmyer also refers to C. Spicq's commentary on Hebrews (*L'Epitre aux Hebreux*, 2 vols., Paris: Gabalda, 1952-53), in which Spicq points out that the Jewish midrashic haggadah "also identified Melchizedek with Shem, the eldest son of Noah, because from Adam to Levi the cult was supposed to have been cared for by the first-born" (vol. 2, 205).

includes Abraham as well (cf. Gen. 11:10-26). Abraham, after
receiving the blessing from Shem-Melchizedek, is designated to
become the new chief priest and patriarch over all his descendants.

The identification of Melchizedek as Shem is found in many
Christian exegetes as well. Saint Ephrem the Syrian, a fourth-cen-
tury doctor of the Church, writes in his *Commentary on Genesis*:

> Melchizedek is Shem, who became a king due to his greatness;
> he was the head of fourteen nations. In addition, "he was a
> priest." He received this from Noah, his father, through the
> rights of succession.[15]

Saint Jerome is also familiar with the identification, as seen in his
commentary on Gen. 14:18:

> They say that he [Melchizedek] was Shem, the son of Noah,
> and calculating the years of his life, they declare that he lived
> to the time of Isaac, and that all the first-born [from] Noah,
> until Aaron exercised the priesthood, were high priests.[16]

The identification of the royal priesthood of Melchizedek
with the priesthood of first-born sons also has significance later
in the Old Testament, even after the Levites have replaced the
first-born sons as priests. After the development of the Israelite
monarchy, the king is referred to as the first-born son (Ps. 89:27;
cf. 2 Sam. 7:14, Ps. 2:7). King Solomon, the son of David, functions as a priest at the dedication of the Temple (1 Kings 8).
According to Ps. 110:4, he is a priest "after the order of
Melchizedek" not only because Jerusalem is identified with the
Salem of Gen. 14 (cf. Ps. 76:2), but also because he has received
the title of first-born son.

---

[15] Saint Ephrem the Syrian, *Commentary on Genesis*, section XI, in *The Fathers of the Church*, vol. 91 (Washington: The Catholic University of America Press, 1994), 151.

[16] Saint Jerome, op. cit., 19: "*Aiunt huc esse Sem filium Noé, et supputantes annos uitae ipsius ostendunt eum ad Isaac usque uixisse, omnesque primogenitos [a] Noe, donec sacerdotio fungeretur Aaron, fuisse pontifices.*" See also Jerome's Epistle 73 to the Presbyter Evangelum on the identification of Melchizedek as Shem (*Patrologia Latina*, vol. 22, 676-81).

There is yet another connection between the pre-Levitical priesthood and first-born sonship. Up to now, we have considered the priesthood and first-born sonship on an individual level. Several texts in the Old Testament make it possible to establish a connection on a collective level as well. In Ex. 4:22-23, the Lord instructs Moses to tell Pharaoh:

> Thus says the LORD, Israel is my first-born son, and I say to you, "Let my son go that he may serve me"; if you refuse to let him go, behold, I will slay your first-born son (cf. Deut. 14:1-2; 32:5-9; Jer. 31:9; Hos. 11:1).

Sarna comments as follows:

> The relationship of Israel to God is expressed poetically, in filial terms. All peoples are recognized as being under the universal fatherhood of God, but Israel has the singular status of being the first to acknowledge YHVH [Yahweh] and to enter into a special relationship with Him. As such, Israel enjoys God's devoted care and protection. . . . The first-born son in Israel was regarded as being naturally dedicated to God and in early times had certain cultic prerogatives and obligations.[17]

In Ex. 19:6, we find that the whole nation of Israel is called to be a "kingdom of priests and a holy nation." Sarna comments:

> [T]he priest's place and function within society must serve as the ideal model for Israel's self-understanding of its role among the nations. The priest is set apart by a distinctive way of life consecrated to the service of God and dedicated to ministering to the needs of the people.[18]

Just as the first-born sons within Israel have a fatherly, priestly role in the community towards the younger children, so the whole nation of Israel, as God's first-born son, is called to exercise a priestly role with respect to the other children-nations of

---

[17] Sarna, 24.
[18] *Ibid.*, 104.

God (cf. Deut. 32:8-9). Hence, the priesthood of first-born sons operates on both the individual and collective levels. On the individual level, Jacob/Israel—the first-born rather than Esau— becomes the priestly father of the twelve tribes of the nation of Israel. On the collective level, the nation of Israel—descended from the patriarch Jacob/Israel—is called to be a kingdom of priests. However, the priesthood of the people of Israel is contingent on their obedience to the covenant (Ex. 19:5).

> But the Old Testament declares many times that this condition [obedience to the covenant] has never been fulfilled (Deut. 9:7; Jer. 7:25-26). It follows logically, therefore, that the priesthood promised to the people remained, so far as the Old Testament is concerned, an ideal never attained.[19]

On the individual level, the priesthood associated with the first-born sons also does not reach its fulfillment in the Old Testament. The first-born sons of all the tribes of Israel are "desacralized" through the process of redemption[20] and are replaced by the Levitical priests. The traditional explanation of why the first-born sons are replaced is because of their idolatrous worship of the golden calf:

> Then Moses stood in the gate of the camp, and said, "Who is on the LORD's side? Come to me." And all the sons of Levi gathered themselves together to him. . . . And the sons of Levi did according to the word of Moses. . . . And Moses said, "Today you have ordained yourselves for the service of the LORD" (Ex. 32:26, 28-29).

Sarna comments as follows:

> [The Levites] remained faithful to the covenant and loyally maintained the purity of Israel's worship. This note, as v. 29 and Deut. 10:8 imply, is intended to provide a background for the election of the tribe of Levi to be in charge of the

---

[19] Vanhoye, 28.
[20] Sarna, 66-67.

Tabernacle [Num. 1:48-54; 2:17; 16:9] and to be surrogates for the first-born [Num. 3:40-51]. It is quite likely that the first-born played a leading role in the worship of the golden calf and for that reason were displaced as cultic officiants.[21]

The Book of Numbers indicates in various places how the Levites replaced the first-born (Num. 3:11-13; 8:14-19). Chapter three of Numbers also explains that a census was taken of the existing number of non-Levitical first-born sons (22,273) so that they could be redeemed by the Levites (22,000). The extra 273 non-Levitical, first-born sons were redeemed by a redemption price of five shekels (cf. Num. 3:40-51).[22] With the change to the Levitical priesthood came a change in the law (cf. Heb. 7:12). This law which "was added because of transgressions" (Gal. 3:19) could not give life (cf. Gal. 3:21; Ezek. 20:25), but served as a "custodian" or "*paidagogos*" (Gal. 3:24) until Christ came to give us a new covenant, a new law, and a new priesthood.

---

[21] *Ibid.*, 208-09. Evangelical scholar John Sailhamer explains that "God had a claim to every Israelite first-born who had been 'passed over' in the Exodus (Ex. 13:1-2, 11-13). God's claim on the first-born of Israel was apparently intended at the start to be the means of establishing the priesthood in Israel. . . . Every first-born son was to be a priest. Because of the Levites' faithfulness at the time of the golden calf, however, God now moved to relinquish his right to all first-born Israelite males and put in their place the tribe of Levi (Num. 3:11-13). Once again, it is evident that the sin of the golden calf marked a decisive change in Israel's relationship with God in the Sinai covenant" *The Pentateuch as Narrative* (Grand Rapids, MI: Zondervan Publishing House, 1992), 373. For a fuller discussion of the consequences of the worship of the golden calf, see the article by Jewish scholars L. Smolar and M. Aberbach, "The Golden Calf Episode in Postbiblical Literature," *Hebrew Union College Annual* 39 (1968), 91-116. Among the punishments they associate with the incident are the loss of sacerdotal privileges of the people of Israel (cf. Ex. 19:6) and of the first-born sons.

[22] Jewish scholar J. Milgrom explains that the "replacement of the first-born by the Levites implies that the former originally held a sacred status. This is supported by the biblical laws regarding the human first-born that utilize the phrase 'dedicate [*natan*] / sanctify [*kiddesh*] / transfer [*he'evir*] to the Lord' (Ex. 13:1, 12; 22:28) as well as 'redeem [*padah*] from the LORD' (Num. 18:15). . . . Thus the Bible may be preserving a memory of the first-born bearing a sacred status; his replacement by the Levites may reflect the establishment of a professional, inherited priestly class. . . . The rabbis also maintained that the first-born originally held a priestly status" *The JPS Torah Commentary: Numbers* (Philadelphia: The Jewish Publication Society, 1990), 17-18.

The Priesthood of Christ

Our discussion of the Old Testament priesthood has prepared us to consider now the priesthood of Christ in the New Testament. A possible point of contact with the Old Testament priesthood of first-born sons considered above is the description of Jesus in the Gospel of Luke as the "first-born" son of Mary (Lk. 2:7, 2:23). Catholic biblical scholar Joseph Fitzmyer points out that the use of "first-born" in Lk. 2:7 indicates that Jesus is "entitled to have all the privileges and status of the first-born in the Mosaic Law (see Ex. 13:2; Num. 3:12-13; 18:15-16; Deut. 21:15-17)."[23] The use of the term "first-born" also prepares for the narrative of the Presentation in the Temple, which cites Ex. 13 concerning the consecration of the first-born (Lk. 2:23). Luke is unmistakably presenting Jesus in the narrative as a priest—a priest not in virtue of his being a Levite, but in virtue of his being a first-born son.

Support for this idea comes from noticing that Luke does not mention the payment of the redemption fee of five shekels (Num. 8:15-16), by which a first-born son was "desacralized" and replaced in the service of the Lord by a Levite.[24] Catholic biblical scholar Raymond Brown indicates that "it has been argued that the reason why Luke does not mention the redemption of the child Jesus through the payment of the five shekels is that he wants the reader to think that Jesus *stayed* in the service of the Lord" as

---

[23] Joseph Fitzmyer, *The Gospel According to Luke I-IX*, Anchor Bible, vol. 28 (Garden City, NY: Doubleday & Co., Inc., 1980), 407.

[24] Raymond Brown, *The Birth of the Messiah* (Garden City, New York: Doubleday & Co., Inc., 1979), 447, explains the redemption payment as follows: "Exodus 13:1 and 13:11f demand the consecration of all first-born males to the Lord: 'the first to open the womb.' This is traditionally related to the Lord's sparing the life of the Israelite first-born when He slew the first-born of the Egyptians. The original idea was that the first-born should then spend his life serving the Lord in a special way; but in fact the tribe of Levi eventually took over the special service of the Lord in cult and thus effectively replaced the first-born. This change was recognized by the legal provisions in Numbers 18:15-16 which allowed the first-born to be bought back from the service of the Lord for five shekels (twenty denarii), while the Levites remained in His service."

a priest.[25] Brown himself does not agree with this idea because Jesus was not a Levite and therefore, apparently, not a priest.

Jesus indeed is of the house of Judah, not Levi (Mt. 1:2; Lk. 3:33; Heb. 7:14), but Luke may nonetheless be indicating that Jesus *is* a priest—not a Levitical priest, but a priest "after the order of Melchizedek" (Ps. 110:4), a priest by virtue of being a first-born son. Jesus, as the Son of David (cf. Lk. 1:27; 1:32; 1:69; 2:4; 2:11), is a first-born son (Lk. 2:7; Ps. 89:27) and a royal priest like Solomon (1 Kings 8) in the Temple of the Lord. Jesus is not redeemed, but remains in the service of the Lord as a priest.

While this brief treatment of allusions to the priesthood of Christ in the Gospel of Luke can be expanded,[26] let us return to our discussion of the priesthood of Christ in the Letter to the Hebrews. We have now discovered, with the help of our treatment of the Old Testament, the links between brotherhood, fatherhood, and priesthood. As we saw above, the author of Hebrews understands the priesthood of Christ in terms of the twofold relationship of Christ as Son of God and brother of mankind. He presents Christ the Priest precisely in terms of the familial priesthood of first-born sons. By establishing the New Covenant, Christ brings about a change in the law and a change in the priesthood as well (cf. Heb. 7:12). Christ abolishes the Levitical priesthood and restores—on a supernatural level—the priesthood of the first-born sons. In the new family established by the New Covenant of Christ, Jesus is the "first-born" son (Heb. 1:6), the oldest brother who brings His many younger "brethren" (Heb. 2:17; cf. Rom. 8:29), who are other "sons," to glory (Heb. 2:10). Christ's status as first-born son allows Him to be a

---

[25] *Ibid.*, 449.

[26] For example, more support for the idea that Luke is presenting Jesus as a priest can be discovered by drawing from the many connections between the Lucan infancy narrative and the narrative concerning Samuel in 1 Sam. 1-2. Consider, for example, the messianic prophecy about a priest in 1 Sam. 2:35: "And I will raise up for myself a faithful priest, who shall do according to what is in my heart and in my mind; and I will build him a sure house, and he shall go in and out before my anointed for ever."

"merciful and faithful high priest" (Heb. 2:17). He is faithful "over God's house"—that is, over God's New Covenant family of which we are a part—as a son (Heb. 3:6) and as a priest (Heb. 10:21).

As first-born son and priest, Christ receives fatherly authority over those in the New Covenant family. His younger brothers are also His children (Heb. 2:13-14; cf. Jn. 21:5). Jesus, who is the image of God the Father (Col. 1:15) and "bears the very stamp of his nature" (Heb. 1:3), images God's fatherhood by becoming the Father of the new creation (2 Cor. 5:17). As Adam was father over the created human race, Christ the new and last Adam (1 Cor. 15:45) is the father of the redeemed human race. Given the view explained above identifying Melchizedek with Shem (a view which it is reasonable to think the author of the Letter to the Hebrews also held),[27] the identification of Christ as a "high priest after the order of Melchizedek" (e.g., Heb. 5:10; 6:20) corresponds to the identification of His priesthood in terms of the relationships of first-born son, brother, and father. Christ is a priest after the order of Melchizedek not only because of the foreshadowing of the Eucharist in the offering of bread and wine (cf. Gen. 14:18), but also because He is the first-born Son of God as Shem-Melchizedek is the first-born son of Noah; He is the eldest brother in the family of the children of God as Shem-Melchizedek is the eldest in the family of mankind descended from Noah; He is the patriarch or father figure who blesses the "descendants of Abraham" (Heb. 2:16) as Shem-Melchizedek is the patriarch who blesses Abraham.

---

[27] The text of Heb. 7:3 ("He is without father or mother or genealogy, and has neither beginning of days nor end of life") would seem to argue against the identification of Melchizedek as Shem (since Shem's father is known to be Noah). However, it can be shown that Heb. 7:3 actually refers to technical priestly qualifications associated with the Levitical priesthood (cf. Num. 8:24-25), qualifications which do not apply to the priesthood after the order of Melchizedek. In other words, Melchizedek's priesthood is without beginning or end, while the Levitical priesthood begins at age twenty-five and ends at fifty, and necessarily is applicable only to those who can trace their lineage to Levi.

Christ, the priest after the order of Melchizedek, restores in a transcendent way the priesthood of first-born sons when He introduces the New Covenant, which is accompanied by a change in the priesthood and a change in the law (cf. Heb. 7:12).

The Christian Priesthood

The restoration in Christ of the priesthood of first-born sons can now be applied to the Christian priesthood. We will first consider its application on the collective level, wherein we discover the roots of the "priesthood of all believers." Contrary to a widespread misunderstanding, Catholics not only believe in a ministerial priesthood of individual priests but also believe, like their Protestant brethren, in a common priesthood of all the faithful (LG 10). Again, it is not a question of *"either* common priesthood *or* ministerial priesthood" but of *"both* common priesthood *and* ministerial priesthood." As we saw above, in the Old Testament, Jacob/Israel receives the "first-born" priestly blessing and the nation of Israel is then called to share in that first-born sonship and priesthood (Ex. 4:22; 19:6).

In the New Testament, Jesus, the new Israel (cf. Jn. 4:6, 11-12), confers first-born priestly status on the Church, which is the true and new Israel of God (Gal. 6:16), "the assembly of the first-born" (Heb. 12:23). "Jesus Christ the faithful witness, the first-born of the dead, . . . loves us and has freed us from our sins by his blood and made us a kingdom, priests to his God and Father" (Rev. 1:5-6; cf. Rev. 5:10; 20:6; 1 Pet. 2:5, 9). The Church shares in Christ's first-born sonship and thus becomes the elder brother to those outside the Church, who can be viewed collectively as the younger brother. As elder brother, the Church as the Body of Christ has a priestly mission similar to that of Christ the Head.

We are now in a position, finally, to get back to our original question of why Catholics refer to priests as "father." We apply the priesthood of first-born sons, restored by Christ, to the individual level. Within the family of the Church, Christ instituted the ministerial priesthood, in which individual priests are the elder brothers and father figures of the faithful. As seen above, the New Testament portrays the Church as the new Israel, inheriting the promise to be a kingdom of priests. Within this new Israel, Jesus established His twelve apostles as the new patriarchs of the twelve tribes of the new Israel (Mt. 19:28; Rev. 21:12-14). Like the patriarchs of old, the apostles are priests and fathers. Unlike the patriarchs of old, they are not priests and fathers over their own natural families, but over the supernatural family of the Church. This new Church family, like the natural family, exists at various levels: from the "nuclear" family or local Church to the extended family or universal Church. The chief priest and father figure over the universal Church is the apostle Peter, who received a special priestly blessing from Christ (Mt. 16:17-19). In the Acts of the Apostles, we read that the apostles passed on their ministry by appointing elders or presbyters in every church (Acts 14:23). In this way, they as priest-fathers passed on the priesthood "over God's house" to the "first-born" sons, the "elder brothers" (cf. Acts 15:23). Saint Augustine explains this apostolic succession in the priesthood in his commentary on Ps. 45:16 ("Instead of your fathers shall be your sons"):

> What does that mean? The apostles were sent as fathers; to replace those apostles, sons were born to you who were constituted bishops. . . . The Church calls them fathers, she who gave birth to them, who placed them in the sees of their fathers. . . . Such is the Catholic Church. She has given birth to sons who, through all the earth, continue the work of her first Fathers.[28]

Theologian Henri De Lubac comments that

> the authority of the bishop has an essentially paternal character. If he is head, it is because he is father. And every priest charged with a ministry participates at his own level in this authority and exercises it with the same character.[29]

---

[28] Saint Augustine, *In Ps. 44*, 32 (*Corpus Christianorum*: Series Latina, 38:516); quoted in Henri De Lubac, *The Motherhood of the Church* (San Francisco: Ignatius Press, 1982), 90.

[29] *Ibid.*, 105.

On the parish level, the priest is the father figure over the local Church family entrusted to his care. On the diocesan level, the bishop is the priestly father figure over the diocesan Church family. On the worldwide level, the Bishop of Rome, the Vicar of Christ, is the Holy Father or Pope ("*il Papa*") over the Catholic Church on earth. Jesus Christ, "who is seated at the right hand of the throne of the Majesty in heaven" (Heb. 8:1) is still our great High Priest, exercising a fatherly authority as first-born son over all of God's house—the Church triumphant in heaven, the Church suffering in purgatory, and the Church pilgrim on earth—until the end comes, "when he delivers the kingdom to God the Father" (1 Cor. 15:24), "from whom all fatherhood in heaven and on earth is named" (Eph. 3:15).

The fatherly identity of the priest gives us a good perspective to examine issues related to the priesthood, such as priestly celibacy and the ordination of women. First, with regard to celibacy, it is entirely fitting that the priest, as a spiritual father and following the example of Christ the great High Priest, be wholly dedicated through celibacy to his spiritual family, the Church, without being the father of a natural family.

Second, with regard to women's ordination, just as God has created specific relationships for men and women in the natural family as fathers and mothers—relationships that cannot be interchanged—so too in the supernatural family there exist relationships for men and women as spiritual fathers and mothers that cannot be interchanged. Priesthood is associated with spiritual fatherhood and, as such, requires a male person. Therefore, the ordination of women to the priesthood is not possible. It should always be remembered, however, that the fatherly authority exercised by the Pope, bishops, and priests is essentially one of service to the "younger" brothers and sisters in God's family. Priests are called to be like Christ, who "came not to be served but to serve" (Mk. 10:45).

I have never had a chance to go back to my old colleague from work to discuss more fully the priesthood and spiritual fatherhood in God's plan. Perhaps some day I will have the opportunity to do so. In the meantime, I can focus on serving, as a brother and father, the portion of the Family of God entrusted to my care. Through Baptism, I bring about the birth of new children of God by water and the Spirit (Jn. 3:5). Through the Eucharist, I nourish the children with the Bread of Life (cf. Mt. 7:9). Through Confession, I forgive the sins of the children so that through discipline they may grow in righteousness (cf. Heb. 12:7-11). Through the Anointing of the Sick, I lay my hands on the sick children and pray that they may be saved (Jas. 5:14-15). Through my preaching, I instruct the children in the law of God (Mal. 2:7).

In the priesthood, I have the example of many holy priests— many holy fathers—to inspire me. In particular, there is the example of the Holy Father, Pope John Paul II. The fatherly character of the priest was especially evident to me when, nine days after my ordination to the priesthood, I had the opportunity to meet Pope John Paul II in Rome. With my natural father standing next to me, I, a newly ordained father, was able to spend a few minutes with my spiritual father, the Pope. Thanks be to God the Father, "from whom all fatherhood in heaven and on earth is named" (Eph. 3:15)!

CHAPTER XI

The "Real Presence"
of the Marriage Bond

LEON J. SUPRENANT, JR.

When we hear someone tell us something that applies directly to us, and even challenges us to reexamine some aspect of our lives, we say that the speaker is "hitting home" or speaking to us "where we live."

The courageous witness of the Church to Christ's teaching on marriage and family issues literally "hits home." Not only does the Church's teaching reveal to us the "great mystery" of Christ and His Church (Eph. 5:32), but it challenges us at the core of our daily lives. As was the case with Jesus' teaching on the Eucharist, many people today, upon hearing the Church's teaching on marriage, say, "This is a hard saying; who can listen to it?" and they walk away (cf. Jn. 6:60, 66).

The witness of the Church is the witness of Christ, and the pivotal teaching of Christ upon which all the other sexuality issues hinge, including contraception, fornication, and homosexuality, is Christ's teaching on marriage.

A Trap

There are several New Testament passages that provide Christ's teaching against divorce and remarriage (e.g., Mt. 5:31-32; Mk. 10:2-12; Lk. 16:18; 1 Cor. 7:10-11). However, the fullest presentation is found in Mt. 19:1-12.

The passage begins with Jesus' entering "the region of Judea beyond the Jordan" (Mt. 19:1). This places Jesus within the jurisdiction of King Herod, who imprisoned and executed Saint John the Baptist for speaking out against the king's adulterous union with his brother's wife (cf. Mt. 14:1-12).

The Pharisees, the Jewish religious leaders at the time, wanted Jesus to be arrested and killed (cf. Jn. 11:45-57). And so they ask Jesus the provocative question, "Is it lawful to divorce one's wife for any cause?" (Mt. 19:3). Clearly, this was a "trick question" designed to trap Jesus (cf. Mt. 22:15-18; Jn. 8:3-6). If He answers "no," then He would be implicitly criticizing Herod, because Herod's divorce and remarriage was not justifiable under any reputable interpretation of Jewish law.[1] Jesus would then be subject to the same fate as John the Baptist. But if He answers "yes," He would be espousing in essence a "no-fault" system. Such a wimpy, compromised stance would destroy any credibility He might have as a moral teacher.

Jesus' response involves a return to the basics. He answers,

> Have you not read that he who made them from the beginning made them male and female, and said, "For this reason a man shall leave his father and mother and be joined to his wife, and the two shall become one"? So they are no longer two but one (Mt. 19:4-6).

He quotes from the first two chapters of Genesis to remind the learned Pharisees of God's plan for married life.

---

[1] The principal rabbinical schools at the time were those of Shammai and Hillel. The former interpreted Deut. 24:1-4 as meaning that one could divorce and remarry only in the case of adultery. The latter interpreted "something indecent" (Deut. 24:1) more loosely, so as to permit divorce and remarriage in a variety of circumstances.

But the Pharisees protest: "Why then did Moses command one to give a certificate of divorce, and to put her away?" (Mt. 19:7). Jesus' simple—but not simplistic—response not only lacks the "nuance" of the contemporary rabbinical teaching, but it even seems to contradict Moses himself. Explain yourself, Jesus!

First, Jesus clarifies Moses' teaching on divorce: "For your hardness of heart Moses allowed you to divorce your wives, but from the beginning it was not so" (Mt. 19:8). Moses did not "command" divorce, as the Pharisees claimed, but allowed it in certain circumstances because of the people's "hardness of heart." The phrase "hardness of heart" immediately brings to mind Pharaoh in the Book of Exodus (e.g., Ex. 7:2-4), who was notorious for his rejection of God's law and his enslavement of the chosen people. However, the tragic irony of Israel's post-Exodus history is that the Israelites manifested this same "hardness of heart." Moses' concession in Deut. 24 was designed to keep public order among a people that was still spiritually enslaved. But it did not reflect God's noble plan "from the beginning."

Jesus then adds, "[W]hoever divorces his wife, except for unchastity, and marries another, commits adultery; and he who marries a divorced woman, commits adultery" (Mt. 19:9). He definitively teaches that one cannot divorce and remarry. Like Jesus' teaching on the Eucharist in Jn. 6:60, this is a "hard saying," leading the disciples to respond, "If such is the case of a man with his wife, it is not expedient to marry" (Mt. 19:10).

A red herring in the discussion is the phrase "except for *unchastity*" (*porneia*), which some people misinterpret so as to soften Jesus' teaching. We must realize that if Jesus meant that you could divorce and remarry in the case of "unchastity" or "adultery," He would have been adopting the familiar position of the rabbi Shammai, and His teaching would not have elicited the response found in verse 10.[2]

---

[2] The view that Jesus permits divorce and remarriage in the event of *porneia* in Mt. 19:9 was unheard of before Erasmus proposed it in the sixteenth century. That interpretation squarely contradicts Jesus' statements in Mk. 10:2-12 and Lk. 16:18. It is also grammatically unfounded, because "except for *porneia*," given its placement, does not refer to remarriage.

Many Fathers of the Church understood "except for *porneia*" as meaning that in certain cases there may be a separation for a short or indefinite period, but *not a single Church Father* interpreted the phrase as permitting a remarriage. Others held that Jesus' use of *porneia* referred to situations which really were not marriages in the first place, such as incestuous relationships (cf. Lev. 18).

In either case, the Church has always understood Christ's words as requiring strict monogamy, just as Christ would never leave His Church in favor of a new bride (cf. Eph. 5:25). For those who are called to the married life (cf. Mt. 19:10-12), grace is required. Christian marriage is a *sacrament*, a sign of Christ's abiding presence and assistance. The Sacrament of Matrimony gives spouses the grace to love each other exclusively and permanently, and thereby image and manifest the love Christ has for His Church (cf. Catechism, nos. 1615, 1661).

What God Has Joined

Some of us may be wondering what Jesus really means when He says, "Whoever divorces his wife and marries another commits adultery." Adultery means a married person's having intimate relations with someone who is not his spouse. We may reason that if a marriage ends in divorce, then the slate is clean—the person is free to marry a second spouse without committing adultery.

This reasoning would be legitimate if a divorce could end a marriage, if a state or the individuals themselves—or even the Church—possess the authority to do so. But Jesus courageously proclaims that marriage is within God's sole jurisdiction: "What . . . God has joined together, let no man put asunder" (Mt. 19:6). In a valid Christian marriage, the two become one (Gen. 2:24; Mt. 9:6) in a permanent, mutual bond that exists even when the spouses and the state consent to the legal fiction of a divorce.

The Church, then, has constantly and emphatically taught that a Christian marriage cannot be dissolved.[3] In doing so, she has carefully distinguished divorces from annulments. An annulment is a finding by the Church that a genuine marriage never existed. The principal bases for annulments are *lack of form* (it was not really a Christian marriage ceremony), *incapacity* (e.g., the person is under age or already married), or a failure of *consent* (e.g., the person lacks the emotional or psychological maturity to consent to marriage). But if a real Christian marriage exists and has been consummated by the couple's engaging in the marital act, the Church teaches—in fidelity to Christ—that no one has the power to dissolve it.

Consequently, the alarming rise in annulments of consummated Christian "marriages" in recent decades is a source of scandal. Both to those who love the Church and to those who ridicule her, the routine granting of annulments on such a large scale appears to be a development that threatens the Church's pivotal teaching on the permanence ("indissolubility") of marriage. This threat is not explicit, since an annulment is not a divorce in principle. However, if the teaching—embodied by Church (or "canon") law—is easily avoided, its credibility is compromised. To our shame, a skeptic of the Church's claims regarding marriage can point to the annulment process as a convoluted system of "Catholic divorce."

Here it is necessary to set forth some preliminary observations:

(1) Some situations arise that cry out for the granting of annulments. In affirming the indissolubility of marriage, extreme care must be made to avoid a presentation that is insensitive to legitimate annulment claims, as well as the suffering of those who are caught in unhappy—but "real"—marriages.

---

[3] There was with time, nevertheless, a developed understanding that saw indissolubility not only as a moral obligation but also as an ontological reality. See Coriden, *et al.*, *Code of Canon Law: A Text and Commentary*, canon 1056 and commentary thereto (New York: Paulist Press, 1985). The Church does reserve the authority to dissolve a marriage in the unusual circumstance of a marriage in which the married couple has not engaged in sexual intercourse. See also Matthias Scheeben, *The Mysteries of Christianity*, trans. Cyril Vollert, S.J. (St. Louis: B. Herder Book Co., 1946), 596.

(2) Many divorced Catholics feel estranged or separated from the Church, and there is indeed a tremendous need for a concerted pastoral effort to bring healing and reconciliation to these people. Without in any way watering down the compassion of this outreach, it must nonetheless be taken into account that this estrangement from the Church, if actual, is not the result of the Church's imposition of "rules" that are harsh, oppressive, or out-of-date. Further, our passionate desire to reconcile fallen-away Catholics with the Church must not lead us to tolerate the popular mindset that spouses may decide—with the state's approval—to no longer be married.

(3) Marriage must be examined from the perspective of God's Word. Church law is entirely dependent upon and subservient to the Word of God when it comes to regulating marriages.[4] Put most succinctly, the marriage covenant was created by God, and should be examined accordingly.

(4) A related issue is the "ungodly" legalism and apparent gamesmanship involved in the intensive examination of marriage ceremonies, which can seemingly strip the sacraments of their mystery. To a certain extent, this is a necessary evil, since annulment cases create the unique situation of examining a marriage (usually the marital consent) many years after the fact. Further, this inquiry is not conducted at the request of concerned parishioners who want to make sure the sacrament was indeed valid. Rather, the person who is seeking an annulment is claiming that the marriage, often contracted during the course of Mass before a priest and many relatives and friends, was not really a marriage. Evaluation of such a claim requires technical analysis of something that is not merely technical but rather covenantal and holy. A healthy disgust for such an enterprise is not unwarranted, and such disgust can only be redeemed by a constant search for Christ in the midst of the legalese.

---

[4] Cf. Pope John Paul II, Apostolic Constitution *Sacrae Disciplinae Leges* (1983), as reprinted in Coriden, xxv.

(5) Contemporary American society exerts considerable influence not only on married couples but also on members of this country's marriage tribunals and the Church in general. We must take to heart the fact that secularism, the denial or rejection of God's grace and action in the world, is the most serious post-conciliar problem.[5] While accommodation in certain instances needs to be made because of peculiarities of culture, the widespread disregard of sexual morality today must not distort the Catholic response.

(6) The most important principle is what I call the "real presence" of the marriage bond. The bond is a reality that comes into being when a Christian couple gets married. Holy people through the centuries have accepted martyrdom rather than apostasize, that is, deny their baptismal faith. Priests have risked death by continuing to exercise the Sacrament of Holy Orders in prisons, concentration camps, etc. There are also accounts of those who have accepted martyrdom by literally throwing themselves on the Blessed Sacrament to prevent its desecration. An analogous defense of the marriage bond needs to be made. The ongoing presence of the bond following a valid, sacramental marriage is not dependent on the whim of the spouses, the fiat of civil government, or the mores of contemporary society. While annulments may be appropriate in certain situations, the general mindset should be that the sacred bond is presumptively present, and one is well-advised to safeguard it with his very life.

Defining Marriage

Spouses confer upon each other the Sacrament of Matrimony by expressing their consent before the Church, the household of God (cf. Catechism, no. 1621). We must understand that this mutual consent of the man and woman during the marriage ceremony is what makes a marriage. It is the doorway that leads to marriage *in facto esse*—marriage as a vocation to be lived during

---

[5] Cf. 1985 Extraordinary Synod (Boston: Daughters of St. Paul), 44, as well as Cardinal Law's introduction, 12.

the days, weeks, years, and decades to come. Once the threshold is crossed, the marriage irrevocably begins and an indissoluble marriage is formed.

To carry this analogy further, what does marriage look like from the inside? Why does this structure exist? Answering these questions requires a look at what marriage is (its *essence*) and what it is for (its *ends* or purpose).

The Catechism defines marriage as a covenant by which a man and a woman establish between themselves a partnership for life, and is by its nature ordered toward the good of the spouses and the procreation and education of offspring; this covenant between baptized persons has been raised by Christ the Lord to the dignity of a sacrament (no. 1601). This definition is taken from canon 1055 of the 1983 Code of Canon Law. It is drawn from the teaching of the Second Vatican Council (cf. GS 48), which in turn drew on the rich biblical and theological patrimony of the Church. Let's take a closer look at this definition.

Marriage as Covenant

It is no accident that the above definition of marriage uses the term "covenant" rather than the perhaps more familiar term "contract." The terms are not mutually exclusive; marriage is also in a real sense a contract. But the term "covenant" more fully captures the sacramental dimension of marriage, reflecting the totally faithful relationship of Christ and His Church that was brought into being by a new and everlasting covenant (cf. Lk. 22:20; Heb. 13:20). The Church's use of the term covenant points to the fact that husbands are to love their wives "even as Christ loved the Church" (Eph. 5:25)—to the point of laying down their lives for their beloved (cf. Jn. 15:12-13).

God made a series of covenants with His people in the Old Testament that were ultimately fulfilled in Christ. These covenants were not treated by God as something transitory or unimportant. Rather, they transformed Israel into His family (cf. Is. 61:10-62:12). Listen to what God thinks of His covenant with King David:

> I will not violate my covenant,
> or alter the word that went forth from my lips.
> Once for all I have sworn by my holiness;
> I will not lie to David.
> His line shall endure for ever,
> his throne as long as the sun before me.
> Like the moon it shall be established for ever;
> it shall stand firm while the skies endure (Ps. 89:34-37).

Of the many distinctions to be made between covenants and contracts, the most important consideration is that a covenant is an eternal pact, not subject to dissolution because of a reversal of fortune, change of heart, or the failure of a marital partner to fulfill his or her end of the covenant. Contracts, on the other hand, are "made to be broken." They are entered into precisely because breach is anticipated, and they typically set forth the respective rights of the parties in the event of such a breach. While contracts typically relate to an exchange of *goods* or *services* ("I'll give you X if you give me Y"), covenants create family bonds, and thus relate to the total, unconditional exchange of *persons* ("I am yours and you are mine").

Because of the common understanding of what a contract is, the term "covenant" should be used for reasons beyond the superior theological accuracy of the term. The more marriage is understood as a mere contract, the more people will primarily—if not exclusively—look to legal principles rather than biblical principles, and with disastrous ramifications. Already it is evident that many Christians at least implicitly believe that only the state has jurisdiction over their marriages, and they are divorcing at a rate comparable to that of society as a whole. No-fault divorce, prenuptial agreements, and non-heterosexual unions are natural progressions of an understanding of the marriage bond informed by the law of contracts, without regard to Scripture and apostolic Tradition.

We need to recognize that the term "marriage" has two distinct but intimately related meanings. It refers both to the marriage ceremony (i.e., the wedding) and to the lifelong relationship that began with the wedding. The term "contract" tends to emphasize the wedding ceremony, where there was an "exchange" of vows. The term "covenant," on the other hand, tends to emphasize the permanence of the marital relationship. Its distinctive force and beauty as applied to marriage is what it says about the lived sacrament—a "community of life and love" that images the mystery of the Family of God: "Authentic married love is caught up into divine love" (GS 48; cf. Catechism, no. 1639).

Baptism

Christian marriage presupposes that the spouses are "Christian," that they have become members of the Family of God through the waters of Baptism. Marriage should be honored by all Christians (cf. Heb. 13:4) and, for those of us who are called to marriage, it is the means by which God desires to sanctify us.

It should also be noted that, at the beginning of His public ministry, Jesus performed His first "sign"—at His mother's request—at a wedding feast in Cana (cf. Jn. 2:1-11). The Church has always seen in this passage a confirmation of the goodness of marriage and Jesus' desire to bless those entering married life (cf. Catechism, no. 1613).

And yet we recognize that not all who profess the name "Catholic" have a living faith. Some people are baptized at infancy but have long since stopped practicing their faith. They want a Church wedding but they really do not want the Church. Should they be able to present their dusty baptismal certificates to the priest, much like a teenager would present a birth certificate to obtain a driver's license? Since sacraments not only presuppose faith, but are also intended to nourish, strengthen, and express it (cf. SC 59), should not more than mere proof of Baptism be required?

All Christians should have a living faith animated by charity. When a fallen-away Catholic approaches the Church for marriage, the pastor must seize this "teachable moment" as an opportunity to rekindle the faith. No one would argue that the marriage in the Church of a person without a living faith should be accepted without question or reservation, especially when that person is already cohabitating with his or her fiancé(e), which is the grave sin of fornication (cf. Mt. 15:19-20; Catechism, no. 2353).

But on the other hand, an infant who is baptized and then left to the "dogs" of society is still marked for life as a child of God. He is a prodigal *son* (cf. Lk. 15:11-32), not a stranger or alien.

Further, sacramental grace is conferred freely by Christ and is not dependent on the merits of the minister. Hence, a sinful priest is still able to celebrate a valid Mass. Likewise, baptized Christians are able to confer on each other a valid Christian marriage. As is the case with all sacraments, the ministers need only to intend to accomplish what the Church intends. To apply a more vigorous standard would involve accepting the Donatist heresy, which dates back to the fourth century. Simply stated, Donatism involves the mistaken belief that the effectiveness of the sacraments depends on the worthiness or holiness of the ministers, rather than on the unmerited grace of Jesus Christ.

This does not mean that faithless people can fully access the grace of the Sacrament of Marriage, any more than a recipient of Holy Communion who is without faith or who knows that he is in a state of grave sin is open to receiving the life-transforming grace that is always available through the Eucharist. Unworthy reception of sacraments is not only a grace-less encounter, but a sacrilegious act, as Saint Paul describes:

> Whoever, therefore, eats the bread or drinks the cup of the Lord in an unworthy manner will be guilty of profaning the body and blood of the Lord. Let a man examine himself, and so eat of the bread and drink of the cup. For any one who eats and drinks without discerning the body eats and drinks judgment upon himself (1 Cor. 11:27-29; cf. Catechism, no. 2120).

More likely, the situation involves parties whose faith is weak rather than nonexistent. For these, the fact that the sacrament "works" through the unmerited grace of Christ does not mean that the prospective spouses should be neglected. It is crucial that the abundant grace that Christ wishes to bestow on the couple through the sacrament be maximized, because this grace is absolutely necessary for growth in holiness and fidelity to the marriage covenant.

One who does not take his or her Catholicism seriously, or who has not been catechized well, may not know what the Church teaches about marriage "in the Lord" (cf. 1 Cor. 7:39). Yet, imposing criteria beyond Baptism involves serious risks, including (1) the risk of making unfair judgments concerning who is "eligible" for a Christian marriage; (2) the risk of causing doubts about the validity of marriages already celebrated, including marriages of separated brethren; (3) the danger of further secularizing the West by closing off the Church to the ignorant and weak, thereby furthering an elitist model of the Church; and (4) the risk of distorting marriage from being a means of grace for those who need it into a "reward" for those who are already "faithful" (cf. Mk. 2:15-17).[6]

Notwithstanding these concerns, a pastor cannot admit a couple to the sacrament where they reject explicitly and formally what the Church intends to do when the marriage of baptized persons is celebrated.

What this situation calls for is a renewed commitment to proclaiming and explaining the teachings of Jesus Christ, especially at this critical moment when the couple is actually coming to the Church asking for the sacrament. It also calls for a healthy optimism that God—who made the world out of nothing—can do great things with faith the size of a mere mustard seed (cf. Mt. 13:31-32).

The Ends of Marriage

All of Christ's disciples are called to deny themselves, take up their cross, and follow Him (cf. Lk. 9:23). Many of those who are following Jesus are called to live this Christian vocation in the married state. Why? How does marriage "in the Lord" fit into God's plan to restore all things in Christ (cf. Eph. 1:10)?

---

[6] *Familiaris Consortio*, no. 68; Peter Elliott, *What God Has Joined* . . . (New York: Alba House, 1990), 198.

The Church has traditionally taught that there are three ends of marriage. These "ends" or purposes of marriage are deeply rooted in Scripture, and their identification as such dates back at least as far as Saint Isidore of Seville in the seventh century.[7]

Perhaps the most surprising—if not offensive at first blush— is *remedy for concupiscence*. This end is derived from 1 Cor. 7:9: "But if they [the unmarried and widows] cannot exercise self-control, they should marry. For it is better to marry than to be aflame with passion." Concupiscence refers to our wounded, sinful nature as a result of original sin (cf. Catechism, nos. 1264, 1426).

This does not mean that one purpose of marriage is to provide a permissible "outlet" for sexual drives. Such a view would only perpetuate the brokenness that Christ came to heal. If spouses are "outlets," then they are being treated as objects or functions, not as persons created in the image and likeness of God (cf. Gen. 1:28). Rather, Christian marriage redeems and elevates sexuality by directing the spouses away from themselves and toward each other.[8] Selfishness gives way to self-gift, which continues to point us to the great mystery, to Christ's sacrificial love for His bride, the Church (cf. Eph. 5:21-33).

The next end or purpose is closely related to the first: *mutual assistance*. This end is rooted in the second chapter of Genesis: "Then the Lord God said, 'It is not good that the man should be alone; I will make him a helper fit for him'" (Gen. 2:18). But the relationship is much stronger than a mere partnership or even friendship. Later in the chapter the sacred author writes, "Therefore a man leaves his father and his mother and cleaves to his wife, and they become one flesh" (Gen. 2:24). This latter passage is quoted four times in the New Testament: twice by Jesus to emphasize God's plan for marriage "from the beginning" (cf. Mt. 19:4-6; Mk. 10:5-9); once by Saint Paul to emphasize the sacredness of sexual intercourse (cf. 1 Cor. 6:16); and

---

[7] Most Rev. Geoffrey Robinson, "Unresolved Questions in the Theology of Marriage," as published in Doogan, ed., *Catholic Tribunals* (Newtown, Australia: E.J. Dwyer, 1991), 62.

[8] Elliott, 70-71; cf. Catechism, no. 1609.

later by Saint Paul in explaining the relationship between Christ the bridegroom and His beloved bride, the Church (cf. Eph. 5:29-32).

Christian marriage enables a man and woman, through the abiding grace of the Holy Spirit (cf. Rom. 5:5), to overcome the domination and lust that have characterized human relations since the fall (cf. Gen. 3:16), and so form a partnership of life and love that manifests to the world the faithful, self-emptying love of Christ for the Church. This partnership is so intimate that the two have become one in a permanent, exclusive, and complete union.

The third end is the *procreation and education of children*, which is traceable to God's first command to man, found in the first chapter of the first book of the Bible: "Be fruitful and multiply" (Gen. 1:22). The Church has definitively referred to this end as "primary" while the other two are "secondary."[9] For some, this end seems to reduce the institution of marriage to being a "baby factory." Others may read into this the Church's constant condemnation of acts that deliberately frustrate this purpose, such as contraception and sterilization, and either leave the Church or at least push for a change in the Church's "outdated" teaching. But the question remains: Why does the Church consider the procreation and education of children the primary end of marriage?

First, the primary end of marriage is not merely the procre-

---

[9] There is overwhelming tradition in support of this position, up to the promulgation of the decree of the Holy Office (the forerunner of the Congregation for the Doctrine of the Faith) in 1944, which unequivocally affirmed in response to a formal question (*dubium*) that the procreation and education of children is the one and only "primary end" of marriage. Vatican II, the 1983 Code of Canon Law, the Catechism, and the popes since Pius XII have refrained from using this terminology. Some argue that this silence amounts to a change of teaching, despite the fact that there is nothing in these documents that directly contradicts the traditional teaching. Vatican II probably avoided the "primary end" formulation because of the pastoral character of GS and that document's audience (all of humanity). In any event, the magisterial documents of the past fifty years do not justify the conclusion that the "procreation and education of children" is no longer the "primary end" of marriage, even if such formulation has fallen into relative disuse.

ation of children without the responsibility that accompanies such parentage. Education, as commonly understood, is not a sufficient addition to the equation. The end of marriage is to produce saints, not Harvard graduates. That is why the traditional understanding of this end has always been "the procreation and education of children *for the worship of God.*" But while this has always been what the Church assumed, it is important to clarify this vision, especially in societies where the family is assaulted and devalued.

All people share in the mission of the Church—to make disciples of "all nations" (Mt. 28:19) in every generation. The primary end of the Church, so to speak, is to evangelize the world.[10] Within this general missionary purpose, married couples are especially concerned with extending Christ through time,[11] by producing a new generation that will worship God in spirit and in truth (cf. Jn. 4:24). As will be discussed further below, married couples form the domestic Church, and thus are the first heralds of the Gospel to their children.[12] Christian families are truly the living cells (cf. 1 Cor. 12:27; Col. 2:18-19) that build up the Body of Christ.

All married couples are called to bear fruit, and this involves being open to the gift of children, who are called "the supreme gift of marriage" (GS 50). Yet without exception all married couples—from those who carry the cross of being childless to those blessed with a large family (cf. Catechism, no. 2373)—are called to be spiritually fertile. This fertility can include adoption, foster parentage, acts of hospitality, and myriad forms of active apostolate. If such fertility were not an essential purpose of marriage,

---

[10] Vatican II teaches: "The Church on earth is by her nature missionary since, according to the plan of the Father, she has as her origin the mission of the Son and the Holy Spirit" (AG 2). Pope Paul VI and Pope John Paul II have written that the Church "exists in order to evangelize." See Pope John Paul II, Encyclical Letter On the Gospel of Life *Evangelium Vitae* (1995), no. 78.

[11] Pope Pius XI, Encyclical Letter On Chaste Wedlock *Casti Connubii* (Boston: Daughters of St. Paul, 1930), 9; *Familiaris Consortio*, nos. 13, 38.

[12] LG 11, 35; GE 3; *Familiaris Consortio*, no. 39.

why would the Church, which exists to birth new members in the saving waters of Baptism (cf. Mt. 28:19), see in Christian marriage the definitive image of the fruitful union of Christ and His Church?

Christ repeatedly emphasizes that a tree is known by its fruit (e.g., Mt. 7:16-20; Lk. 13:6-9). If a marriage may be likened to a tree, Christ would not say either have a healthy tree (i.e., marriage) *or* bear good fruit. One assumes the other. As Christ says, "A sound tree cannot bear evil fruit, nor can a bad tree bear good fruit" (Mt. 7:18). The ends of marriage are thus so intimately connected that it is useless to try to separate them.

Another biblical analogy is Saint Paul's preaching. One of his ends was to save himself—preaching was his vocation in life, so that not preaching would be a denial of God's will for him. He writes, "Woe to me if I do not proclaim the Gospel!" (1 Cor. 9:16). Stated positively, he preaches so that he may share in the Gospel's blessings (cf. 1 Cor. 9:23). Yet, by living out his specific Christian vocation, he can also say that he was not just seeking his own advantage, but the advantage of many, "that they may be saved" (1 Cor. 10:33). Saint Paul saved his soul by saving others. Similarly, when laying down their lives for each other in imitation of Christ, spouses will save themselves *and* bear much fruit for the Church (cf. Jn. 12:24-25).

Another way of understanding the primary and secondary ends of marriage is to see that each end relates to a person or class of persons who will benefit from the marriage: the spouse (remedy for concupiscence), the spouse's partner (mutual assistance), and the couple's children (procreation and education). Following the lead of Jesus, who emptied Himself for us (cf. Phil. 2:5-11), we need to exist for others. The grace we receive is not meant for us to hoard, but to give freely to others (cf. Mt. 10:8). Baptism and each of the successive sacraments necessarily involve mission.

Mutual assistance is a more sublime end than remedy for concupiscence, because by its nature it is other-directed. However, the two have become one, so even in mutual assistance there is at least in principle a possibility of self-enclosure. When this "two-become-one" unselfishly begins to go out of itself in worship and ministry, the couple strives toward its perfection in its "two-ness" (i.e., sanctity of individuals) and its "one-ness" (i.e., sanctity of family) and this love between them is so palpably real that it brings forth new life.

The Moment of Truth

As noted, the Church teaches that the exchange of consent between the spouses is what makes the man and woman "one flesh" (Catechism, no. 1626; cf. Gen. 2:24). This consent involves a total gift of self—"I take you to be my wife"—"I take you to be my husband" (Catechism, no. 1627). The Code of Canon Law uses the following definition: "Matrimonial consent is an act of the will by which a man and a woman, through an irrevocable covenant, mutually give and accept each other in order to establish marriage."[13] What are some characteristics of this "irrevocable covenant"?

As discussed above, consent in covenantal terms does not, properly understood, blur the distinction between the wedding ceremony and married life. Some difficulty does arise from misconstruing "covenant" as merely expressive of married life, so that the object of consent is improperly confused with future (i.e., post-consent) expectations that cannot possibly be met in their entirety. The exchange of vows makes each of them the other's spouse, irrespective of whether they ever have the "perfect" house, the "perfect" job, and the "perfect" number of "perfect" children.

At the wedding ceremony, by means of a public, liturgical act (cf. Catechism, no. 1631), the spouses-to-be are forever changed. Such a lifelong, life-changing commitment requires a truly human "I do," free from any coercion or fear (cf. Lk. 1:68-75). To survive, the marriage covenant must be built on a firm foundation— Jesus Christ (cf. Mt. 7:24-27; Eph. 2:19-22). This points to the vital role that the Church—especially the Christian formation of the spouses—plays in preparing a couple for marriage.

---

[13] Canon 1057 (2).

The marriage ceremony produces the marriage covenant that in turn is the seed of married life. Consent, then, belongs to the realm of the marriage ceremony, with the immediate effect of producing a marriage, the happiness and fruitfulness of which is left to God's goodness and human cooperation.

The object of marital consent is much simpler than what most people realize. A couple need not be particularly holy people or even theologians to effect a sacramental marriage! What *is* required is that the couple intend to do what the Church intends by the sacrament. This fact is presumed by the saying of the words of consent provided in the marriage vows, and doubts are resolved in favor of the sacrament. Mistaken notions of marriage do not prevent Christians from becoming the ministers of this sacrament to one another as they make their consent, provided they are free and have a general intention to marry as Christians. That being said, the simple consent does envision a big act of faith and abandonment to divine providence. It is only with grace that couples can live the sacrament, especially at those times when they might be tempted to stray. God asks couples to say "yes" before they literally know what they have gotten themselves into. But if the "yes" at the altar rail becomes a "no" ten years later, one must recognize that the subsequent refusal does not change the effect of the original "yes," as though subsequent events (i.e., the marriage as experienced) can have any bearing on the absolute, binding nature of marital consent.

It should be evident by now that covenants are not to be entered into lightly. The account of the covenant between the Gibeonites and the Israelites in Josh. 9 provides several insights. In that episode, the Gibeonites deceive the Israelites into entering a covenant, so that the Gibeonites will not be destroyed by the more powerful Israelite forces. In Josh. 9:14, the sacred author notes that the Israelites "did not ask direction from the LORD" in making the covenant. The clear implication is that, had they sought the Lord's will and blessing, they might have avoided entering an unfavorable covenant. This is in stark contrast to Tobias and Sarah, who prayed for—and received—the Lord's mercy and blessing before coming together as husband and wife (cf. Tob. 8:4-9).

Josh. 9 also teaches that covenants must be honored. Upon learning of the Gibeonites' dishonesty, the Israelite leaders advised the people that they could not make void the covenant and destroy the Gibeonites:

> But all the leaders said to all the congregation, "We have sworn to them by the LORD, the God of Israel, and now we may not touch them. This we will do to them, and let them live, lest wrath be upon us, because of the oath which we swore to them" (Josh. 9:19-20).

Later, King Saul incurs bloodguilt for putting the Gibeonites to death, in violation of the covenant (cf. 2 Sam. 21:1-4). This incident demonstrates that God holds us accountable to our covenantal promises.

It is useful to compare marital consent to taking an oath in court. A person cannot avoid conviction for perjury by saying that he internally did not mean to publicly take an oath. Similarly, the public language of matrimonial consent is decisive in creating the marriage. Assuming capacity to consent and freedom from coercion, a party should not be able to say after the fact that he or she "didn't mean it." Such a case is an instance of a person ministering a sacrament unworthily, but ministering it just the same.[14]

Conversely, if a person really does mean what he or she says in taking an oath, is not a subsequent repudiation a lie?

Creation of the Marriage Bond

The immediate effect of marriage is the matrimonial bond. Canon 1134 expresses the Church's teaching that the natural matrimonial bond is by its nature *perpetual* and *exclusive*, while also recognizing that Christian marriage is a special sacrament in

---

[14] While "internal consent" is presumed to be in agreement with the words used in the marriage ceremony, it is still possible under canon law to show that consent was lacking: "But if either or both parties through a positive act of the will should exclude marriage itself, some essential element or an essential property of marriage, it is invalidly contracted" (Canon 1101(2)).

which the parties are "consecrated":

> Thus *the marriage bond* has been established by God himself in such a way that a marriage concluded and consummated between baptized persons can never be dissolved. This bond, which results from the free human act of the spouses and their consummation of the marriage, is a reality, henceforth irrevocable, and gives rise to a covenant guaranteed by God's fidelity. The Church does not have the power to contravene this disposition of divine wisdom (Catechism, no. 1640, original emphasis).

What is this bond? To answer this question requires some understanding of what sacraments are.

Most people accept that in nature some things are signs or symbols of other things. For example, water may symbolize cleansing, bread may symbolize nourishment, and a hug may symbolize warmth, friendship, love, etc. In addition, those with some religious sensibility are willing to grant that God can act in human lives, that people can be touched through prayer, grace, etc., and indeed "be saved." The problem is accepting that the earthly and the heavenly, the physical sign and the spiritual reality, can actually converge. This problem is traceable to the sublime mystery of the Incarnation, and is also analogous to the "human yet divine" nature of Scripture and even the Church herself. To understand the marriage bond, it is necessary to understand that it shares in this "human yet divine" mystery, by which God transforms the family of man into the Family of God.

Just as those who are baptized really become God's children (cf. 1 Jn. 3:1; Rom. 8:14-17), those who enter Christian marriage are united in a real bond that is neither fictitious nor simply external. They are "two consecrated members of Christ's body" who are entering into a "union for the purpose of dedicating themselves to the extension of this body."[15] This union, or bond, images the bond between Christ and His Church, which is so real that Christ would ask Saint Paul—who was persecuting

---

[15] Scheeben, 599.

Christians, not the glorified Christ—"Why do you persecute *me?*" (Acts 9:4; cf. Eph. 5:28-32).

The marriage bond sets the couple apart for each other and for God. This special consecration includes the vocation to worship and to acts of service[16] as a domestic Church, and is preeminently manifested in the act of sexual intercourse. Why? Because sexual intercourse, which at least implicitly renews the marital covenant, is a quasi-liturgical act, in that it recalls, celebrates, and anticipates not only the union produced by the mutual self-gift of the spouses, but also the fruitfulness of this union. In turn, this act gives us a penetrating glimpse of the self-emptying, fruitful love of the Trinity.

Vatican II beautifully describes marital intercourse:

> [T]he acts in marriage by which the intimate and chaste union of the spouses takes place are noble and honorable; the truly human performance of these acts fosters the self-giving they signify and enriches the spouses in joy and gratitude (GS 49).

To be sure, sexual intercourse in itself, even between married people, does not confer grace automatically. However, it rightly occurs as a sacred act within the grace-filled context of married life. In fact, the union formed by the consent of the spouses is sealed upon its consummation, when the spouses give themselves to each other in the sacred, symbolically rich act of sexual intercourse. Subsequent acts of sexual intercourse renew the marriage covenant in a manner perhaps even more profound than the renewal of vows that spouses sometimes make on their anniversary or other special occasions. The marital act says, "I am forever totally yours." This understanding should prevent us from having

---

[16] One way of looking at the marriage bond is as a quasi-character, analogous to the permanent "character" of Baptism, Confirmation, and Orders (cf. Elliott, 144). Among other features of the sacramental character is the setting apart for "divine worship" and "service of the Church" (Catechism, no. 1121). In other words, the sacramental character refers to our participation in Christ's sonship, which enables us to be faithful "to the deepest vocation of the Church": loving one another (service) and praising the Most Holy Trinity (worship) (LG 51).

a distorted view of sex as being dirty or sinful on the one hand, or casual or recreational on the other.

Again, the marital act is ordered to the "procreation and education of offspring for the worship of God"—in other words, the formation of saints.[17] All children are conceived and born with original sin, but Catholic parents do not have the mere generation of offspring as the goal, and indeed it is the faith of the parents that brings the child to Baptism and creates the "domestic Church" for the faith to grow.[18] An analogy may be made to a great missionary like Saint Francis Xavier. Not a single person was saved by his preaching apart from reception of Baptism. Yet, the fact that Baptism was still required after his preaching does not mean that the preaching was morally neutral or otherwise not ordered to the formation of saints. The marriage bond sets the couple apart for quasi-liturgical acts that are fruitful naturally and, properly understood, supernaturally, inasmuch as the spouses are instrumental causes of the children's regeneration in Christ. Through this process, the spouses form not only a natural family, but a supernatural family—a domestic Church, the Family of God in miniature.

Real Presence

John Kippley aptly describes the connection between the Eucharist and the marital act, which further suggests its quasi-liturgical function.[19] Without repeating the points made therein, there are also analogies to be drawn between the abiding reality of the two sacraments, the marriage bond and the Blessed Sacrament:

---

[17] *Familiaris Consortio*, no. 38; Saint Thomas Aquinas, *Summa Contra Gentiles*, IV, 58; see also 1 Tim. 2:15—this process is also the means of salvation for the mother.

[18] See note 12, *supra*.

[19] John F. Kippley, *Sex and the Marriage Covenant* (Cincinnati: Couple to Couple League, 1991), 76-86.

(1) Both realities involve an objective presence that is rejected by those who understand the "real presence" subjectively. In marriage, such people would say that the bond lasts so long as they both shall "love," rather than "live." The corresponding Eucharistic heresy is transignification and its relatives, which make Christ's presence dependent on our own subjective awareness of Him. This error attempts to go from the natural symbol to the divine action without the critical mystery of faith, the Real Presence of Christ in the Eucharist.

(2) The "real presences" are ordered to communion but not dependent on it. A marriage that is not yet consummated already has a sacramental bond. Similarly, when the consecration at Mass is completed, the sacrifice is effected and the Real Presence is there, irrespective of whether the Eucharist is consumed.

(3) Conversely, there is a sense of potency in both sacraments ordered toward consummation. A marriage does not become extrinsically indissoluble until consummation (cf. Catechism, no. 1640). Likewise, the Blessed Sacrament is a source of grace and devotion outside of Mass, but is nonetheless ordered toward Holy Communion, at which time the communicant receives the sacramental grace.

(4) Unworthy reception, like unworthy ministers, detracts only from the grace that is received and does not by that fact interfere with the reality of the sacramental presence, which comes into being through the action of Christ.

In addition to these points, it is also interesting to note that although a person can receive the Eucharist many times but is only married (to a particular spouse) once, there is yet a further connection between first Holy Communion and the consummation of marriage. The former is a sacrament of initiation, while the latter has a singular effect on the nature of the bond. In both instances there is a sense of transition, a sense in which the neophyte has become a communicant. It is like a sacramental loss of virginity that cannot be repeated or undone, but certainly renewed.

Necessary Ingredients

Back in the fifth century, Saint Augustine identified three "goods" of marriage, namely *proles* (offspring), *fides* (faith), and *sacramentum* (sacrament). Unfortunately, the goods of marriage are often confused with the ends of marriage.[20] The goods, rather, are the characteristics of marriage as redeemed and elevated by Christ (cf. Catechism, no. 1643). Since they are essential aspects of marital love, spouses must consent to these "goods" in order to effect a Christian marriage.

Fides refers not to the theological virtue, but to that aspect of justice whereby a spouse remains faithful to the other in a monogamous covenant. *Sacramentum* has special reference to indissolubility, but also refers to all those things that result from marriage's being a sign of Christ's union with the Church. These two goods are duly recognized as "properties" of marriage in canon 1056 of the Code of Canon Law.

Indissolubility means that the two become one for the entirety of their lives. There is nothing that can separate what God has joined (cf. Mt. 19:6). The perpetual love of the spouses images God's perpetual presence with His chosen—or espoused—people (cf. Is. 54:5-8; Ps. 89:3-4), as well as Christ's marriage to His Church, with whom He will always be (cf. Mt. 28:20; Rom. 8:35-39).

Fidelity means that the marriage bond is not only perpetual, but exclusive. If I have made a total gift of myself to my wife, how can I then give myself to someone else? Marital infidelity—adultery—is a grave injustice against one's spouse and family. To leave one's spouse for an adulterous relationship is a counter-witness to the faithful love of Christ and His Church. It reflects the lingering effects of sin, not unlike the notorious infidelities of Israel to their God (cf. Ex. 32:1-8; Jer. 5:7; Catechism, no. 2381).

---

[20] See e.g., Janet E. Smith, *Humanae Vitae: A Generation Later* (Washington: Catholic University Press, 1991), 47-54; Kevin Matthew, "Essential Elements and Essential Properties of Marriage," as published in Doogan, *supra*, 115-18.

Here we must emphasize the grace of Christ that is given to spouses who unite in a lifelong commitment, and the mercy and reconciliation that is available to those who call upon the Lord. And it is sometimes necessary for spouses to separate. Yet, even if they are no longer living together, they are still husband and wife and are called to live in fidelity to their indissoluble marriage bond (cf. Catechism, no. 1649).

The third ingredient is "openness to fertility" (Catechism, no. 1643). Since children (*proles*) are the "supreme gift" (or "good") and "crowning glory" of marriage (GS 48, 50), spouses must not despise their fertility. Scripture clearly provides that every child is a gift of God, a "good" of marriage (cf. Ps. 127:3-5; 128:3-4). The same God who "hates divorce" desires "godly offspring" (cf. Mal. 2:13-16). Those couples who carry the heavy cross of sterility are still called to manifest generosity and openness to life through prayer and acts of Christian charity, including the possibility of adoption (cf. Catechism, nos. 1654, 2379).

In examining the "ingredients" of a marriage, we must remember that marriage is a mystery (Gk. *mysterion*). In fact, it is a mystery caught up in the even greater mystery Saint Paul describes in Eph. 5:32. The ancient maxim "faith seeking understanding" implies a faith that acknowledges the limitation—as well as the potential—of deepening our understanding of marriage. Having given our lives to Christ and in a secondary sense to our spouses, the lives we live are not our own (cf. Gal. 2:20), but subject to God's loving providence. Spouses, like all Christians, are pilgrims who will not be "home" in the truest sense until we take our places at the marriage supper of the Lamb, in heaven (Rev. 19:9; cf. Rom. 8:18; Phil. 3:13-14).

Marriage as Mission

Patterned after the marvelous example of Joseph and Mary, every married couple is called to create a "holy family" with Jesus as its center. In calling the family the domestic Church, the Church recognizes the fact that every married couple has a significant role to play in the Church. Their "partnership of life and love" forms a microcosm of the Church and bears much-needed witness to a society hungering for Good News.

Part of the mission of the domestic Church is to raise godly children (cf. Prov. 22:6; Mal. 2:15) through prayer, word, and example. In the Book of Acts, we frequently read that when someone converted to Christ, the whole household became believers (cf. Acts 11:14; 16:31; 18:8). But the mission of the domestic Church does not end with baptizing the children. Rather, that is where in a real sense it begins! The family is a spiritual incubator, preparing children to accept generously their vocation in life, to follow Christ where He leads.

The domestic Church shares in the mandate to evangelize, to make disciples of all nations (cf. Mt. 28:19-20; Mk. 16:15), urged on by the love of Christ (2 Cor. 5:14). The spiritual incubator must not become a spiritual bomb shelter, unwilling to share the gift of faith freely with others in their neighborhood, parish, or extended family. The light must shine not only to "all in the house" (Mt. 5:15), but before all, so that they may give glory to Our Heavenly Father (cf. Mt. 5:16).

The Catechism (no. 1655) teaches that "[t]he Church is nothing other than the family of God." Where our family is, there is home. The charity and hospitality of families enable the Church to reach the poor and those without families, helping them to find the wonderful home that the Father has prepared for them (cf. Jn. 14:2-3; Ps. 84: 1, 10).

And so Christian families as domestic Churches are vital to the missionary dynamism of the Church. Every Christian family is founded on a Christian marriage. And every Christian marriage hinges on the marriage bond—the abiding love of the Holy Spirit that enables the two to become one. This is truly a teaching that hits home.

Leon J. Suprenant, Jr. is the vice president of Catholics United for the Faith and the editor of Lay Witness, *a monthly magazine for lay Catholics. He received his law degree from the University of Missouri-Kansas City School of Law and his master's degree in theology from Franciscan University of Steubenville. He resides in Steubenville, Ohio, with his wife Maureen and their four daughters.*

CHAPTER XII

Sacraments of Healing
A Return from Exile and a Healing of Heart

KRIS GRAY

Nothing can describe the priceless gift we receive in Baptism, when the Most Holy Trinity comes and dwells in our souls. This new life in Christ, however, does not abolish the frailty and weakness of our human nature. As a result, we may harden our hearts, turn away from God, and sin. Sin is like a cancer that eats at our souls and, if left unchecked, can extinguish the life given us in Baptism. The only sure remedy for the disease of sin is offered to us by the divine physician, Jesus Christ, through the sacraments of healing.

During His ministry in Galilee, Jesus was known not so much for who He was or what He said, but for the healings He performed. Saint John tells us that the "multitude followed him, because they saw the signs which he did on those who were diseased" (Jn. 6:2). According to the Gospels, Jesus spent much of His time giving sight to the blind, hearing to the deaf, mobility to the lame, life to the leprous, and even resurrection to the dead. Given the spiritual aim of His mission, why did Jesus make the healing of physical illness a major focus of His ministry? The answer, in short, is that in Scripture sickness signifies the crippling effects of sin and, at the heart of Jesus' mission, is the objective of forgiveness of sin and the healing of its wounds. Jesus' power and desire to heal sickness are signs of His power and even greater desire to forgive sin. For this reason, Saint John describes Jesus' healings as "signs" and not "miracles" in order to point to the deeper significance of Jesus' deeds. Jesus, the divine physician, wants to perform open heart surgery on us, so that our hearts, hardened by sin, may be open to His grace and love.

We shall examine God's plan for healing sin in three stages: first, sin and its effects on Israel in the Old Testament; second, the release and healing brought by Jesus in His messianic mission; and finally, how the mission and power of Christ to heal is continued in His Body, the Church. The sacred Scriptures provide us a poignant illustration of the disastrous consequences of sin through the life of Israel. Israel finds herself exiled as a result of her sin and her breaking of the Old Covenant. Into this disastrous situation, Jesus brings release and freedom from sin in the form of a new jubilee. This release is not only for the Jews, but for all mankind. Release from sin, restoration of our communion with God, and healing were at the heart of Jesus' mission while He was here on earth, and they continue to be at the heart of the Church's mission today. This new jubilee inaugurated by Christ is eternally celebrated in His heavenly kingdom, and lived out in a special way here on earth through the Church's sacraments of healing.

Sin and Its Devastating Consequences

God desires that we share in the communion of love that exists in the Holy Trinity. When we sin, we turn away from this communion and experience the "3-D" effects of sin: a widening *distance* between us and God, a growing enslavement to sin's *dominion*, and ultimately *death*. The truth that these are consequences of sin is evident not only in our own experience, but is also clearly taught in the New Testament writings.

Saint Paul speaks of the *distance* or separation between us and Christ as a result of our sin:

> [R]emember that you were at that time separated from Christ, alienated from the commonwealth of Israel, and strangers to the covenants of promise, having no hope and without God in the world (Eph. 2:12).

This idea of distance between men and God as a result of sin is graphically portrayed in the Gospel parable where a chasm separates the rich man from Lazarus, who rests in Abraham's bosom (cf. Lk. 16:19-31).

Saint Paul also speaks of our enslavement to sin and the *dominion* it has over us prior to the grace of Christ: "For sin will have no dominion over you, since you are not under law but under grace" (Rom. 6:14). He says that when we yield ourselves to sin we become its slaves (cf. Rom. 6:16).

Finally, Saint Paul is clear that the ultimate fruit of sin is *death* when he says that "the wages of sin is death" (Rom. 6:23). Thus the powerful lens of Scripture gives us a focused picture of sin's consequences in 3-D: Distance, Dominion, and Death.

That sin leads to distance, dominion, and death is already alluded to in the opening chapters of Genesis, where the first sin results in expulsion from the garden of Eden and the curse of mortality (Gen. 3), where Cain's sin results in ostracism and exile to the land of Nod away from the presence of the Lord (Gen. 4:8-16), where Ham's crime leads to the enslavement of one nation to another (Gen. 9:20-27), and where the building of the tower of Babel results in the dispersion of the peoples through the confusion of tongues (Gen. 11). These opening examples set the tone and expectation for the consequences of sin in the life of Israel and in the lives of all men.

Israel's Covenantal Communion with God

The Old Testament recounts how God, after having freed the Israelites from their enslavement in Egypt and having "baptized" them in the waters of the Red Sea (cf. 1 Cor. 10:2), then entered into a covenant with His people. This covenantal relationship was much more than a simple contract where one exchanges services for goods or wages. Rather, Israel and God swore an oath—

giving their word and their very selves to each other. In effect, they became "family."

God entered into a covenant with Israel because His desire was for intimate communion with His people. In the marriage covenant, recall that the husband and wife give themselves to one another and the two become one, creating a new family. The two are so completely joined that only death itself can break the covenantal bond between them. Just as the marital covenant takes two individuals and joins them so as to become one flesh, so too God desired that Israel would be one with Yahweh.

To this end, God dwelt in the midst of His people, first in what was known as the tent of meeting, and later in the Temple in Jerusalem. The Book of Exodus tells of Moses' going into the tent of meeting and speaking with Yahweh as one speaks to a friend. When Moses would leave the tent of meeting, he would have to wear a veil over his face because it shone so brightly with the radiance of God. It was this intimate relationship that God desired not only with Moses, but with all His people.

The relationship, which in the beginning stages of the covenant was described as that between a father and a son, was to grow and deepen so as to become the communion signified between spouses in marriage. God's desire was to take Israel as His bride, and to share with this bride the very radiance of His own life and blessedness.

Israel's Sin and the Need for Forgiveness

Israel, however, would not remain so faithful to her covenantal oath. During the course of the Old Covenant, God blessed Israel with great fruitfulness and many riches. Over time, however, Israel became prideful and foolishly saw her richness as her own doing, not as a gift from God and the result of His presence among them. In her pride, Israel turned away from the intimate covenantal relationship she shared with Yahweh and turned to other gods. The Lord speaks of Israel:

And she did not know that is was I who gave her the grain, the wine, and the oil, and who lavished upon her silver and gold which they used for Ba'al (Hos. 2:8).

Israel took God's gifts with which He had blessed her and used them not for God's glory, but for her own sinful purposes. Rather than turning to God with thankfulness and deepening her love for Yahweh, Israel turned away from God and sought communion with pagan nations and their false gods. Much to God's sadness, Israel chose to live as an unfaithful spouse: "[A]s a faithless wife leaves her husband, so have you been faithless to me, O house of Israel" (Jer. 3:20). The more Israel sinned, the greater the distance she put between herself and God, breaking the covenantal communion she had enjoyed and to which she had sworn to be faithful.

Yahweh continued to call after Israel through the prophets, desiring her to turn back to Him and repent from her sinful harlotry, so that the communion she shared with Him might be restored. God even used the prophet Hosea as a visual sign of Israel's waywardness. The Lord spoke to Hosea saying, "Go, take to yourself a wife of harlotry and have children of harlotry, for the land commits great harlotry by forsaking the LORD" (Hos. 1:2). So Hosea took Gomer as his wife. In her unfaithfulness to Hosea, Gomer showed Israel how Israel herself had turned from God and been unfaithful to Him and the covenant. At the same time, Hosea bore witness to God's steadfast love for Israel and His desire for reunion. But, rather than responding to Yahweh's calls for her return, Israel continued down a path that only widened the distance between herself and God, and only increased sin's dominion over her.

Because of her infidelity to the covenantal relationship and her unwillingness to repent and turn back to God, Israel brought upon herself the curses of her covenantal unfaithfulness. Ironically enough, Israel was given what she desired. She went after the gods of the other nations, and so God allowed her to go to them, but not as she expected. God allowed the Babylonians to conquer Jerusalem and destroy the Temple. Israel was taken into captivity and bondage in Babylon and exiled outside the Promised Land. Babylon's dominion over Israel, and Israel's distant exile from the Promised Land, Jerusalem, and especially the Temple where Yahweh's presence dwelt, were signs of her enslavement to sin and the spiritual distance that Israel had created between herself and God. God allowed the Israelites to suffer physically what they were already suffering spiritually, not because He wanted Israel to suffer, but because He wanted His people to see in their physical suffering the spiritual suffering that their sin had caused and to which they had grown blind. God did not desire Israel's physical suffering, but rather her spiritual healing. He longed for Israel to repent and return to Him so that He could heal her:

> I, even I, will rend and go away, I will carry off, and none shall rescue. I will return again to my place, until they acknowledge their guilt and seek my face, and in their distress they seek me, saying, "Come, let us return to the LORD; for he has torn, that he may heal us; he has stricken, and he will bind us up" (Hos. 5:14-6:1).

One thing stood in the way of this healing and return: Israel's sin. Years later, even though many would be allowed to return from Babylon to the Promised Land, the captivity and exile did not fully end. After the Babylonians, the Jews were still under the rule of other nations: first the Medo-Persians, then the Greeks and, in the time of Christ, the Romans. Israel had come back to the Promised Land and had rebuilt the Temple in Jerusalem, but the Shekinah, the glory cloud that dwelt in the Temple's inner sanctuary and witnessed to the very presence of Yahweh dwelling in Israel, had not returned. In addition, the ultimate curse of their covenantal unfaithfulness, that of death, still loomed over the people of Israel. The exiles were home, but the exile had not yet ended (cf. Neh. 9:36). The prophets had made it clear that Israel's exile was caused by her sins, and that return from exile could only come with forgiveness of sins (cf. Jer. 33; Ezek. 36; Is.

40). It was sin that had caused Israel's disastrous situation; only repentance and the forgiveness of sin would set her free. There was only one way out for Israel, and that was the hope of the promised messiah.

At this point, it should strike us that Israel's predicament is analogous to our own situation when we sin. Israel entered into the Old Covenant after passing through the waters of the Red Sea. Through the waters of Baptism, we enter the New Covenant Family of God. The Holy Spirit comes to dwell within each of us, incorporating us into the very Body of Christ so that we become true sons and daughters of the Father. This is so true that Saint Paul says, "God has sent the Spirit of his Son into our hearts, crying, 'Abba! Father!'" (Gal. 4:6). Our relationship with the Holy Trinity is so intimate that we each become as the bride of Christ, clothed in the pure, fine linen that is our righteous deeds (cf. Rev. 19:7-8).

When we sin, rather than living as faithful brides of Christ, we become prodigal sons and unfaithful spouses. We intentionally turn and walk away from our loving heavenly Father and Bridegroom, distancing ourselves from the Family of God into which we had been incorporated. We exchange the riches of our family inheritance for our own sinful desires. If we do not repent, we eventually find ourselves captive under sin's dominion. Like Israel, who in Babylon found herself enslaved due to her sins, we find ourselves once again enslaved to our sins just as we were before our entry into the Family of God through Baptism. It is at this point that we experience the disastrous situation that sin causes, and realize the incredible gift God has given us in the sacraments of healing. Through these sacraments, we experience the mercy of God given through Jesus Christ, the Messiah. Until Christ's coming, Israel, however, waited and hoped for the messiah who would come bringing forgiveness of sin and release from its consequences.

The Good News of Jesus' Mission to Forgive Sins

At this point in Israel's history, the opening chapters of the Gospels begin. The messiah was the one who would lead Israel out of exile and restore her relationship with God. But restoration and the end of exile could not occur without putting an end to sin. Thus Jesus, as the long-awaited Messiah, is revealed in the Gospels as the one who takes away sin. From the outset, the Gospels tell us that Jesus' very name is given because "he will save his people from their sins" (Mt. 1:21). Further, Zechariah prophesied that his son, John the Baptist, would herald Christ's coming, so as to "give knowledge of salvation to his people in the forgiveness of their sins" (Lk. 1:77). John the Baptist is described as "preaching a baptism of repentance for the forgiveness of sins" (Mk. 1:4) and, upon baptizing Christ, John declares, "Behold, the lamb of God, who takes away the sin of the world" (Jn. 1:29). The one who would save Israel from her sins, as the prophets had promised, had now arrived.

According to Saint Luke, Jesus begins His ministry from His hometown of Nazareth. On the sabbath, in the synagogue where He learned the Torah, Jesus stands up and reads this passage from Isaiah:

> The Spirit of the Lord is upon me, because he has anointed me to preach good news to the poor. He has sent me to proclaim release to the captives and recovering of sight to the blind, to set at liberty those who are oppressed, to proclaim the acceptable year of the Lord (Lk. 4:16-19; cf. Is. 61:1-2).[1]

After reading this passage, Jesus stuns those in attendance by making these prophetic words His own: "Today this scripture has been fulfilled in your hearing" (Lk. 4:21).

---

[1] These next few paragraphs draw heavily on the article written by my husband, Timothy Gray, "A New Lease on Life: Saint Luke's Vision of Jesus' Jubilee Year," *Lay Witness* (December 1997), 10-12.

Isaiah wrote this passage as he envisioned the day of "release" from Babylonian captivity for Israel. Anticipating this coming redemption, he used the term "release" to describe Israel's return from captivity in Babylon in terms of the Old Testament year of jubilee (cf. Lev. 25; Deut. 15). During the year of jubilee, slaves were freed, all debts were canceled, the land was fallowed, and forfeited land was returned, according to the Mosaic distribution. Throughout the Old Testament's recording of the jubilee legislation, there is one word that is continually repeated: *release* (in Heb. *deror* and in Gk. *aphesis*). The slaves were "released," the debts were "released," and the land was "released." Quite simply, the jubilee was the year of "release."

In His reading from Isaiah, Jesus omits the phrase, "the day of vengeance of our God" (Is. 61:2b), and replaces it with "to set at liberty those who are oppressed" (Lk. 4:18; cf. Is. 58:6), thus accentuating the theme of release. In addition, after reading the prophetic passage of Isaiah and declaring its fulfillment, Jesus suggests that the poor who are to be liberated will be like the widow and leper of Elijah's day (cf. Lk. 4:23-27). This declaration scandalizes the Jews in Jesus' audience (cf. Lk. 4:28-29). The scandal is not that the jubilee liberation would benefit widows and lepers, but rather that Jesus is making the radical claim that among the widows and lepers experiencing the jubilee would be *Gentiles*. According to first-century Jewish thinking, the long-awaited jubilee would bring about the vindication of Israel, which would certainly include God's avenging judgment upon Israel's enemies—in particular the Roman rulers. Jesus' extension of release to Gentiles, along with His passing over of divine retribution, flies in the face of Jewish expectation, which longed for vengeance as much as restoration.

Why does Jesus make the claim that the Gentiles are not the enemy, but rather fellow recipients with the Jews of the jubilee liberation? Is Jesus overlooking the problem of Roman injustice and domination of Israel? No. Jesus' point to His listeners is not that things are not as bad as they think, but rather that they are much worse. The Jews have not seen the depth of their plight.

Israel's bondage is far stronger than iron chains or Roman soldiers; it consists of a much stronger slavery to sin. Their captivity is not simply a captivity which keeps them from possession of their homeland, but a captivity of the heart which keeps them from possessing Yahweh Himself. They are not as much under the rule of the Romans as they are under the dominion of the devil. Jesus' declaration of a new jubilee year is ultimately not to proclaim an end to Roman Gentile rule over Israel, but rather to proclaim an end to Satan's rule and sin's dominion over Israel's heart. Roman rule, just like Babylonian rule, was simply a sign pointing to the far more serious enslavement to sin.

Thus, the Gentiles and the Jews share a common enemy, and both will need the liberation and redemption that Jesus offers. The jubilee program of release that Jesus will carry out needs to be seen in a new light. The slaves to be freed are those enslaved to sin. The debts to be canceled are the sins of both Jews and Gentiles. The familial land to be restored is not Palestine, but the original patrimony of Adam and his children, the garden of paradise.[2] The land to which Jesus will lead His people is the Promised Land of heaven. This release from sin is at the heart of Jesus' messianic mission and, for this reason, Jesus begins His mission by proclaiming release, healing, and liberty not from Rome, but rather from sin.

Jesus reveals His mission of releasing the people from their sins through His words and His deeds. Saint Luke's Gospel records Jesus as using *aphesis* not only in the above quotation from Isaiah, but also in His teaching of the Our Father (Lk. 11:4) and His description of the woman who, having been forgiven much, also loved much (Lk. 7:47). By using "release" (*aphesis*) to describe forgiveness, Jesus takes the jubilee image of release from debt and slavery, and the return of the family inheritance of land, and uses it as a metaphor for the release from the debt and bondage of sin, and the return of our heavenly inheritance which is lost through sin.

---

[2] In Is. 58:10-12, God promises that, if the jubilee is truly practiced and the poor are taken care of, then the Lord will bless the land such that it will be like a new Eden.

In addition to His words, Jesus' actions also speak of the release from sins that Jesus is proclaiming in His ministry. Three examples from Saint Luke's Gospel will illustrate the "release" that Jesus brings.

Forgive Us Our Debts

While Jesus is sitting at table with Simon the Pharisee, a "woman of the city, who had been a sinner" comes to Him and begins to weep at His feet. She washes His feet with her tears, wipes them with her hair, kisses and anoints them with oil. When the Pharisee sees Jesus' approval of her actions, he doubts that He is an authentic prophet, for a real prophet would have known "what kind of woman this was." Jesus responds by telling a parable:

> A certain creditor had two debtors; one owed five hundred denarii, and the other fifty. When they could not pay, he forgave them both. Now which of them will love him more? (Lk. 7:41-42).

Simon rightly responds that the one forgiven more loves more (cf. Lk. 7:43). Jesus then explains that the woman's welcome of Him was far greater than Simon's. He concludes by saying, "Therefore I tell you, her sins, which are many, are forgiven, for she loved much; . . . And he said to her, 'Your sins are forgiven'" (Lk. 7:47-48).

By choosing to tell the story of the two debtors, Jesus shows that the sinful state of the woman is analogous to being in debt. The debt owed, however, is more serious than money owed to a creditor. Rather, it is the debt owed to a holy and righteous God because of our sin. Isaiah, finding himself before the throne of God, realizes the weight of such sin and cries out,

> Woe is me! For I am lost; for I am a man of unclean lips, and I dwell in the midst of a people of unclean lips; for my eyes have seen the King, the LORD of hosts! (Is. 6:5).

In ancient societies, when one found himself unable to pay his debts, he was often thrown into debtor's prison and/or sold into slavery until the debt was paid. The only way out was payment of the debt.

In a similar way, we find ourselves indebted as a result of our sin. Through the forgiveness of sins that Jesus brings, we are released from our sin, our debt is canceled, and we can share in the new jubilee that Christ has inaugurated. Thus, we continually cry out as Jesus has taught us in the Our Father, "And forgive us our debts, As we also have forgiven our debtors" (Mt. 6:12).

Release and Freedom from Slavery

A few chapters later, Saint Luke recounts the story of the woman healed on the sabbath. Saint Luke carefully describes the woman as "bound" to accentuate the release and freedom that Jesus brings to her. She is a slave who is set free as a part of Jesus' jubilean mission:

> Now he was teaching in one of the synagogues on the sabbath. And there was a woman who had had a spirit of infirmity for eighteen years; she was bent over and could not fully straighten herself. And when Jesus saw her, he called her and said to her, "Woman, you are freed from your infirmity" (Lk. 13:10-12).

The leader of the synagogue was indignant, because Jesus had healed on the Sabbath. Jesus responds to this indignation, saying,

> You hypocrites! Does not each of you on the sabbath untie his ox or his ass from the manger, and lead it away to water it? And ought not this woman, a daughter of Abraham whom Satan bound for eighteen years, be loosed from this bond on the sabbath day? (Lk. 13:15-16).

It was not simply the infirmity that had bound the woman, but rather Satan, who had enslaved her those eighteen years. To this woman, bound and enslaved by Satan, Jesus proclaims release and a new jubilee.

Ultimately, it is spiritual, not physical, ailments that truly bind us. It is slavery to sin that holds us captive, and from which only God can set us free. Jesus makes this clear when He says, "Truly, truly, I say to you, every one who commits sin is a slave to sin. . . . So if the Son makes you free, you will be free indeed" (Jn. 8:34-35). As Saint Paul proclaims, it is through the forgiveness of sins that this freedom comes:

> Let it be known to you therefore, brethren, that through this man [Jesus Christ] forgiveness of sins is proclaimed to you, and by him every one that believes is freed from everything from which you could not be freed by the law of Moses (Acts 13:38-39).

The Return of Our Inheritance

Saint Luke also recounts how Jesus describes the release and restoration of inheritance in the parable of the prodigal son (Lk. 15:11-32). Prodigal means recklessly extravagant, lavish. The wayward son in the parable is called prodigal because he throws away a great fortune and, even worse, a great father. The son goes to his father and asks for his portion of his father's inheritance. In effect, he says to his father, "I wish you were dead, so that I could receive what is to come to me once you die!" The father, in all humility and selfless love, grants his son his wish. The son then proceeds to travel away from the father to a distant land, where he squanders his family inheritance on sinful ways. Forced to feed and eat with the swine, the son desires to return home to his father. Dying to himself, he returns to the house of his father, not as his father's son, but simply with the desire to be a servant. The father, seeing him from afar and thinking not of himself and his own dignity, but only of his desire for his son's return, runs out to welcome him home. Taking hold of his son, he proclaims, "[T]his my son was dead, and is alive again" (Lk. 15:24). The father resurrects the son from death to life, from servitude to the sonship that was his in his father's home.

The father not only welcomes his son back into the family,

but restores his inheritance, which is signified in the father's clothing of his son: "[T]he father said to his servants, 'Bring quickly the best robe, and put it on him; and put a ring on his hand, and shoes on his feet'" (Lk. 15:22). The family inheritance and communion lost by the prodigal son's sin is restored by the father's merciful and loving forgiveness.

In these three accounts, Saint Luke highlights how Jesus' forgiveness of sins must be understood in light of a new jubilee, bringing release from the bondage of sin. The goal of this new release and forgiveness of sins is the reunion of God's family (cf. Catechism, no. 1443).

The Healing of the Leper

Isaiah prophesied that with the jubilee the blind would receive their sight and the lame walk, lepers would be cleansed and the deaf hear, and the dead would be raised up (cf. Is. 35:5-6; Mt. 11:2-6). The Old Testament recognized a close connection between sickness and sin. The Catechism makes this observation when it says, "It is the experience of Israel that illness is mysteriously linked to sin and evil" (Catechism, no. 1502).

What is the cause of this mysterious association between sin and illness in Scripture? The first reason is that there was no illness in Eden. Disease and death come only after the sin of Adam and Eve (cf. Catechism, no. 405). The first references to illness in Scripture are to that of the Pharaoh of Abraham's day and Abimelech, who are afflicted with plagues as signs of divine disapproval of their plans to take Abraham's wife Sarah (Gen. 12:17; 20:17).

The second reason is that God's covenant with Israel promises health and prosperity for obedience, and disease and affliction for disobedience:

If you will diligently hearken to the voice of the Lord your
God, and do that which is right in his eyes, and give heed to
his commandments and keep all his statutes, I will put none
of the diseases upon you which I put upon the Egyptians; for
I am the Lord, your healer (Ex. 15:26).[3]

Does this mean that when we are sick it is solely the result of
sin we have committed? By no means. In Scripture, illness generally enters into human life because of sin; but it does not follow
that, in individual cases, sickness is caused by personal sin. Jesus
Himself makes this clear in His response that the man born blind
was not born blind due to sin, but rather that the glory of God
might be manifested (cf. Jn. 9:1-3). But since the life of the body
and the life of the soul are analogous, the sickness of the body,
which is felt and seen, can be used as a sign to teach us of the illness of the soul that is often unfelt and unseen. In the Old
Testament, God not only taught Israel of her sinfulness through
captivity, but also through sickness and disease. So when Jesus
proclaims a new jubilee, the release from sickness and disease is
a sign of the greater release from sin and Satan.

In Mark's Gospel, the first person to feel Jesus' healing touch
is a leper. Leprosy was then what AIDS is today, a terrifying,
deadly disease that often meant for its victim a life of suffering
and abandonment. Because of his disease, the leper was exiled to
the outskirts of the town, left to "dwell alone in a habitation outside the camp" (Lev. 13:46). Here he was left to beg for his sus-
tenance because he was broken off from the daily life of the community. Declared "unclean" as a result of his leprosy, he was not
only cast out from his village and family, but he was even barred
from entering the Temple and participating in Israel's liturgical
worship. To be ritually unclean was to be socially and religiously
exiled. The state in which the leper found himself because of his
physical sickness is analogous to the state in which we find ourselves

---

[3] Deut. 28 sets forth in even more graphic detail the devastating, temporal curses Israel
will suffer if she does "not obey the voice of the Lord [and is not] careful to do all his
commandments" (Deut. 28:15).

because of the spiritual disease of sin. Sin makes us spiritually what the leper is physically: exiled and cut off from God.

Recognizing Jesus' healing power, this leper kneels before Jesus and begs, "Lord, if you will, you can make me clean" (Lk. 5:12). The leper's carefully worded request to Jesus is, surprisingly, not to be healed, but rather to be *clean*. In this brief request, the heartfelt desire of the leper is revealed. His first desire is not simply to be physically healed, but to be made ritually (spiritually) clean, not simply to return to the village and his people, but to return to the Temple and his God. This leper realizes what Jesus desires all Israel to understand, that the healing most needed is the healing that comes from the forgiveness of sins, the healing that will end Israel's exile and restore her relationship with God.

Jesus, moved with pity for the leper, touches him and replies, "I will; be clean" (Lk. 5:13). In an astonishingly bold move, Jesus, who is clean, touches the unclean leper. According to the Torah and Jewish custom, when the clean touches that which is unclean, it too becomes unclean, defiled. This had been the case throughout the history of Israel: Sin, which is signified by the notion of uncleanness, had spread like a cancer without a cure. Is this compassionate rabbi from Nazareth now unclean, defiled? No, for now a new power is revealed in the Person of Jesus. Now when sin and the unclean encounter Jesus, the unclean becomes clean, sin is expelled, and the spiritual cancer is cured. This man, now healed of his leprosy, is able to return and participate in the daily life of his family and the worshipping community.

The Healing Power of Christ in the Church Today

Old Testament legislation called for a jubilee year to be celebrated only once every fifty years. The new jubilee that Jesus inaugurated, however, extends beyond His earthly ministry to the present day. Jesus' ministry of healing and reconciliation was entrusted to the apostles, and through apostolic succession, down to the Church in all ages: "Truly, I say to you, whatever you bind on earth shall be bound in heaven, and whatever you loose on earth shall be loosed in heaven" (Mt. 18:18). This saying of Jesus comes in the context of correcting a brother for his sin, thereby making it clear that the binding and loosing relates to sin (cf. Mt. 18:15-17).

Some, however, are scandalized by the notion that a man may have the power to forgive sins, saying, "Who can forgive sins but God alone?" However, this is not the first time the objection has been raised. When Jesus told the paralytic that his sins were forgiven, the Pharisees question in their hearts, "Who can forgive sins, but God alone?" (Mk. 2:7).

Jesus responds by asking,

> Which is easier, to say to the paralytic, "Your sins are forgiven," or to say, "Rise, take up your pallet and walk?" But that you may know that the Son of Man has authority on earth to forgive sins . . . (Mt. 9:6).

Jesus uses the physical healing of paralysis to illustrate the spiritual healing that results from the forgiveness of sins. Jesus makes explicit not only that He has authority to forgive sins, but that He has authority "on earth" to forgive sins. Matthew emphasizes this earthly dimension by noting that the crowds gave glory to God, "who had given such authority to men" (Mt. 9:8). The crowd rejoices and gives glory that this authority was given not only to the Son of Man, but also to the sons of men, as is illustrated in their use of "men" in the plural. Therefore, the crowd, like a Greek chorus, chants the key theme of the story in their refrain, "Glory to God who has given such authority to men!"

If some would still question whether God would give such authority to men, Jesus' words in the Gospel of John should remove all doubt. Saint John explicitly tells how Jesus gave this divine power to forgive sins to His apostles by breathing on them the divine power of His Holy Spirit and saying: "Receive the Holy Spirit. If you forgive the sins of any, they are forgiven; if you retain the sins of any, they are retained" (Jn. 20:22-23). No man, on his own authority, has the power to forgive sins. But, those who are successors to the apostles and ordained by the

power of the Holy Spirit have the divine authority to forgive sins
in Christ's name. Why go to a priest to have your sins forgiven?
Because this is what Jesus has commanded. He told His apostles,
"He who hears you hears me, and he who rejects you rejects me,
and he who rejects me rejects Him who sent me" (Lk. 10:16).
Thus when we hear the priest say that we are to go in peace for
our sins are forgiven, we do not simply hear the priest, but rather
He who sent him, Our Lord and Savior Jesus Christ.

That God chooses to involve a representative in the pardon-
ing of sins is not something new with the New Testament. In the
section of the Book of Exodus that is referred to as the "Book of
the Covenant," God tells Moses,

> Behold, I send an angel before you, to guard you on the way
> and to bring you to the place which I have prepared. Give heed
> to him and hearken to his voice, do not rebel against him, for
> he will not pardon your transgression; for my name is in him.
> But if you hearken attentively to his voice and do all that I say,
> then I will be an enemy to your enemies and an adversary to
> your adversaries (Ex. 23:20-22).

The voice of the angel carries the very words of God, so much so
that when the angel speaks, it is God's words that the people
hear. In addition, according to God Himself, it is the angelic mes-
senger who will withhold pardon if the people transgress and
rebel. What is it that gives this angel the power to bestow or withhold pardon for transgressions? The answer appears to be that
God's "name is in him." Because the very name of God has been
set upon this angel, he has the authority to execute God's judgment. This authority is not his own, but from God.

Interestingly, Jesus uses similar language in reference to the
apostles at the Last Supper. Saint John, the beloved disciple,
recounts Jesus' prayer in which He says,

> I have manifested thy name to the men whom thou gavest me
> out of the world; . . . And now I am no more in the world, but
> they are in the world, and I am coming to thee. Holy Father,
> *keep them in thy name*, which thou hast given me, that they

may be one, even as we are one. While I was with them, *I kept them in thy name*, which thou hast given me (Jn. 17:6; 11-12).

According to Christ, He has kept the apostles that the Father has given Him in the Father's name. Only three chapters later, Christ will breathe on these apostles and give them authority to forgive sins. The Church recognizes that, while God alone pardons sins, He chooses to work through the words of absolution which the priest speaks in His name. This truth is clearly evident in the very words of absolution that the priest speaks during the Sacrament of Penance:

> God, the Father of mercies, through the death and the resurrection of his Son has reconciled the world to himself and sent the Holy Spirit among us for the forgiveness of sins; through the ministry of the Church may God give you pardon and peace, and I absolve you from your sins in the name of the Father, and of the Son, and of the Holy Spirit.[4]

The priest does not absolve sin in his own name, but "in the name of the Father, and of the Son, and of the Holy Spirit." This authority to forgive sins is not limited to Baptism alone, as Saint James states in connection with the Sacrament of Anointing of the Sick,

> Is any one among you suffering? Let him pray. Is any cheerful? Let him sing praise. Is any among you sick? Let him call for the elders of the church, and let them pray over him, anointing him with oil in the name of the Lord; and the prayer of faith will save the sick man, and the Lord will raise him up; and if he has committed sins, he will be forgiven (Jas. 5:13-15).

Saint Paul, too, in his letter to the baptized saints in Corinth, exhorts them to be reconciled to God and speaks of the "ministry of reconciliation" given to the apostles from God (2 Cor. 5:16-20). Both apostles speak of a ministry of reconciliation and forgiveness of sins to those who are already baptized:

---

[4] Ordo *paenitentiae*, no. 46, (formula of absolution); cf. Catechism, no. 1449.

Christ's call to conversion continues to resound in the lives of Christians. This *second conversion* is an uninterrupted task for the whole Church who, "clasping sinners to her bosom, [is] at once holy and always in need of purification, [and] follows constantly the path of penance and renewal" (Catechism, no. 1428, quoting LG 8, original emphasis).

This teaching of a second conversion is an ancient teaching of the Church, as illustrated not only by the writings of the apostles, but also by the writings of the early Church Fathers, such as Saint Ambrose, who speaks of the two waters of repentance: "[T]here are water and tears: the water of Baptism and the tears of repentance" (Catechism, no. 1429). In addition, Tertullian understands the Sacrament of Penance as "the second plank [of salvation] after the shipwreck which is the loss of grace" (Catechism, no. 1446). These sources bear witness to the authority given to the Church by Christ to forgive sins—not only through Baptism—but also through the sacraments of healing.

Conclusion

Jesus Christ began His messianic mission by inaugurating a new jubilee for the forgiveness of sins. This jubilee brings release from the enslavement of sin and restores our relationship with God. By offering to us the Sacraments of Reconciliation and the Anointing of the Sick, our prodigal Father cries out to His erring children as He did through the prophet Ezekiel:

> Repent and turn from all your transgressions, lest iniquity be your ruin. Cast away from you all the transgressions which you have committed against me, and get yourselves a new heart and a new spirit! (Ezek. 18:30-31).

When we have sinned, let us turn back to God and make use of the gifts He has given us in the sacraments of healing. Let us confess our sins and repent, as did David, and then we will receive in the sacraments of healing "a clean heart" and a "new and right spirit" (Ps. 51:10). These sacraments provide us with grace and strength so that we can turn away from evil and return to communion with the Triune God. Through them, we partake here on earth of the first fruits of the tree of life at the center of the heavenly Jerusalem, whose leaves are for the healing of the nations (cf. Rev. 22:1-5). These fruits not only heal our souls, but also restore and deepen our relationship with Our Heavenly Father:

> Indeed the sacrament of Reconciliation with God brings about a true "spiritual resurrection," restoration of the dignity and blessings of the life of the children of God, of which the most precious is friendship with God (Catechism, no. 1468).

Kris Gray studied theology at Franciscan University of Steubenville and Hebrew at the Hebrew University of Jerusalem. She has a bachelor's degree in electrical and computer engineering from the University of Wisconsin-Madison. She and her husband Timothy reside in Alexandria, Virginia.

CHAPTER XIII

The Burning Truth
About Purgatory

CURTIS A. MARTIN

Of all the misunderstood Catholic teachings—and there are a few of them—purgatory is often seen as the most embarrassing. Thousands of Catholics leave the Church every year. Their faith is questioned and their religious education doesn't rise to the challenge. You've probably heard these questions yourself: "Where in the Bible does it say you have to go to a priest to confession?" "Where does it say that the pope is infallible?" "That Mary was conceived without original sin?" And, "Where in the world did you Catholics get the teaching on purgatory?" These are tough questions. But as good as they are, they don't compare to the great answers that Scripture and apostolic Tradition have to offer.

The typical conversation goes something like this:

Non-Catholic: "So you're a Roman Catholic?"

Roman Catholic: "That's right. I'm even a Notre Dame fan."

NC: "Do you believe everything the Church teaches?"

RC: "Well, yeah, I guess so."

NC: "Even purgatory?"

RC: "I think so."

NC: "Well, let me get this straight. You believe in an all-loving God, don't you?"

RC: "Yeah!"

NC: "Do you believe that this God sent His only begotten Son to die for you?"

RC: "Sure!"

NC: "So let me get this straight: You believe in an all-loving God, who loved you so much that He sent His only begotten Son to die for you, just so you can go to heaven when you die. Yet, this loving God first sticks you in a 'cosmic oven' and bakes you for a couple hundred years or so until you're done?"

RC: "Well, I've never really thought about it that way."

NC: "Where in the Bible does it say 'purgatory'?"

About this time, our Catholic friend is looking for someplace to hide! He seems to have three equally unsatisfactory options. Option number one is blind faith: "I don't know why I believe it, but I'm going to keep right on believing it anyway. After all, I'm Catholic, and don't confuse me with the facts!"

Option two is an over-confident triumphalism: "Silly Fundamentalist! Where in the Bible really!"

The third option is to run for the hills.

Each of these options fails to take the situation seriously. Blind faith ignores the importance of an answer. Triumphalism ignores the importance of the question. And running away fails to see the importance of reality.

There is, however, another way: the way of constructive apologetics, which takes the question and the answer very seriously, and prayerfully begins to search the sacred texts and the storehouses of apostolic Tradition to find the truth about these important issues. "What is needed is a calm, clear-sighted, and truthful vision of things."[1]

First, let's look at the question. The case against purgatory seems to be based on three major objections. First, the teaching

---

[1] Pope John Paul II, Encyclical Letter On Commitment to Ecumenism *Ut Unum Sint* (1995), no. 2.

of purgatory seems to contradict the finished work of Christ and offend the basic understanding of God as a loving, all-caring, all-merciful God who has forgiven us our sins in Christ Jesus. Second, purgatory seems to offer a "second chance" for those who did not follow Christ in this life. Third, purgatory does not appear to be a biblical teaching.

Sacred Scripture stresses the truth of God's love and Evangelical Protestants have frequently had a powerful experience of Christ's forgiveness. Saint John explains in his First Epistle: "In this is love, not that we loved God but that he loved us and sent his son to be the expiation for our sins" (1 Jn. 4:10). Jesus Christ Himself stresses mercy over judgment, stating,

> Truly, truly, I say to you, he who hears my word and believes him who sent me, has eternal life; he does not come into judgment, but has passed from death to life (Jn. 5:24).

Sacred Scripture teaches of a God who "so loved the world that he gave his only Son, that whoever believes in him should not perish but have eternal life" (Jn. 3:16). The Christian believer is called to accept the mercy of God as all-powerful, capable of overcoming all sin, and yet the Catholic who holds the teaching of purgatory seems to belittle God's forgiveness. From this perspective, God appears almost schizophrenic, wanting to forgive our sins and yet meticulously holding us accountable for them, at one time cleansing us from all unrighteousness (cf. 1 Jn. 1:9) and then later deciding to "fry us" for displeasing Him. Have we "passed out of judgment" (cf. Jn. 5:24) or haven't we? Has Christ forgiven our sins, or hasn't He?

This is no small issue, particularly for the non-Catholic who believes that faith in the sufficiency of the death and resurrection of Jesus Christ is the key to salvation. To minimize that belief in any way is to undermine saving faith. So, to an Evangelical, the doctrine of purgatory appears to be an attack on the efficacy on Christ's unique and saving sacrifice. The doctrine of purgatory collides with the Protestant doctrine of *sola fide*, that we are saved by faith alone.

The second objection against purgatory is that it is a manu-factured second chance. If you don't really want to follow Christ, you can still get to heaven through the "back door." This offends against Christ, who called us to stand with Him or against Him. Scripture is clear that spiritual mediocrity is unacceptable:

> "I know your works: you are neither cold nor hot. Would that you were cold or hot! So, because you are lukewarm, and neither hot nor cold, I will spew you out of my mouth" (Rev. 3:15-16).

Jesus calls for complete commitment. He is either Lord of all, or He isn't Lord at all. There is no second chance; we are either for Christ or against Him (cf. Lk. 11:23). The doctrine of purgatory seems to be an "end run." But Jesus said, "I am the way, and the truth, and the life; no one comes to the Father, but by me" (Jn. 14:6).

The third argument against the doctrine of purgatory flows from the other main dogma of Protestant theology, *sola scriptura* ("the Bible alone"). After all, where in the Bible do we find purgatory? A quick word check in any concordance will demon-strate that the word is nowhere to be found in Scripture. Saint Paul seems to teach clearly in Hebrews: "[I]t is appointed for men to die once, and after that comes judgment" (Heb. 9:27). There is no discussion of some third place between heaven and hell. Surely something as important as purgatory would be clearly taught in the pages of sacred Scripture! The biblical case for pur-gatory seems impossible to make.

Purgatory also appears to be "guilty by association": The doc-trine is caught up in the "Catholic collection" of the intercession of the saints, indulgences, the sacrifice of the Mass, and other items that are perceived as "unbiblical" and the fruit of mere human tradition. Yet Christ warns, "[F]or the sake of your tradi-tion, you have made void the word of God" (Mt. 15:6).

In summary, many Catholics find themselves defending a teaching that they don't understand, which seems to undermine the work of Christ, and which also apparently lacks all biblical support. It shouldn't come as a surprise that many Catholics begin to feel uncomfortable with their beliefs, and the simplicity and confidence of Evangelical Christianity understandably begins to look very attractive.

These views are held by very sincere Christians, men and women with whom we are united in Baptism. Catholics have an obligation to take these questions seriously. These are good people, and these are good questions. Good questions deserve great answers!

When I began to investigate the teaching of purgatory, I did so as a fallen-away Catholic and an Evangelical Protestant. I used the tools my Evangelical friends had given to me: sacred Scripture, prayer, and Christ-centered friendships. I knew that it wasn't enough to simply stop with the question, "Where in the Bible is purgatory?" As a Christian, the two most fundamental truths that I held were the Trinity—three Persons in one God: Father, Son, and Holy Spirit—and the Incarnation, that the eternal Son, at a point in history, took on human nature and became man like us in all things but sin. And yet the word "Trinity" and the word "Incarnation" were nowhere in Scripture. That is to say, the words weren't, but the teachings were.

I now needed to go to the Bible and examine whether the *teaching* of purgatory—whether the word was there or not—was to be found in the teachings of Christ and the apostles. I knew enough about Catholic teaching to know that Catholics frequently cited 2 Mac. 12:45: "[I]t was a holy and pious thought. Therefore he made atonement for the dead, that they might be delivered from their sin."

While this was interesting, it proved nothing to me, because 2 Maccabees was one of the books I, as an Evangelical Protestant, did not accept as being part of the canon of Scripture. I began to search the Gospels to see if Jesus gave any teachings concerning judgment or purification at the end of our earthly life. I began to see that several of our Lord's teachings, far from disproving purgatory, seemed to point to the possibility that there might be some debt of justice that would be paid after our earthly life. As

Christ teaches about the importance of forgiveness, He gives the example of a king who wished to settle accounts with his slaves. He brought in a man who owed a great deal of money and forgave him the debt. The forgiven man in turn went out and met one of his fellow slaves, who owed him but a fraction of the amount, and demanded repayment. The just king summoned his slave back and said,

> "You wicked servant! I forgave you all that debt because you besought me; and should not you have had mercy on your fellow servant, as I had mercy on you?" And in anger his lord delivered him to the jailers, till he should pay all his debt (Mt. 18:32-34).

What was Jesus talking about? Scripture clearly teaches, "There is therefore now no condemnation for those who are in Christ Jesus" (Rom. 8:1). And yet Our Lord Himself gives the example of a man who had been forgiven, afterward acted unjustly, and finally was handed over to repay all that he owed. Again in Saint Luke's Gospel, Our Lord challenges His followers to make peace with one another, so that they will not be handed over to the magistrate who should throw them into prison: "I tell you, you will never get out till you have paid the very last copper" (Lk. 12:59; cf. Mt. 5:26). Christ calls the believer, who has passed out of condemnation—the sentence of hell—to live a life of justice which will be exacted to the last cent. If this is not the case, then the teachings of Jesus make no sense. The Catholic teaching about purgatory is that if, at the end of our earthly life, this debt of justice was not satisfied, we shall be purified in purgatory before entering heaven. The teachings of Christ did not seem to contradict this. But lack of contradiction is still a long way from proof.

In Saint Matthew's Gospel there is a tremendous confrontation between Christ and the Pharisees, in which they accuse Him of exercising authority over demons by the power of Beelzebul, the "prince of demons" (Mt. 12:24). Jesus then warns them of the sin against the Holy Spirit and states,

Therefore I tell you, every sin and blasphemy will be forgiven men, but the blasphemy against the Spirit will not be forgiven. And whoever says a word against the Son of man will be forgiven; but whoever speaks against the Holy Spirit will not be forgiven, either in this age or in the age to come (Mt. 12:31-32).

If this sin cannot be forgiven either in this age or in the age to come, some sins might be able to be forgiven in the age to come. Without using the word "purgatory," Jesus is presenting teachings that seemed in harmony with the Catholic teaching on purgatory and were a bit difficult to interpret from an Evangelical perspective. While I was far from ready to accept that Jesus was referring to purgatory, I was finding myself hard-pressed to come to any other conclusion. This "forgiveness of sins" and "the age to come," the reference to a prison in which we would not be released until we had "paid the last cent"—this is certainly not heaven or hell. We never get out of hell, and heaven is certainly no prison.

I pondered what Our Lord might mean as I continued to read through the remainder of the New Testament. I came across a passage in Saint Paul's First Letter to the Corinthians that I found very surprising. While addressing the very issue of sin within the Christian community—those who were believers and had accepted the Lordship of Jesus Christ into their lives—Saint Paul says,

For no other foundation can any one lay than that which is laid, which is Jesus Christ. Now if any one builds on the foundation with gold, silver, precious stones, wood, hay, stubble–each man's work will become manifest; for the Day will disclose it, because it will be revealed with fire, and the fire will test what sort of work each one has done. If the work which any man has built on the foundation survives, he will receive a reward. If any man's work is burned up, he will suffer loss, though he himself will be saved, but only as through fire (1 Cor. 3:11-15).

Saint Paul is clearly speaking to the Christians here. The notes in my *Ryrie Study Bible*—a Protestant Study Bible in no way sympathetic to Roman Catholicism—affirmed the fact that the passage refers to believers. The works of gold, silver, and precious stones refer to works of faithfulness performed in obedience to Christ by the power of the Holy Spirit, while those works of wood, hay, and stubble refer to those carnal acts in which we refuse to accept the Lordship of Christ.

The passage is quite clear: Gold and silver, when placed into a furnace, would be purified; wood and hay would be burned away. As this is done, the Scripture says we will suffer loss, but be saved "as through fire." The image of purgatory was becoming more vivid as I read. What else could Saint Paul be referring to? He can't be referring to hell, because it's clear that the people who undergo this "purifying fire" will be saved, while those who are in hell are lost forever. And yet he can't be referring to heaven, because he mentions the suffering of loss, while in heaven every tear will be wiped away (cf. Rev. 21:4).

Scripture teaches that God is a "consuming fire" (Heb. 12:29). The point Saint Paul seems to make is that, as God draws us to Himself after death, there is a process of purification in the fire of God's holy presence. God Himself purifies us of those imperfect deeds: the wood, hay, and stubble. And those works that are performed in faithfulness and obedience to Christ by the power of the Holy Spirit, those of gold and silver, are purified. This purification is necessary because, as Scripture teaches of heaven—the new Jerusalem—and the temple within it, "Nothing unclean shall enter it" (Rev. 21:27). The biblical images of the purifying fire through which the believer is saved, while suffering loss, were now beginning to sound more and more like purgatory.

But where is the word "purgatory?" I began to see that this question revealed an ignorance on my part. The Scriptures were written in Hebrew and Greek. "Purgatory" comes from the Latin word *purgatorium*. In Scripture, we do find references to an afterlife that is neither the hell of the damned nor heaven. In the Old Testament, the Hebrew word *sheol* is used to describe this condition; in the New Testament, the Greek term is *hades*. I had always thought that *hades* was hell, but Scripture teaches very clearly that *hades* is not hell; it is distinct from *gehenna*, or the lake of fire which is the hell of the damned. In fact, the Book of Revelation describes how, at the end of time, death and *hades* are thrown into hell (*gehenna*). This is the second death, the lake of fire. Scripture teaches that at the end of time, there is no more death; once the purification of all souls has taken place, there is no more need for *hades*. These two realities, death and *hades*, are destroyed in hell, while the damned will remain there forever (cf. Rev. 20:14-15). This same concept of *sheol* (in Hebrew), *hades* (in Greek), and *purgatorium* (in Latin) is purgatory as we have come to know it today (cf. Catechism, nos. 1030-32).

Searching Scripture, I had come to see that the teaching of purgatory did not contradict the sacred page, but I still wasn't convinced that purgatory was part of the orthodox faith. Where else could I turn? Oddly enough, I received the answer to that question from a well-known Evangelical teacher, Josh McDowell.

I was attending a conference sponsored by Campus Crusade for Christ in Daytona Beach, Florida, and we were discussing the reliability of the biblical text. McDowell presented clear teachings from history that the books we held as sacred Scripture had been reliably passed on throughout the ages so that we could trust that the New Testament we read today was an accurate reflection of the sacred texts authored nearly 2,000 years ago. One of the key arguments that McDowell employed was the testimony of history and external sources. He explained that while we do not have the original manuscripts of sacred Scripture, the testimony of the Church Fathers and the early Christians bore witness to the accuracy of our present text. He made the simple claim that the perspective of the Fathers provided solid grounds for confidence. After all, some of them had known the apostles; others were second and third-generation disciples. Because they were closer to the event, their opinions were less susceptible to error and confusion.

As I listened to McDowell speak about the reliability of Scripture, I realized that what he was saying about the translations of Scripture also applied to the interpretation of Scripture.

If I wanted to know whether purgatory was a biblical doctrine, I should look to the Church Fathers and see whether or not they maintained that purgatory was part of the faith which Jesus Christ gave to the world. I didn't realize it, but I was rediscovering sacred Tradition.

It became so obvious: If the early Christians, who were discipled by the apostles, believed in purgatory, then it must be part of that sacred deposit of faith entrusted to the Church by Jesus Christ. Scripture is clear that Jesus taught many things that did not find their way into the Bible. Saint John closes his Gospel by stating,

> There are also many other things which Jesus did; were every one of them to be written, I suppose that the world itself could not contain the books that would be written (Jn. 21:25).

Many of these teachings were widely known by the early Christians. This is evidenced, for example, in the Book of Acts, when Saint Paul encourages the Christians in Ephesus—who had been taught by Saint Peter, Saint John, the Blessed Virgin Mary, and other prominent first-century Christians—to remember "the words of the Lord Jesus, how he said, 'It is more blessed to give than to receive'" (Acts 20:35). He thus reminds them of a statement by Jesus that must have been familiar to them, but that statement appears nowhere in the Gospels. Saint Paul freely draws upon the spoken Tradition and, in fact, affirms it in sacred Scripture when he exhorts the Christians in Thessalonica: "So then, brethren, stand firm and hold to the traditions which you were taught by us, either by word of mouth or by letter" (2 Thess. 2:15).

Josh McDowell helped me to see that the early Christians were the first and best witnesses to what Christ taught: Authentic Tradition would never contradict sacred Scripture, but rather shed more light on it. So, with questions about purifying fire and the forgiveness of sins in the next life, I turned to the Fathers to see what they believed.

As I turned to extra-biblical sources, I discovered a new way of looking at the world. Up until this time, I had read the Scriptures with great profit, but not without struggle. At times I felt like the Ethiopian eunuch on the road to Gaza who, while reading a passage from Isaiah, was met by Philip, who asked him, "'Do you understand what you are reading?' And he said, 'How can I, unless some one guides me?'" (Acts 8:30-31). I longed for this sure guide. Many times I had prayed, "O Lord, if you could just come and explain this passage to me. I seek the truth, and you, Oh Lord, are the truth. You've given me your words; now give me an understanding of what they mean." At first it didn't seem as though Our Lord had heard my prayer. But then I began to discover that, while He wasn't going to come and explain the Scriptures to me miraculously, He would send teachers to me.

While I trusted in Scripture as a sure foundation, I did not hesitate to turn to my godly friends and proven Christian teachers to help me unlock the truths of Scripture. The first Christian disciples were taught by Christ and the apostles, and they wrote books. And the first step in this new hermeneutic, this new way of understanding, was to recognize that Tradition was not necessarily opposed to Scripture. Rather, apostolic Tradition was, in fact, the context from which we could come to understand Scripture with the mind of Christ. Apostolic Tradition is nothing more than the fulfillment of the great commission in time: "Go therefore and make disciples of all nations" (Mt. 28:19). Those disciples form an unbroken chain throughout history.

How did the early Christians reconcile purgatory with the life, death, and resurrection of Jesus Christ? The major objection to purgatory is that somehow it undermines the finished work of Christ. Is Christ's death sufficient? Of course it is! It is sufficient to win our redemption and to allow the Holy Spirit to sanctify us. The work of the Holy Spirit in the life of the believer, however, is the work of purification and sanctification. It is the application of the divine life won by Christ. Purgatory in no way should be viewed as a "second chance," by which those who did not believe in and follow Christ can somehow "suffer their way into heaven," despite their rejection of the Christian life. Jesus is clear that those who refuse to follow Him are guilty: "[H]e who does not believe has been judged already, because he has not believed in the name of the only Son of God" (Jn. 3:18). Spiritual purification is possible only for those who have been reconciled to God in this life (cf. 2 Cor. 5:18-20).

The reality of spiritual purification, which takes place either in this life or in the state of purgatory, must be a Trinitarian act, the act of an all-holy community of divine Persons working to purify the soul of the believer. This much must be true if we are to find the doctrine of purgatory in the writings of the early Christians.

The concept of purification after death dates back to the Jews of pre-Christian times. Evidence of this can be seen in the Second Book of Maccabees. Catholics will quickly cite this as scriptural evidence for the reality of purgatory, but we must remember that Protestants do not accept 2 Maccabees as scriptural. Nevertheless, objective readers will have to note that, even if the seven books of the Old Testament accepted by Catholics and rejected by Protestants are not biblical, they are godly writings and worthy of our consideration. In 2 Maccabees, following a battle, the faithful Jews found out that their fallen comrades each carried with them sacred tokens of idols, which the law forbade the Jews to wear:

> [T]hey turned to prayer, beseeching that the sin which had been committed might be wholly blotted out. And the noble Judas exhorted the people to keep themselves free from sin, for they had seen with their own eyes what had happened because of the sin of those who had fallen. He also took up a collection, man by man, to the amount of two thousand drachmas of silver, and sent it to Jerusalem to provide for a sin offering (2 Mac. 12:42-43).

The sacred text notes that this was an honorable deed, and the passage closes with the statement, "Therefore he made atonement for the dead, that they might be delivered from their sin" (2 Mac. 12:45).

What is striking about this passage is not what it asserts, but what it takes for granted. This episode is not told in an apologetic style, as if to prove that prayer for the dead was a pious act, but rather assumes it. Moreover, once the Catholic Church is accepted as the Church that Christ founded, and thus as the Church that defines the canon of Scripture, the teaching in Maccabees takes on greater weight as inspired Scripture (cf. 2 Tim. 3:16).

What is clear and undeniable is the solidarity the early Christians felt with the deceased. Many of the first churches grew up around the burial site of the great saints. The Church entrusted themselves to the prayers of those alive in Christ and also commended the faithful to God's mercy. Many ancient Christian monuments call out for prayer. For example, the epitaph of a bishop named Abercius, composed toward the end of the second century, provides: "Standing by, I, Abercius, ordered this to be inscribed; truly, I was in my seventy-second year. May everyone who is in accord with this and who understands it pray for Abercius." This practice of prayer for the deceased predates clear theological explanations.

Lex orandi, lex credendi—"the law of praying is the law of believing." Hundreds of years before the Church clearly defined that Jesus Christ was one divine Person with two natures—a divine nature and a human nature—Saint Thomas exclaimed in the Upper Room, "My Lord and my God!" (Jn. 20:28). This profession of faith in Christ's divinity predates a clear theological understanding of how Thomas could worship the man Jesus and not be guilty of idolatry. The truth was only gradually distilled into definitions when various heresies arose that attacked either Christ's divinity or His humanity. So, too, prayer with and for the dead predates a fully developed defense of this practice, which was provided at the ecumenical councils of Lyons II (1274), Florence (1439-45), and Trent (1545-63).

Nevertheless, the Fathers of the Church do bear witness to the reality of purgatory. In the third century, Saint Cyprian of Carthage, a bishop and martyr, extols the benefits of martyrdom for the sake of Christ, writing:

It is one thing to stand for pardon; another to arrive at glory.
It is one thing for one put in prison not to come out from there
until he has "paid the last penny"; another thing to receive
immediately the reward of faith and virtue. It is one thing, tor-
tured by long sorrow for sins, to be cleansed and purged for a
time by fire; another thing to have purged all sins by suffering.
It is one thing, finally, to wait on the day of judgment for the
sentence of the Lord; another thing to be immediately
crowned by the Lord.[2]

Writing in the next century, Saint Augustine, a bishop and
doctor of the Catholic Church, encourages the faithful to seek
holiness in all things, so as to be purified in this life:

"Lord, rebuke me not in Your indignation, nor correct me in
Your anger." In this life may You cleanse me and make me such
that I have no need of the corrective fire, which is for those
who are saved, but as if by fire. . . . For it is said: "He shall be
saved, but as if by fire." And because it is said that he shall be
saved, little is thought of that fire. Yet plainly, though we be
saved by fire, that fire will be more severe than anything a man
can suffer in this life.[3]

Some years later in another work Saint Augustine would further comment on 1 Cor. 3:10-15, in light of Mt. 25:31-46:

But if the fire of which our Lord speaks is the same as that of
which the apostle says, "Yet so as by fire," then both—that is to
say, both those on the right as well as those on the left—are to
be cast into it. For that fire is to try both, since it is said, "For
the day of the Lord shall declare it, because it shall be revealed
by fire; and the fire shall try every man's work of what sort it
is." If, therefore, the fire shall try both, in order that if any
man's work abide—i.e.[,] if the superstructure be not consumed
by the fire—he may receive a reward, and that if his work is

---

[2] Saint Cyprian of Carthage, *Letter 55* (251 A.D.), as translated in *Saint Cyprian:
Letters* (1-81), The Fathers of the Church Series, vol. 51 (Washington: The Catholic
University of America Press, 1964), 146.

[3] Saint Augustine of Hippo, *Explanation of the Psalms V* (395 A.D.), as translated in
William A. Jurgens, ed., *The Faith of the Early Fathers*, vol. 3 (Collegeville, MN: The
Liturgical Press, 1979), Ps. 37(3), 17.

burned he may suffer loss, certainly that fire is not the eternal
fire itself. For into this latter fire only those on the left hand
shall be cast, and that with final and everlasting doom; but that
former fire proves those on the right hand. But some of them
it so proves that it does not burn and consume the structure
which is found to have been built by them on Christ as the
foundation; while others of them it proves in another fashion,
so as to burn what they have built up, and thus cause them to
suffer loss, while they themselves are saved because they have
retained Christ, who was laid as their sure foundation, and
have loved Him above all.[4]

A century later, Saint Caesarius of Arles, in commenting on
1 Jn. 5:16-17, describes the sins and imperfections that plague
the faithful Christian through his life:

Although we do not believe that the soul is killed by [venial]
sins, still they make it ugly by filling it with some kind of blis-
ters and, as it were, a horrible scab. For this reason they allow
the soul to come to the embraces of that heavenly spouse only
with difficulty or with great confusion[.]. . . [I]f we neither
give thanks to God in tribulations nor redeem our own sins by
good works, we will have to stay in that fire of purgatory as
long as those above-mentioned slight sins are consumed like
wood and hay and straw. Perhaps someone may say: It makes
no difference to me how long I will have to stay, as long as I
pass on to eternal life. Let no one say this, dearest brethren,
because that fire of purgatory will be more difficult than any
punishment in this world can be seen or imagined or felt.[5]

At the close of the sixth century, Pope Saint Gregory the
Great teaches how Scripture points again and again to the reality
of purification, both in this life and in the life to come:

In the Gospel our Lord says, "Finish your journey while you
still have the light." And in the words of the Prophet He

---

[4] Saint Augustine of Hippo, *City of God* (426 A.D.), as translated by Marcus Dodds,
D.D. (New York: Random House, 1950), Book XXI, 802-03.
[5] Saint Caesarius of Arles, *Sermon 179* (535 A.D.), as translated in *Saint Caesarius of
Arles: Sermons Volume II* (81-186), The Fathers of the Church Series, A New
Translation (Washington: The Catholic University of America Press, 1964), 451-53.

declares, "In an acceptable time I have heard thee, and in the
day of the salvation I have helped thee." Saint Paul's comment
on this is: "And here is the time of pardon; the day of salvation
has come already." Solomon, too, says, "Anything you can turn
your hand to, do with what power you have; for there will be
no work, nor reason, nor knowledge, nor wisdom in the nether
world where you are going." And David adds, "For his mercy
endures forever." From these quotations it is clear that each
one will be presented to the Judge exactly as he was when he
departed this life. Yet, there must be a cleansing fire before
judgment, because of some minor faults that may remain to be
purged away. Does not Christ, the Truth, say that if anyone
blasphemes against the Holy Spirit he shall not be forgiven
"either in this world or in the world to come?" From this statement we learn that some sins can be forgiven in this world and
some in the world to come. For, if forgiveness is refused for a
particular sin, we conclude logically that it is granted for others. This must apply, as I said, to slight transgressions, such as
persistent idle talking, immoderate laughter, or blame in the
care of property, which can scarcely be administered without
fault even by those who know the faults to be avoided, or
errors due to ignorance in matters of no great importance. All
these faults are troublesome for the soul after death if they are
not forgiven while one is still alive. For, when Saint Paul says
that Christ is the foundation, he adds: "But on this foundation
different men will build in gold, silver, precious stones, wood,
grass, or straw . . . and fire will test the quality of each man's
workmanship. He will receive a reward, if the building he had
added on stands firm! [I]f it is burnt up, he will be the loser;
and yet he himself will be saved, though only as men are saved
as passing through fire" [cf. 1 Cor. 3:12-15]. Although this
may be taken to signify the fire of suffering we experience in
this life, it may also refer to the cleansing fire of the world to
come, and, if one accepts it in this sense, one must weigh Saint
Paul's words carefully.[6]

[6] Saint Gregory the Great, *Dialogues* (593 A.D.), as translated in *Saint Gregory the Great: Dialogues*, The Fathers of the Church Series, A New Translation (New York: Fathers of the Church, Inc., 1959), IV, 41, 247-49. See also Saint Basil the Great, *Commentary on Isaiah* (375 A.D.), 10, 20; Saint Maximos the Confessor, *Questions and Doubts on the Church, the Liturgy, and the Soul of Man* (649 A.D.), question 10; Lactantius, *The Divine Institutes* (305 A.D.), 7, 21.

As I began to read these and other passages, I was struck not only by the confidence of these holy men and the reality of the purifying fire (cf. 1 Cor. 3:15), but also by how deeply the teaching was rooted in the apostolic Tradition. The historic evidence clearly pointed to a belief in a state of purification that would later be called "purgatory." This term corresponded to the Hebrew concept of *sheol*, and to the Greek term *hades* in the New Testament. This third and temporary state is biblical, apostolic, historical and, most of all, true and completely reconcilable with the teachings of Jesus Christ in the Gospels.

My new perspective helped me to see why so many people had difficulty with the concept of purgatory. It was because they misunderstood what the teaching was all about. The Christian God is not schizophrenic, at one point desiring our salvation and giving His Son to die on the Cross, and in another moment baking us in an oven. Rather, the doctrine of purgatory is completely reconcilable with a loving God who is a consuming fire. As we are drawn up into His love, into His very divine life, Father, Son and Holy Spirit, we begin to burn with that same divine fire, and those impurities to which we have clung in this life must be burned away. This will inevitably involve suffering, as we let go of those imperfect things to which we are attached.

The hidden mystery behind the teaching of purgatory is our calling to live in God for all eternity, which requires us to give perfectly of ourselves (cf. Mt. 5:48). Even with deep faith, the Christian life is difficult. We are called to manifest heroic generosity, and yet generosity hurts in this life. No matter what we're asked to give, we seem to run out—of time, of energy, of money. God calls us to acknowledge this weakness, this poverty, and to turn to Him and cry out for help that He might fill us with His grace.

In heaven, generosity will not hurt; the lack of generosity will hurt. That is because in heaven God will give Himself to us fully and completely, holding nothing back. Our ability to receive from Him will be completely contingent upon our ability, in turn, to immediately give back. Otherwise, the gift of God would destroy us. Like strapping a water balloon onto a fire hydrant nozzle, we

would explode! It is only when we learn the habit of complete
and total self-giving that we will be able to experience the joy of
heaven.

This is the encouragement of Saint Paul, who says,

> Have this mind among yourselves, which was in Christ Jesus,
> who, though he was in the form of God, did not count equal-
> ity with God a thing to be grasped, but emptied himself (Phil.
> 2:5-7).

This is the vocation of the Christian faithful: to accept the finished work of Jesus Christ, and to allow that work to be applied
to our lives by the work of the Holy Spirit, so that those who are
justified will be sanctified. For us it is impossible. But with God,
all things are possible.

*Curtis A. Martin is the president of Catholics United for the Faith, an inter-
national lay apostolate committed to evangelization and catechesis, and the
executive director of the Fellowship Of Catholic University Students (FOCUS).
He received his bachelor's degree in communications from Louisiana State
University and his master's degree in theology from Franciscan University of
Steubenville. He resides in Steubenville, Ohio, with his wife Michaelann and
their five children.*

CHAPTER XIV

Conclusion
Heaven as Homecoming

SCOTT HAHN

Whenpeople say "heaven," what comes to mind? White-robed saints, glorious angels, shining clouds, celestial choirs, gold harps? All of these are fine, but there's much more to it.

Without going into great detail, there is one dominant theme that unites the many images found in Scripture and Christian art: Heaven is one glorious family reunion of all God's children.

Indeed, Jesus is the one who taught us to see heaven this way: "I am ascending to my Father and your Father" (Jn. 20:17). So he tells us:

> In my Father's house are many rooms; if it were not so, would I have told you that I go to prepare a place for you? And when I go and prepare a place for you, I will come again and will take you to myself, that where I am you may be also (Jn. 14:2-3).

Saint Paul uses similar family language:

> We know that the whole creation has been groaning in travail together until now; and not only the creation, but we ourselves, who have the first fruits of the Spirit, groan inwardly as we wait for adoption as sons, the redemption of our bodies (Rom. 8:22-23).

For Saint Paul, this puts our earthly life in perspective, for we are pilgrims heading home to heaven: "[O]ur commonwealth is in heaven, and from it we await a Savior, the Lord Jesus Christ, who will change our lowly body to be like his glorious body" (Phil. 3:20-21).

If heaven is our homeland, then death must lead to a true homecoming: "For to me to live is Christ, and to die is gain" (Phil. 1:21). Saint Paul describes this "gain" in family terms, as our filial inheritance (cf. Rom. 8:9-17; Eph. 1:3-18).

A similar family outlook is reflected in the Epistle to the Hebrews:

> For it was fitting that he, for whom and by whom all things exist, in bringing many sons to glory, should make the pioneer of their salvation perfect through suffering. For he who sanctifies and those who are sanctified have all one origin. That is why he is not ashamed to call them brethren (Heb. 2:10-11).

In closing, the author reminds his readers of their heavenly call:

> You have come to Mount Zion and to the city of the living God, the heavenly Jerusalem, and to innumerable angels in festal gathering, and *to the assembly of the first-born who are enrolled in heaven* (Heb. 12:22-23).

These family images of heaven converge in John's spectacular visions in the Book of Revelation. The heavenly Jerusalem is where all of the elect saints and angels gather as one glorious company of royal priests to worship before the throne of the Lamb (Rev. 4-5). We are united as brothers and sisters in Christ. At the climax of these prophetic visions, John is shown our eternal

communion with Christ, which he describes in the most remark-
ably intimate terms, as "the marriage supper of the Lamb" (Rev.
19:9). As the bride of Christ, the Church will be revealed in all
her bridal beauty and splendor, which is nothing less than the
eternal glory of the blessed Trinity (cf. Rev. 21:1-10, 22-23).

This nuptial bond between Christ and His Church reveals
the profound symbolism of the Sacrament of Marriage. In fact,
for Saint Paul the marriage between Christ and the Church is
more than symbolism; it is the everlasting reality of marital
love, of which our earthly marriages are but dim and temporary
shadows (cf. Eph. 5:21-32). That is the same way Saint Paul sees
God's fatherhood—as the eternal reality and perfect archetype
that far surpasses human fatherhood (cf. Eph. 3:14-15).

Of course, most of this is probably familiar territory to you.
By now, you've read enough to grasp the basic theory and biblical rationale behind this vision of the Family of God.

Perhaps the only thing remaining at this point, besides the
theory, is the practice. For if you're anything like me, you find
it much easier to think and talk about being a child of God than
to believe it from the heart—and live it. Nowhere is the struggle greater—or more vital to our spiritual well-being—than the
issue of personal assurance. In other words, how can we be fully
assured that God loves us as His children?

Rock-Solid Grounds:
The Assurance of Our Father's Love

God's gift of children confers the dignity of fatherhood upon
men. My heavenly Father has blessed me so far with five wonderful kids: Michael, Gabriel, Hannah, Jeremiah, and Joseph. I
must say, words can't begin to express how much I love and
delight in them.

God has also used my children to offer another gift to me—
full assurance of His love. Why? Because I am absolutely certain
of one thing: I am *not* greater than God. So I can't possibly love
my kids more than He loves His.

It does me a lot of good to think about that, long and hard. It seems these days that we need all the help we can get. And there may be none greater than the deep, abiding awareness of our own status as God's beloved children. What confidence this grace brings, for it roots us in the eternal love of the only perfect Father.

I admit that I've doubted God's fatherly love for me at times. On occasion, I've had to ask: How do I know that I am God's child?

The Holy Spirit will then prompt me to ask a similar question: Well, how do my kids know that they're mine?

That's easy.

First, they live in my house. Second, they are called by my name. Third, they sit at my table. Fourth, they share my flesh and blood. Fifth, my bride is their mother. Sixth, we've always celebrated birthdays, anniversaries, holidays, and vacations together. Seventh, they receive instruction and discipline from me. These are rock-solid grounds to assure my children that they'll never have to wonder to whom they belong.

Has Our Heavenly Father given us any less?

Well, if you put it that way . . . that's exactly the way Our Father *has* put it. And we call it the Catholic Church. (By now, you probably know where this logic is leading, especially if you've read the previous chapters with attention.)

First, we live in His house. As members of the Catholic Church, we live in the house which Christ promised to build—as a wise man does—upon the rock (cf. Mt. 16:17-19; 7:24-27). "Christ was faithful over God's house as a son. And we are his house if we hold fast our confidence and pride in hope" (Heb. 3:6).

> So then you are no longer strangers and sojourners, but you are fellow citizens with the saints and members of the household of God, built upon the foundation of the apostles and prophets, Christ Jesus himself being the cornerstone (Eph. 2:19-20).

Second, we are called by His name. In Baptism, we are marked for life in the name of the Father, Son, and Holy Spirit (Mt. 28:18-20). We "were sealed with the promised Holy Spirit, who is the guarantee of our inheritance until we acquire possession of it" (Eph. 1:13-14). Our family unity is thus based upon

> the unity of the Spirit in the bond of peace. There is one body and one Spirit, just as you were called to the one hope that belongs to your call, one Lord, one faith, one baptism, one God and Father of us all (Eph. 4:3-6).

Third, we sit at His table. We "partake of the table of the Lord" (1 Cor. 10:21)—as God's children—in the Eucharist, which Jesus instituted in the presence of His disciples "as they were at table eating" (Mk. 14:18).

Fourth, we share His flesh and blood. In Holy Communion, we come to share in Christ's flesh and blood, according to His command:

> Truly, truly I say to you, unless you eat the flesh of the Son of man and drink his blood, you have no life in you; he who eats my flesh and drinks my blood has eternal life, and I will raise him up at the last day. For my flesh is food indeed, and my blood is drink indeed. He who eats my flesh and drinks my blood abides in me, and I in him (Jn. 6:53-56).

Fifth, His bride is our mother. The Church is Christ's bride, the heavenly Jerusalem (cf. Eph. 5:21-32; Rev. 21:1-10, 22-23), and also our mother. "But the Jerusalem above is free, and she is our mother" (Gal. 4:26). Even more, Jesus gave us His mother, the Virgin Mary, to be our mother:

> When Jesus saw his mother, and the disciple whom he loved standing near, he said to his mother, "Woman, behold, your son!" Then he said to the disciple, "Behold, your mother!" And from that hour the disciple took her to his own home (Jn. 19:26-27).

Sixth, we celebrate as a family. We gather together as the children of God to celebrate, most especially in the Eucharistic banquet: "Christ, our paschal lamb, has been sacrificed. Let us, therefore, celebrate the festival" (1 Cor. 5:7-8). For this reason, God calls us to "be filled with the Spirit, addressing one another in psalms and hymns and spiritual songs, singing and making melody to the Lord with all your heart" (Eph. 5:18-19). As Catholics, we celebrate different feast days to honor our Blessed Mother and our spiritual brothers and sisters, the saints—not only for their holy lives, but also their glorious deaths, which marked their own joyous homecomings.

Seventh, we receive instruction and discipline from Him. Our Heavenly Father even uses our labors and sufferings to instruct and discipline us.

> "My son, do not regard lightly the discipline of the Lord, nor lose courage when you are punished by him. For the Lord disciplines him whom he loves, and chastises every son whom he receives." It is for discipline that you have to endure. God is treating you as sons; for what son is there whom his father does not discipline? . . . For they disciplined us for a short time at their pleasure, but he disciplines us for our good, that we may share his holiness (Heb. 12:5-7, 10).

Our Heavenly Father's omnipotent love is the most fundamental reason why the Roman Catholic Church exists. More than just using it to maintain unity of doctrine, morals, and worship, God empowers the Church as His family for the purpose of blessing His children and establishing the *communio* of His family—down through the ages and all around the world.

In sum, Our Heavenly Father has given to us rock-solid grounds for assurance, more than any earthly father has ever provided. And so we can exclaim: "See what love the Father has given us, that we should be called children of God; and so we are" (1 Jn. 3:1). Not only can we know that we are God's children, but we can be confident that our omnipotent Father will get us home safely: "I am sure that he who began a good work in you will bring it to completion at the day of Jesus Christ" (Phil. 1:6).

Postscript: In Memory of My Earthly Father

It was a sacred moment when my heavenly Father called me to surrender my earthly father. Words utterly fail to capture the mixture of sorrow and joy that I felt in giving up a father—in the hope of being reunited as brothers in heaven.

Standing at his hospital bedside, I gazed into the fading eyes of the man that God chose to give me life, to teach me baseball and so much else. Indeed, here was the person who first introduced me to the meaning and mystery of a father's love.

Only now he was teaching me the most difficult and ultimate lesson in life—how to suffer and die. For the first time in our life together, he asked me to pray with him and read to him from the Scriptures. God's abundant mercies were evident.

In the midst of his suffering, my father was also discovering death's deepest and most wonderful secret: the glorious conversion that can be wrought in the humbled souls of God's beloved children through the paternal prescription of pain.

After hearing his final belabored breath, I shut his eyes and knelt beside the bed and worshipped. For the first time in my life, I had no other father but God.

Since that day six years ago, I've thought about heaven more than in all thirty-five years that I lived before my father died. I have never stopped praying for him—or longing for our heavenly reunion, as brothers in Christ. *Requiescat in pace.*

By becoming an Emmaus Road
Companion or Founder, you will help
promote *Catholic for a Reason*
as a means of evangelization world-wide.

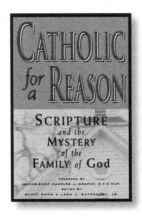

To order *Catholic for a Reason*, or to become an
Emmaus Road Companion or Founder and receive a
signed copy of *Catholic for a Reason*, call:

Emmaus Road Publishing
800-398-5470

or write to:

Emmaus Road Publishing, Inc.
827 North Fourth Street
Steubenville, Ohio 43952

Order three or more copies of *Catholic for a Reason*
and Emmaus Road Publishing Inc. will waive the shipping.
Bulk copies are available for groups, bookstores and wholesale.

EMMAUS
ROAD
PUBLISHING,INC